British Secret Service
During the Great War

British Secret Service During the Great War

Accounts of Espionage &
Counter-Espionage 1914-18

Nicholas Everitt

LEONAUR

British Secret Service During the Great War
Accounts of Espionage & Counter-Espionage 1914-18
by Nicholas Everitt

First published under the title
British Secret Service During the Great War

Leonaur is an imprint of Oakpast Ltd

Copyright in this form © 2013 Oakpast Ltd

ISBN: 978-1-78282-060-4 (hardcover)
ISBN: 978-1-78282-061-1 (softcover)

http://www.leonaur.com

Publisher's Notes

Contents

THIS BOOK
IS DEDICATED TO
VISCOUNT NORTHCLIFFE
WHO
DURING THE THROES OF OUR NATIONAL
CRISIS PROVED HIMSELF THE GREATEST
OF ALL LIVING ENGLISHMEN

Not Heaven itself upon the past has power;
But what has been, has been, and I have had my hour.

Dryden

Foreword

There is something so mysterious and thrilling about Secret Service that the subject must inevitably appeal to the public, and especially to the more imaginative section of it. Secret Service is the theme of Mr. Nicholas Everitt's book, in which he describes the exciting adventures that he met with whilst in quest of information of use to his country during the Great War.

In carrying out his task he proved himself to be a keen observer and a man of resource. His experience gives point to the old saying that a man's ability is shewn less in never getting into a scrape, for *humanum est errare*, than in knowing how to get out of one! There is perhaps no vocation in which it is easier to get into a tight corner and more difficult to get out again than in the Secret Service, where the sword of Damocles often hangs over one's head.

Besides giving an account of his adventures, Mr. Everitt devotes no small part of his work to criticism of the Foreign Office and its overseas branches—the Diplomatic and Consular Services. He draws attention to what he conceives to be their defects and suggests how they might be remedied.

While not concurring with everything said by the Author in regard to politics and politicians, I am sufficiently in agreement with the main features of his book to recommend it to the British Public, because I believe that publicity is the most potent instrument of Reform.

Northcliffe.

February, 1920

Introduction

This book is not published with the sole idea of increment to its builder; it presumes to venture beyond.

When old machinery is continued in use year after year with no thought for wear and tear, no effort to repair defective parts, and no attempt to modernise or keep pace with the times, a smash usually follows.

The British Consular Service is a concrete example of such short-sighted folly. It is so glaringly defective in its all-British efficiency that a thorough and complete overhaul, with drastic reforms, should be put in hand without further delay.

The British Diplomatic Service is little better. Its highest positions are filled by men appointed (in many instances) by influence and not by merit.

The exaggerated dignity, arrogance, and egotistical self-importance of some ministers abroad is such that the mere mention of trade sets their teeth on edge, the name of money is too vulgar for their personal contemplation; while if any matter arises in which their authority or actions are questioned they tender their resignations like sulky, petulant children spoilt beyond measure by misguided parents.

Attached to each Chancellery abroad should be a business or commercial expert, paid a fair and reasonable salary, who should make a study of British trade interests and who should control the whole consular service in the country to which he is attached. He should make it his special business to see that every consul is a born Englishman and that each is paid a salary commensurate with his position and duties.

Secret Service (if it is to be continued) should be a fully authorised and recognised department having a real business minister at its head with absolute control of its organisation, work, and finances. Service men would naturally be appointed for each separate service department, whilst civilians should be utilised in useful spheres. Such a re-organisation would do much to stop the friction which arises when military, naval, air-service, and other interests overlap, clash, or are required to work in double harness. The pitiable jealousies with which Whitehall is saturated have to be seen to be believed. Among the rank and file this canker-worm has no existence. The affection of one arm of the service for another is overwhelming, but the higher one investigates upward in rank and officialdom, the more deep-seated are the roots of the pernicious evil found to be.

At home our politicians have ever been much too interfering. Our government has for all too long been overridden by a multitude of lawyers who have pushed aside the more efficient business man, while they interfere with, and attempt to control, colossal matters which they do not and could not properly be expected to understand, and which ought to have been left entirely to experts whose lives had been devoted to the attainment of efficiency therein.

That the navy should have been deliberately prevented from making our so-called blockade really effective throughout the war is as unjustifiable as it has been exasperating to the British public, whilst it has been detrimental to the interests of the Empire. More than half the nation believe that had this matter been treated with a firm, courageous hand, the war would have been over in eighteen months at least. Almost the entire nation believed that the war would continue to drag its disastrous weary course until the blockade was made really effective.

Part of this book is devoted to this most important issue.

The public of the whole world believe we have a thoroughly active and efficient Home Secret Service Organisation, working as a separate independent unit. That is just what we ought to have had and for which there has ever been an urgent want. This omission is a defect in our armour which has been directly responsible for the undoubted loss of valuable lives and the destruction of vast property.

Much too much is left in the hands of the police. It is true our British Police Force is the best, the most efficient, and the least corrupt in the whole world. But it is not fair to place upon it more than it can properly attend to; whilst in any event its powers should be enlarged and a more elastic discretion extended. In comparison with the police of other nations, words quite fail the author with which to express his admiration for our noble and exemplary police administration. Yet its work could be made more effective if we had a separate and properly organised Home Secret Service branch, working conjointly with the police, which could at a moment's notice send down its agents, drawn from any station in society, with full powers to act and to commandeer all and every assistance that occasion might require.

Take a simple example in order that the matter may be the better understood. It is admitted that for many years our East Coast had been overrun with spies. There are places where two or more counties meet. A member of the police force for one county has no power, authority, or discretion enabling him to enter into and to act in another. Thus he cannot follow a suspect over the county border. In 1916 a certain female, whose cleverness was only equalled by her personal charms and powers of fascination, started a tour of our great camps along the Eastern seaboard. Her movements were reported by non-authorised observers. Such a case was obviously one requiring delicate investigation. Owing to lack of the necessary department under notice, the case automatically devolved into the hands of the police.

Our lady fair is watched and followed. It matters not to her; she can gaily slip over the county-border by automobile. Long reports have to be made out and passed through slow and devious channels before the police in the next county can act. By the time this becomes operative, the elusive one has returned to the county she left, or she has entered another one—an evolution which could happen several times in a very short period and much mischief be done under the nose of authorities absolutely powerless to act—until too late. It is not difficult to imagine how a home Secret Service agent, with a private motor-car, would handle such a case; more particularly when working in conjunction and perfect harmony with the police generally.

Take another case.

On April 13th, 1916, the author wrote to Whitehall as follows:

In a certain naval base of considerable importance on the East Coast in the autumn of 1914, a complete plant of wireless installation was discovered in the private house of an English merchant who was known to have business connections abroad, which plant was forthwith removed.

Some months after, a second visit was paid to the same premises and further parts of wireless telegraphy were found and taken away, and an assurance was given that everything in any way connected with wireless had been handed over.

In the month of March, 1916, the premises were once more visited and another complete plant was found to have been installed, which was immediately removed.

In April, 1916, a fourth surprise visit was made upon the same premises, when a very ingenious and complete portable wireless plant was discovered.

My information records that the latter of these respective plants controlled a radius of only about twenty miles, that they were in perfect order and that they had been repeatedly used.

The man and the occupiers of this house are said to be still at large! These facts have given me much food for reflection.

Yours, etc.

The powers-that-be took a *whole week to consider* this report, the result of private enterprise; then they suggested a meeting with the author at any convenient time, for which they added there need be *no hurry whatsoever*.

Meanwhile on Monday, April 24th, 1916, the manipulator of these terribly dangerous and unlawful instruments arrived at another naval base—Lowestoft—*on the eve of its bombardment* by the German Fleet, *actually staying at the Royal Hotel, which overlooks the whole sea-front* and which was occupied by most of the officers in command of the base.

Private agitation alone seemed to account for this gentleman's eventual removal from the East Coast; but it took an unpardonably long time in its successful accomplishment.

Another ridiculous muddle, which was undoubtedly dangerous to the welfare of the nation, was the Petrol Fiasco.

Such people as rag-and-bone merchants of possible alien extraction were permitted petrol in such quantities that they could dispose of it at good profit, whereas the police, even those in control of big and important areas, with enormous added responsibilities piled upon their too willing shoulders, were actually cut down to unworkable limits (one tin per week, equal to about forty miles)—not enough to cover a journey of consequence. Furthermore the author was informed by the head of our then Secret Service that "he himself was quite unable to move in the matter." His supply appeared to have been insanely limited.

No one ever doubted but that we should successfully pull through the war, or that our heroic, unconquerable and magnificent active service man would prove victorious in spite of all the mistakes, the clogs on the wheels, and the disastrous blundering of interfering politicians—those Grand Old Muddlers who so persistently blocked their ears to the motto, "It is never too late to mend," and who so obstinately declined to "get a move on" until positively spurred into seemingly reluctant action by the patriotic Northcliffe Press voicing the fierce indignation of the long suffering British nation.

I venture to predict that Lord Northcliffe will go down in history as the one man amongst men who has done most towards the winning of the war and the safeguarding of the future welfare of our beloved British Empire.

Regarding the chapters in this book which recount actual experiences of Secret Service work, I can assure my readers that nothing has been divulged which touches even the fringe of the important secrets that every Secret Service agent would proudly guard with his life. Those things are sacred and would never be intentionally divulged. On the other hand the records of adventure are not mere efforts at fiction. They are actual experiences, faintly tinted, maybe, in *couleur de rose* to raise bald facts into readable narrative. They are also scenes which are enacted every day on the stage of Life's Theatre, often much nearer to the circle in which the reader moves than he or she may realise, imagine, or dream about. They are given in order the better to excite interest, to exemplify the work which has to be done, and which in the future may still require attention.

Needless to add that a book of this description has not been permitted to go to press without difficulties. Much more has been left unsaid than is said. Much has of necessity been omitted, not only for the sake of the maintenance of the glory of one's own beloved land, but also for the sake of the personal future safety and well-being of others besides oneself.

Some of the readers of the MS., through whose hands it had to pass before publication, have commented upon the political amalgam which has been introduced into the book as not being strictly within the scope of its title. If any apology is due under this head the author can only plead justification by reason of his deep and earnest desire for reform both abroad and at home. In his humble opinion the evils that he exposes or hints at could not have been brought home to his readers had he confined himself entirely to the perhaps more interesting narrative of individual adventure.

So far as the statistics given regarding the blockade leakages are concerned, he feels they are important enough to carry historical interest, and should therefore be collated and put on permanent record. Secret Service agents devoted much time and attention to these details, and our then government was or should have been fully alive to the fact that the so-called blockade was only a ridiculous sham, long before the *Daily Mail* campaign opened. Why our government made no effort to checkmate, stop, or divert these extraordinary supplies going direct into the enemy country, is left to the judgment of my readers.

Twice, between Christmas 1914, and Midsummer 1915, I entered German territory from Denmark and from the sea. After my second visit I was warned that a head-hunter was looking diligently for me in the hope of securing a reward which the Germans had secretly offered. This enterprising individual I sought out, and for a day and a half helped him with another in the hunt for myself, arguing in my own mind that it was my safest occupation at that particular time and in that particular locality. During this short partnership a quarrel ensued regarding the division of the spoils before they were secured, when I learned that the sum at first offered had been 10,000 marks but it had then recently been increased to 25,000. Some compensation remains to me in being able to look back at this attention on the part of the Hun as a compliment of some value to my personal activities.

In the spring of 1916, during our military operations in Belgium, a deep and crafty Alsatian of violent disposition, and of German descent, was captured by our Tommies, and to save his own skin admitted he had been employed in the German Foreign Secret Service since the outbreak of war. Much valuable information was thus obtained; by way of test evidence he stated that *inter alia* he had been ordered to endeavour to hold my trail (I was known to him) during my Baltic wanderings in the late autumn of 1914; and that although he had persisted in various disguises he had been led a terrible dance and had been compelled to abandon the task as hopeless. I was able to corroborate this.

Anyone who has lived a strenuous life of many ups and downs must at times have rubbed shoulders with celebrities. In later years these personal reminiscences invariably provide reflections of more than passing interest.

The author has, from his teens upwards, been swayed with an insatiable lust for travelling in foreign lands. During these peregrinations his experiences have been somewhat unique, his adventures many. An instinctive inquisitiveness has more than once caused his arrest for trespassing in private places of national importance; whilst cosmopolitan habits, imbibed from bohemian associations, may have tended to mould a character adapted for the special work now under consideration.

Owing to a fortunate, or unfortunate, lapse of good manners he was on one occasion—a good many years ago—given ample opportunity to survey at close quarters the *Kaiser*, his empress the *Kaiserin*, little Willie, and the then entire German royal family, from the confines of a guard-room in the grounds of their Imperial *Schloss* at Potsdam. The same year Lord Roberts, with General Wood of the U.S.A. Army, personally escorted him round the most interesting sights of Dresden. The very next day he was arrested in Bohemia for want of a passport.

In 1895 he accompanied Dr. Leyds, then head of the South African Secret Service, when he was on his way to Berlin to interview the *Kaiser* on a mission of most serious menace to Great Britain on behalf of his master Oom Paul Kruger; although the author was unaware at the time of the importance of that mission. Cecil Rhodes he knew as a visitor to his father's house. Dr. Jamieson he has sported with; Dr. Fridjof Nansen is no stranger to him; whilst he crossed the North Sea when the submarine season was in full swing with Ronald Amundsen, that most interesting discoverer of the South Pole. He was within a stone's-throw of Dr. Sun Yat Sen, in the province of Kiang So, when the northern Chinese Army of Yuan Shi Kai surrounded and so nearly captured him during the rebellion of 1918, on the eve of his escape to Japan.

Under the Great Wall of China on the southern limits of the Gobi desert he was within an ace of being captured by the notorious renegade "White Wolf"; whilst part of the band of another equally celebrated bandit, Raisuli, gave him cold shudders down the spine in 1896, despite the scorching heats of the Sahara. He has been an unwilling listener to treason from the lips of one or other of the much-wanted Hardyal or Gardit Singh, who, on the western foothills of the Rocky Mountains prophesied that Germany would declare war in the autumn of 1914; whilst in direct contrast to these unenviable experiences he has been the recipient of hospitality and of sport as the guest of royalty; although the enforced formalities attendant upon such experiences tend to destroy the charm which may be believed to surround the honour.

Variety has been provided by being brought in contact with Nihilists in Russia and Siberia; with anarchists in France and Spain; as a trembling defendant in a stump-head court-martial by backwoodsmen in Western America, where justice is administered with lightning-like rapidity, and fatal mistakes often result through misidentification, as was so nearly the case in his own particularly uncomfortable experience as the unlucky chief actor in a "hold up" on the trail in British Columbia; and more than once he has been lost in the untrodden wilds of vast forests. But these experiences of the ups and downs of life pale and sink into insignificance when compared with the vortex of the rapid, rushing, kaleidoscopic changes, the hair-breadth escapes, the blood-curdling thrills, the risks, the dangers and excitements, which at times are part and parcel of the life of a Secret Service agent.

Secret Service, Intelligence, Reconnaissance, Investigation Strategical or Military Agent—use any name you will—the work of each merely resolves itself for the time being into "the antennæ, or the senses of fighting units;" the seeing, the hearing, the smelling, or the touching of a fleet or an army; of what is before, behind, surrounding, or in its midst. Without its aid few battles could be won and no ultimate victory anticipated.

Military and naval officers endowed with sufficient intelligence, brains, and philological ability are, as a rule, very keen to devote some part of their career to foreign Secret Service. It is believed, with some certitude, to be the surest step to early promotion; to pave the way to future advancement. Amongst those who have risen from such a foundation and who have proved their worth to the British Empire may be mentioned the late Lord Kitchener, who in Egypt, under various disguises, penetrated far into the interior. Colonel Burnaby, Lord Roberts, Sir Richard Burton and hundreds of other distinguished and prominent men may be included in the category; whilst Lt.-General Sir R. Baden-Powell eulogises this branch of the service in a book entitled *My Adventures as a Spy*. He writes:

> It is an undisputable fact that our Secret Service has at all times been recruited from men of unblemished personal honour who would not descend to any act which in their view was tainted with meanness.

No sane, thinking man would condemn Secret Service agents as following a dishonourable calling. If it were so, then it would be equally—if not more—dishonourable to employ, to guide, and to direct them. Yet all commanders of all nations employ them and have done so from time immemorial; and if any nation failed to do so it might as well—as Lord Wolseley said—"*sheath its sword forever.*"

To quote a few well-known names at random, Catinat investigated in the disguise of a coalheaver; Montlue as a cook; Ashby visited the Federal line in the American Civil War as a horse-doctor; whilst General Nathaniel Lyon visited the Confederate camp at St. Louis in disguise before he attacked and captured it. In 1821, George III. granted a pension to the mother of Major André, who, whilst acting as *aide-de-camp* to General Clinton, was condemned as an English Secret Service agent; he further gave a baronetcy to his brother; whilst the remains of the hero were exhumed, brought from America to England, and buried in Westminster Abbey.

The Japanese, one of the proudest nations in the world, whose code of honour is stricter even than our own, accord the highest honours to military or naval intelligence officers, whose bravery and understanding they fully recognise; although they never fail to shoot one whenever and wherever he may be caught acting against them.

It is sometimes puzzling to understand what is the real motive which prompts our military and naval officers to seek so persistently to become enrolled in the Secret Service Department. Is it solely the desire to further their chances of advancement, or is it the bold adventuresome activity of the service, the innate longing to take all risks and to bring back personally the information so essential to the successful conduct of war; or is it the feeling and knowledge that only a brave man is ready to go out alone, unobserved and unapplauded, to risk his life for his country's sake? For let it not be forgotten that to accept an appointment under the Foreign Secret Service in war time is no feather-bed occupation. The smallest slip, the slightest indiscretion, and one's doom is sealed. Only a man to whom life was as nothing if risking it would help his country, would dare to undertake such perilous work.

It is indeed the finest and most thrilling recuperative tonic in the world for anyone weary of life's monotonies. It commands the highest courage, the clearest understanding, the greatest ability and cleverness, never-flagging persistence, and an ever-prevailing optimism. Yet such men and women as these who have striven, laboured, fought alone, and won through against inconceivable difficulties and immense odds, possibly to the permanent ruin of their health or financial status, are, although it seems inconceivable to believe, more often than not overlooked and passed aside by the nation; unobservantly pushed into the cold burial vaults of ungrateful forgetfulness!—the fate, alas! of many an active Secret Service agent, no matter how patriotically loyal, how brave, or how successful he may have been. Such men neither seek nor expect to be bedecked with baubles, or awarded *shekels*, so coveted by those who stay at home. They know the hollowness which quickly fades or is lost in the vortex of political upheaval or changing dynasty. They rest content in the knowledge that they have well and truly served their country, that they have lived in the full realism of existence; whilst they are happy in their memories.

One crowded hour of glorious life
Is worth an age without a name.

Nicholas Everitt.

CHAPTER 1

War and the Introducing of Jim

The year 1914 opened auspiciously. Future prospects looked brilliant. In the past there had been depression owing to political extravagances, but everything pointed to a change in the minds of the people; to an awakening, to future betterment. Money was plentiful and cheap. Labour was an active market with plenty of it. Good business seemed to be in the air. All around there appeared to be a general cheerfulness. Then came the lull before the storm. An ominous calm, a dull, dead, mysterious cloud of invisible, inexplicable, unintelligible danger threatened. No one could penetrate it; no one could fathom what it was; but everyone felt instinctively that something great and terrible was going to happen.

The stock markets sagged and fell away in a most extraordinary fashion, no matter how the bulls or surrounding circumstances supported them. Buyers of properties suddenly stayed their hands. Speculators by natural impulse held aloof. Rumours began to circulate, strange stories passed from mouth to mouth which none believed, but which left an impression of gloom and impending disaster behind them.

The man in the street, the one and only true barometer of England's real feelings, showed an uneasy restlessness which could not be interpreted.

The multitude of German spies, who swarmed like locusts throughout the British Isles, assured themselves that the seditious seeds they had been sowing so energetically during the past years in the receptive and nourishing soil of Radicalism and Socialism, plenteously manured by liberal administrations from the vast financial resources at their disposal, were at last bearing a rich harvest of rare and refreshing fruit. They assured themselves that revolution would devastate Ireland, perhaps part of England, Wales, and Scotland as well. The Unions of the working classes they knew had been nurtured by their fond attentions until they had grown to mighty proportions. Working men of German blood or of strong Teutonic tendencies had agitated amongst the masses again and yet again, for "less time, more pay, and greater and more extended privileges." German Secret Service money had provided the sinews of an underground labour war.

Countless thousands of honest, hard-working British labourers neither knew of, nor recognised, nor even suspected, the traitorous hand which so gently stroked them down the back whilst their ears were being tickled with persuasive suggestions and argumentative reasoning, prompting a greater dissatisfaction the more they were pandered to, and petted, and spoilt, and bribed by the Liberal Government who were the men in power over them. It must not be forgotten that for some years previous to 1914 prominent members of the government of the day had been roundly rated in the Press for encouraging and expressing pro-German sentiments and inclinations; whilst the government itself had been accused of shattering the Constitution of the United Kingdom, of muzzling the House of Lords, of trampling on the rights of Democracy, of humiliating the Crown, and of robbing the Church of England.

Whether there was truth in these accusations the historian will record, but that civil war was a seriously threatened danger there can be no doubt; whilst the proverbial slackness of our phlegmatic British nature is such that Englishmen permitted much to transpire which no other nation in the world would have tolerated. Mr. W. M. Hughes, the Australian Prime Minister, speaking in the London Stock Exchange on March 20th, 1916, more eloquently describes us: "A people slow to anger, unsuspicious of guile in others, foolishly generous in throwing open their land to the world, offering sanctuary to all, even to those who proposed first to exploit and then betray them, before we as a nation awoke to the peril."

It was only too well known to certain members of Scotland Yard, probably others as well, that German Secret Service agents had reported to their respective headquarters, that "the English Radical Government would never dare to intervene in a war waged by Germany." They knew, or rather thought they knew, that England was utterly unprepared for a war of any magnitude; that for years military and naval estimates had been cut down rather than added to, which was substantiated by a collection of innumerable press cuttings showing the violent public agitation in consequence; that the government did not believe a great European war could be possible within the next fifty years; that the United Kingdom was on the verge of revolution over Ulster's dissent from Home Rule; that the Labour Unions had grown so vast, so all-embracing and so powerful that they could and would paralyse the government's action if by any possible chance it did decide on intervening; that Egypt, India, and South Africa were ripe for revolt and only too anxious for an opportunity to shake off British rule; that Australia, New Zealand, and Canada were anxious to declare their respective independence; in fact that the whole British Empire beyond the seas was itching for disintegration, if only "The Day" would dawn giving half a chance of striking a blow for freedom and exemption from control of the hated British yoke; and that the welding together of all these (believed-to-be) irreconcilable nations and peoples in a common battle cause was an unthinkable impossibility.

It was common knowledge to the Secret Service agents of all nations that the Liberal-Radical Government of the United Kingdom of Great Britain and Ireland was tottering to a fall. Its popularity with the masses had waned; its hypocrisy with the middle classes had become a byword; its disloyalty to the Empire with the upper classes had become revolting; its days had become numbered. The German War party saw this and realised the fact better than the English. It knew that it was of vital importance to its world-power dream to make war only when a Liberal, Radical, and Socialist party was in office in England; it would be courting disaster to do so if a Unionist Government were in power.

Yea, verily, the *Kaiser* believed that the harvest of his sowing was ready for the garnering.

All these things were reported in gloating glee by the army of Teutonic spies in our midst to their respective headquarters, thence conveyed to their central office at Berlin with an openness that might have seemed an insult to the intelligence of Scotland Yard and those who direct and control that very effective and efficient department; only our astute police service happened to be much more wide awake than it appeared to be.

The man in power, the one and only being who really knew the truth of what was actually happening over and beyond the horizon of our ken, maintained an impassive silence. His motto throughout was and had been "*Wait and See.*"

The ruler of the waves, the noble and illustrious British bull-dog, Lord Fisher, knew and had known. He had never failed his countrymen. He pushed along all and every preparation for the evil day, which a weak and Peace-at-any-price Government had permitted.

The illustrious martial warrior of previous wars, whose life and loved ones had been sacrificed upon the altar of patriotism and loyalty, knew. He had never failed to lift his voice in warning, both inside and outside Parliament, since he returned from the South African War, imploring support, reformation, and more attention to the army; pleading conscription amongst the youthful masses; working so unselfishly, so energetically and so devotedly, and in feverish anxiety for the protection and welfare of the Motherland and our Empire, right up to the day of his glorious death within sound of the German guns. A fitting dirge for so beloved and valiant a hero.

The man of Foreign Affairs, the man who gained for himself the utmost honour, respect, esteem, and gratitude from all the world, by reason of his unflagging and unceasing efforts to keep and maintain the peace of Europe, he also knew. To the very last hour, yea, even far beyond it, he worked on, hoping against hope that such a terrible calamity as threatened to paralyse the nations of the earth for centuries to come might yet be averted. Noble man, working for a noble cause! History will record your efforts, but no pen can adequately record your meritorious deserts. Oh! the pity of it that you, a true genius in the arts of peace and of peaceful diplomacies, did not retire at the outbreak of war in favour of some more martial, bellicose, and iron-fisted statesman, instead of clinging to office during the awful years that followed, when our enemy not only torpedoed all the laws of nations, but outraged every decent feeling of humanity. Your honourable and gentlemanly nature made it impossible for you to realise, to understand, or to compete with these barbaric and inhuman practices.

The man in opposition, whose duty it is to criticise and restrain the hotheadedness of governmental action, although he is not admitted to share the secrets of the Cabinet, he knew. His instinct told him what was looming behind the electrically charged atmosphere, and he at once showed that he was a true-born Britisher first and foremost before he was a politician.

The man of marvellous organisation abilities, who had been more than once conveniently removed far afield from English politics in order to straighten out our tangled skeins in the East, because such efficient capables as himself, Lord Fisher, Lord Roberts and others did not suit the party system of our modern Democratic Government, also knew. But that man of action without words had to sit and look on, whilst the late friend of the *Kaiser* was kept in office until the unmistakable voice of the people arose in ugly anger to demand the change. Alas, that your precious life should have been sacrificed by treachery which ought to have been checkmated.

The man of mystery, who, although not admitted as a member of the ship of state, clung limpet-like to its bottom and maintained an existence thereon, he knew; perhaps first of all. His knowledge was but a materialisation of reports foreshadowing such an event which had floated to him in *crescendo* numbers. His office was one of semi-independence. He could act with promptness and decision. He did, so far as he was permitted to go.

War was in the air. This seemed to be conceived but not to be real-ised. The very idea was too terrible to be true. A portentous omen had been uttered by a great Silesian nobleman, Count von Oppersdorff, only a few hours before it was publicly known that England would declare war against Germany if the neutrality of Belgium was vio-lated.

He had inquired from Mr. F. W. Wile, an Anglo-American journal-ist in Berlin, if such a contingency could be possible. On being an-swered in the affirmative, he muttered with great seriousness, "There will be many surprises."

The real and concise reason which forced England to join in the war is recorded in the now famous despatch of Sir Edward Goschen, the British Ambassador at Berlin, to Sir Edward Grey, the British Min-ister for Foreign Affairs. It runs as follows:

> August 4, 1914:
>
> I found the chancellor very agitated. His Excellency at once be-gan an harangue which lasted for twenty minutes. He said that the step taken by His Majesty's Government (the ultimatum of war) was terrible to a degree; just for a word—'Neutrality,' a word which in war time had so often been disregarded—just for a *scrap of paper* Great Britain was going to make war on a kindred nation. I said that, in the same way as he and Herr von Jagow (the German Secretary of State) wished me to under-stand that for strategical reasons it was a matter of life and death to Germany to advance through Belgium and violate the lat-ter's neutrality, so I would wish him to understand that it was,

so to speak, a matter of 'life and death' for the honour of Great Britain that she should keep her solemn engagement to do her utmost to defend Belgium's neutrality if attacked.

It was on the 5th of August, 1914, that the British nation was called to arms. It awoke, suddenly, startled as from some horrible nightmare. It was shaken and stirred in a manner unprecedented in its history from the day it had thrown off allegiance to Rome. Without hesitation or delay every patriotic Britisher having no binding ties to hold him, in company with many tens of thousands who had, rushed to seek out recruiting officers or sergeants in order that their services might be proffered in the service of their country. So great and clamorous were the crowds in the big cities that the police had much ado to preserve and maintain order.

The government was not prepared for anything like it. It had made no provision in equipment or supplies to cope with the stream of men so eager to join the colours. Long before arrangements could be made to enrol the first batches of recruits, men from all parts of our empire beyond the seas began to arrive in the Mother Country, all keen, enthusiastic and eager for the fray.

The authorities had their hands more than full and were compelled to refuse thousands, including in some instances, it is said, fully equipped companies of Colonial recruits. Yet posters and stimulating advertisements, appealing for volunteers, continued to be spread broadcast throughout the land, and, as the men rolled up in increasing numbers, confusion became worse confounded. Many went to France in order to join up there; others returned to their homes disgusted and sick at heart by the manner in which they had been treated.

Was the government to blame for this? It had expressed blind faith in Germany and the peaceful sentiments she was alleged to have expressed. Had not Lord Haldane hobnobbed with the *Kaiser*, and had he not related to Parliament what a good fellow the German Emperor really was, and how friendly he meant to be to England? Labour members of Parliament had been to Germany, where they also had been hoodwinked and deceived. Had not the Cabinet argued so strenuously that a European war was unthinkable and impossible for the next century at least, until it seemed to believe it was actually true? *Hence no preparations for such a disastrous calamity had been anticipated, thought out, or provided for.*

"The Day" had dawned.

War with Germany had been declared. Every Britisher, worthy of the name, was individually asking himself, in his heart of hearts or in public, how he best could be of service to his country, to the Empire, and to his king.

In the days to come, when children and children's children will seek by interrogation enlightenment from their forebears as to the part or parts they respectively took in the greatest war the world has ever known, what terrible shame and misgivings will assail the craven, palsied soul of the shirker!

To England's everlasting glory such have been very, very few, and very far between.

★★★★★★

I apologise for the necessity of having to introduce myself, because, as the author, I must also figure prominently in these pages. I am a Bohemian by nature, a Sportsman by instinct, and a Lawyer by training.

Hail, fellow, well met! I believe in the old Scotch proverb, "*Better a fremit freend than a freend fremit.*"

Acquaintances and correspondents I have endeavoured to cultivate in every country I have been in, whilst as a traveller, an author, and a sportsman I believe I am widely known.

At the same time I must confess to being a man of moods, and like most other light-hearted, happy-go-lucky individuals, who seem to be bubbling over with an exuberance of animal spirits, there are times when depression holds down my soul in a hell of its own making. That I never understood myself may explain why so few really ever properly understand me. I am said to be resourceful, ingenious, and so optimistic that I extricate myself from difficulties under which many other people might have capitulated as too overwhelmingly crushing to attempt to resist. My great trouble has been that my restless, rolling-stone disposition makes it intensely distasteful and difficult for me to anchor down for any length of time in any one particular place.

Ever and *anon* there comes to me a call from the wild, a mysterious and irresistible whisper which a true son of nature cannot hope to fight against; an imperative summons from the vastnesses of unknown seas, from deep and pathless forests, from the virgin snows of mountain peaks. Wanderlust has saturated my system, yea, to the very marrow in my bones. It has lured me on, and in obedience to periodical promptings I have travelled the world around and experienced adventure, sport, and fighting in many a foreign land.

Early in 1913-14 I volunteered in the threatened Irish upheavals, with countless thousands of others of my countrymen who felt so strongly the injustice of that matter. When a better and more meritorious chance of "scrapping" presented itself, I was one of the first to offer my services, which were promptly declined, solely because I was over the age limit. Not satisfied with one effort, I made others in various quarters and in various capacities, but all in vain.

It was no consolation to learn later that someone else, an expert engineer, had travelled 7,000 miles, from Hyderabad in India,[1] to help in munition-making, only to be refused a job on arrival in this country; nor that a Tasmanian,[2] with seventeen years' service in the Department of Agriculture in Tasmania, carrying the highest credentials and having obtained six months' leave in order to travel 13,000 miles to the Mother Country to volunteer his gratuitous expert services to our Board of Agriculture, had likewise butted his head against vain hopes of helping to forward encouragement of more home-growing food for the nation.

In the early stages there was a vast army of rejected would-be helpers turned down ignominiously and left to kick their heels in fretful idleness. What a wicked waste of time and good material!

I begin to believe that my American associations have made me a bit of a hustler. Anyway, I approached the celebrated Shikar of many trails, the famed big game hunter, the late Mr. F. C. Selous.[3] I wrote to him suggesting that a corps of Big Game Hunters should be mustered, to consist only of men who had had at least three years' experience of that exciting and dangerous sport; that each man should provide and personally pay for the whole of his individual equipment, including horse, rifle, uniform, and appendages; that Mr. Selous should take command and then offer the services of the corps to the War Office.

Mr. Selous grasped the idea and agreed that a body of quite 500 could probably be raised. He communicated his willingness to take the whole work of raising the troop, but the War Office was neither encouraging to the proposal, nor willing to accept the services of such a body of men when ready to serve. Sorrowful was the tone of the letter from Mr. Selous conveying this news to me, its very much disappointed recipient. He added in the P.S. that he had a friend in command of an infantry regiment who expected soon to be ordered

---

1. *John Bull,* January 29th, 1916.
2. *Ibid.,* February 12th, 1916.
3. This gentleman subsequently died a glorious death in the service of his country. He was shot when on active service in South Africa.

to France, and he had extracted a promise from him to take him along in some capacity or another, in spite of the fact that he was over sixty years of age; and he advised me to look out for a similar loophole through which I might hope to crawl into the catacombs of Yprès and the Meuse, with or without the knowledge or sanction of the Red Tape artists at Whitehall.

About this period many amateur spy hunters were actively on the war-path, and it was suggested to me by friends of high standing in the sporting world that my connection with Northern Europe and my varied experience at home and abroad might be acceptable to the Secret Service; furthermore it was pretty plainly hinted to me that if I wrote a personal letter to Sir Edward Grey it would not be ignored.

Not a moment was allowed to elapse after this. On October 16th, 1914, I wrote, setting out my believed qualifications in concise terms, adding that my age had unfortunately precluded my eagerly proffered services from acceptance in other spheres; that I was keen and eager to be of service to my country; and that I was eating my heart out through inactivity. If there was a chance of my being any use, I prayed that my services might be commanded.

I had been cautioned with impressive seriousness that if my services were accepted it might be only for enrolment in the "Forlorn Hope Brigade" and that my chances of survival might be very remote indeed.

Rather than damping my ardour, this warning merely added fuel to the flames of my desires. In early life I had been most bitterly disappointed. A somewhat sensitive nature had received a shock from which it never properly recovered. With the fatuity of early youth I had placed a whole family upon an idealistic pedestal—including a mere child of thirteen years of age. When that theoristic fabric fell, shattered to a million invisible fragments, at my feet, I could not understand, but I felt for years afterwards that life for me held nothing of worth.

Time heals wounds, and I survived in bodily health. In 1912 I lost a man's best friend on earth—my mother. At Christmas, 1913, my father, my dearest pal, followed her to the grave. I was unmarried. My brother and my sisters had homes of their own, far away. What mattered it to anyone, least of all to myself, if I crossed the Great Divide before my allotted time? I was at best a mere worthless atom of humanity dependent upon no one, with no one dependent upon me.

Here at least was a chance of doing something worth the while.

'Twas a far, far better thing to do than I had ever done.

Yea, indeed. I was ready, and willing, and eager, for the service, whatsoever that service might be, and withersoever it might take me, even to the jaws of death itself.

Having regard to all the circumstances, I do not believe I shall be accused of presumptuousness or of egotism if I say that I fully believed myself to be a fit and qualified person for the service for which I then had volunteered.

On October 17th, 1914, I received a letter from the Under Permanent Secretary of State for Foreign Affairs (Sir Arthur Nicholson— now Lord Carnock), acknowledging my letter of the previous day's date and saying Sir Edward Grey appreciated my offer, although he regretted there were no such appointments at the disposal of his department; but he added that my name had been noted in case my services might be utilised in any capacity at some further date.

On October 19th, I received a letter on War Office paper referring to my letter to Sir Edward Grey of the 16th, saying:

> I should be very glad if you would arrange to come and see me here one morning. If you will let me know when I may expect you I shall arrange to be free.

This letter was signed "P. W. Kenny, Captain"[4] and on its left-hand top corner specified a certain room number. I subsequently ascertained that this gentleman (and a real gentleman in every sense of that embracive word I found him) was the "Acting Buffer" between the Secret Service departments for both the War Office and the Admiralty to anyone who might attempt to approach either of these departments. It will be remembered that his name figured in the public Press as acting in that capacity when Admiral W. R. Hall, C.B., brilliantly defeated and frustrated the clever schemes so carefully yet vainly laid by the then notorious ex.-M.P. Trebitsch Lincoln, whose apparent intention and purpose was to work the double cross against the British Empire

I promptly answered this communication by a special journey to London, of which I gave due notice as requested.

After passing the Police Guards at the entrance to the War Office, I traversed a long corridor to the inquiry room, where a number of

---

4. The author would not have felt at liberty to mention this gentleman by name except for the fact that his connection with the Secret Service was made public in the Press on the Trebitsch Lincoln affair.

attendants were busily engaged issuing forms to be filled up by applicants for interviews. Of course it was impossible to escape the inevitable form, on which I inserted the name of Captain P. W. Kenny, his room number, my name, address, and the nature of my business—private and confidential. It was a bit of a staggerer to hear from the attendant that he did not know Captain Kenny, nor of him, nor did he believe there was any officer of that name in the building. Inquiries, however, from others of his class elicited the information that someone had heard a name somewhat like it and if I went up to the floor on which the room was numbered as before-mentioned, and applied to the porter or commissionaire at the lodge up there, he might be able to locate him for me.

After a wait of some minutes in an ante-room where were collecting a large number of officers and others on errands of various natures, I was sent away in charge of a boy-scout, with about ten other form-fillers, whom he dropped at various floor lodges on the way. The system was for each boy-scout to conduct a whole bunch of followers, who carried their forms in their hands until the desired floors were reached, when the boy-scout guide handed one or more of his followers to the commissionaire in charge of the lodge on each floor sought, who in turn sent them off again in charge of another attendant to the desired room.

I was the last one to depart from our diminutive guide. But when I got to the lodge on the floor on which the room I was seeking was numbered, the commissionaire in charge said he knew nothing of the officer named on my form. After arguing the matter discreetly with him I persuaded him to take me to the room specified on my form, which we found unoccupied, although there were a table and chairs there, as I saw them through the half-open door.

As the *bona fides* of my quest seemed to be doubted I produced the letter I had received, when he politely escorted me to two other lodges on the other floors; but only one of the men in charge could help me at all, and in that he was very vague. He believed there had been an officer, whose name he did not know, using the room so numbered or another room a day or so ago, and he was not certain which it was; he had since changed his room, but where he could not say. Anyway, as he expressed himself, he was a mysterious kind of person, and what he did, or what functions he performed, no one seemed to know. I must confess I was at a loss to understand the position.

Suddenly, however, the thought struck me that it might be a possible stunt to test one's capabilities for a research or investigation; so I listened with interest to the conversations of the various commissionaires and gleaned that the gentleman I sought, if such an individual had any business in the War Office at all, was tall, thin, and aristocratic. The one man who described him thought he knew whom I meant—"A horficer as spent his time a-dodging back'ards and forrards betwixt the War Hoffice and the Hadmiralty, who never said nothink to nobody, so one didn't know which he did belong to; one who 'ardly ever was in 'is room and one who 'ad some queer blokes come to see 'im."

I thanked the commissionaires politely and said I would try another floor on my own account, as once inside the building with a form in one's hand it seemed one could wander anywhere at will and without question.

Accordingly I at once made up my mind what to do. I went to the floor below, to the lodge there, and I asked for Lord Kitchener. There was no hesitation in answering that inquiry; within a few minutes I had reached the desired portion of the building, where I asked to see His Lordship's principal secretary. I have forgotten his name, but I was not kept waiting for a moment. I was accorded an opportunity to explain my mission. I showed him the letter I had summoning me to the War Office, and told him the difficulties I had met with in attempting to locate the elusive "Go-Between." This officer received me very graciously; he smiled at the short description I gave him of my wanderings, and said: "I think I can put you on the right track straight away; please follow me," and getting up he took me to another room at the far end of the corridor we were then in, where we interviewed another officer who also laughed and told us that Captain Kenny had just changed his room and would now be found in room number —— which was on the floor above. Having thanked these officers for their kindly services I ascended once more, and within ten minutes from abandoning my false scent I ran my quarry to earth and was tapping on his oak.

I explained the difficulty I had been placed in to Captain Kenny, who expressed some surprise. Whether he really felt it or not I do not know, but when I showed him the room number given at the top of his letter he admitted the recent change and made apologetic amends for the inadvertence, adding that the attendants in charge of the inquiry bureau below should certainly have known both his name and room number.

Quien sabe, thought I to myself. Anyway, I held my peace and we proceeded to business.

For about an hour Captain Kenny questioned me regarding my knowledge of Northern latitudes, their peoples and my linguistic capabilities. Then he suggested in the most charming and persuasive manner that I should remain awhile in London, like Wilkins Micawber of old, "in the hope of something turning up."

I did so. During this period I called at the War Office at various appointed times and on each occasion was put to further interrogation. Captain Kenny rather reminded me of Dr. Leyds. He seemed to possess that same pleasing persuasiveness which made one feel that one was under deep obligation to him personally for being permitted to relieve him of the smallest matter in hand—indeed, a valuable asset to the person possessing such skill. Within a week of my advent in London a letter came to me from Captain Kenny in which he wrote: "For the moment there are no vacancies in the Intelligence Service, but if you will exercise a little patience I really believe I shall be able to do something for you. I shall see that your name and special qualifications are kept well in view and I trust that we shall be able to make use of your exceptional abilities."

This was followed about the day after by another short note from his private address, asking me to call at the war office next day, adding: "The delay arose through a temporary interruption of certain foreign communications, but he was almost sure he would be able to do something."

I lost no time in answering this letter in person and within half an hour I was fixed for the Foreign Secret Service under the Admiralty in the north of Europe. My remuneration, I was informed, would be rated on the scale appertaining to a naval captain in full commission; in addition to which I should be allowed £1 per day to cover my personal expenses, with a further allowance up to £1 per day to cover travelling expenses; but if I exceeded this amount I must bear the extra payments myself. I was delighted beyond measure: I would gladly have accepted any offer, on almost any terms, I was so keen to "do my bit" to help my country in whatever capacity I could be thought of any use. I subsequently found, however, that these allowances by no means covered one's travelling expenses abroad at that time, which daily mounted higher and higher until they assumed alarming dimensions. True it is, there were times, when one was obscuring oneself from too observant and inquiring persons, that one's expenses could be kept well below these amounts, but at other times, when speed in travelling was of vital importance, expenditure had to be a secondary consideration, and the average daily balances vanished beyond recognition.

At this, last but one, interview with Captain Kenny he produced a large map of Northern Germany and the Baltic. Pointing with his finger to various parts of it he kept asking me whether I could and would go to the places indicated, which included the outskirts of Kiel harbour.

So in order to free his mind from any doubts he may have had as to my venturesomeness, I clinched matters by saying "If you assure me it will in any way benefit my country, I am ready and prepared to go to Hell itself. So why waste breath on these pleasure resorts?"

"Ah!" replied this most exceedingly polite interviewer. "That, my dear sir, is the very answer I have been told, by a certain sporting nobleman who recommended you, I should receive if I pressed you on this. From what he said, and from what I have ascertained about you, I can quite believe it. How long do you require to put your affairs in order?"

"I am ready to start at once," was the reply. I had come to London prepared for such an emergency.

"Good! On Monday at 11 a.m. call upon me again. I shall give you a sealed despatch to deliver at a time and place to be named, and enough money to enable you to reach a certain town. There you will meet a certain gentleman who will give you further instructions. You can now apply for a passport, and I wish you every luck."

"Excuse me, sir. But you do not give me any idea of what my duties will consist—to whom I am to report, or how? I really don't quite follow you; unless, of course, the despatch contains more enlightenment."

"Naturally the despatch will give full instructions to the gentleman you are to meet. He will seek you under the name of Mr. Jim. You will reply by mentioning two other names or words which you must now commit to memory, but not to paper. So far as your duties are concerned, *you have the fullest discretion; remember to use discretion.* You will work entirely on your own initiative. Henceforth you will be known to the service as 'Jim.' And in saying goodbye, I may as well add, if you have not already done so, it might be advisable to seriously consider such testamentary dispositions as you are minded to complete."

CHAPTER 2

Secret Service Organisations, Comparisons, and Incidentals

In earlier times, British Intelligence Agents were attached to the Chancelleries of our Ministers abroad, as is the case today with nearly every nation, except our own. Remuneration was given commensurate with the risks and service. But from the 'sixties the pay diminished and the department faded away from being an asset of much general valuable utility.

The present British Secret Service Department was founded about 1910 by an officer, a man of untiring energy, pluck, and perseverance, who has rendered noble service and willing sacrifice. Since its initiation this department seems to have been harassed, attacked, and shot at by petty jealousies, which, during the agony of the crisis of war were ignoble and contemptible in the extreme. An observer behind the scenes can therefore admire the more the men who ignored this and worked on, unheeding all, with but a single thought, and that the welfare of their king and country.

England never seems to have had any real organisation for Secret Service propaganda which can compare in thoroughness with the German effort. It has had no schools of instruction, nor does it send its members to specialise in any particular branch. It is an unwritten rule of the department that a naval or a military officer must be at the head of every branch or sub-division of any importance; and the service of civilians or of those from other professions than the navy and the army is neither sought nor welcomed, however capable or however clever the persons available may be. The exceptional civilian is soon made to feel this. Whether the idea is to instil discipline, or to impress upon the newcomer the superiority and importance of the right to wear a uniform, it is difficult to imagine.

The main work of the department, however, is on a par with the collection of evidence, the unravelling of secret mysteries, and the study and handling of character—which any man of the world would have probably at once concluded was more fitted to the controlling influence of experienced Criminal and Commercial Investigators rather than to long-service officers who have been strapped to their stool by strict disciplinary red-tapeism from their teens upwards. Admitted that officers must be at the top of the service to direct the information required, and to deal with it when obtained, nevertheless for the direction and control of ways and means of its attainment, the financial part, both inside and out, the selection of the executive staff, the tabulation of facts collected, and correspondence, a member of the government of some standing and with experience of this class of work should be commissioned as Special Minister in full control of the department; because its importance to the State cannot be overstated or exaggerated.

Not only should this department have, as near its chief as possible, a man who has had an extensive experience of active criminal and commercial affairs, but he should also, if possible, be one who has specially qualified himself in the commercial world as a *thoroughly efficient business man.*

It may perhaps be added that it is by no means the only government department which has suffered acutely for want of an efficient business man on its directorate.

So far as office work is concerned, a service officer may understand book routine and discipline, but when it comes to rock-bottom business this war has produced overwhelming proof that a service officer is lost against an efficient business man. Speaking broadly, the former has no idea of the general value of things, or of the worldly side of the business world. How can it be expected of him? He is trained, specially trained, in his profession, which has naught to do with the struggle of the money-makers. He is not accustomed to rub shoulders with the man in the street, whilst there are thousands of minor details which he would probably ignore when brought to his notice, but which a business man would recognise as floating thistledown showing the direction of the wind.

The business man knows that a knowledge of his fellowman is the most valuable knowledge in the world. He is not saddled with fastidious, obsolete forms of etiquette, the waiting for the due observance

36

of which has cost millions of pounds sterling and thousands of much more valuable lives. He is not tied down to the cut-and-dried book routine, probably unrevised for years, which it is an impossibility to keep thoroughly up-to-date.

He is not afraid of the wrath of his immediate superior officers, which, unless being an officer himself he could modify or smooth it over, might put on the shelf for ever all chance of his future success in life. He is not shackled with incompetents whom he dared not report or remove because they hold indirect influences which might be moved to his disadvantage. He is not hampered by the importunities of brother-officers who are pushed at him continually by place-seekers, or by feared or favoured ones. He is not handicapped by the jealous spite of machination of other departments, because an efficient business man will have none of this from anyone, whether above or below him. Should it arise, he eradicates it root and branch at first sight, which an ordinary service officer is generally utterly powerless to do; nor dare he dream of its accomplishment.

It is the existence of this terrible canker-worm of jealousy, false pride, petty spite, or absurd etiquette, which in the past has gnawed into the very vitals of our glorious services, sapping away much of their efficiency and undermining future unity, which always tends to turn victories into defeats or colossal disasters. It is devoutly to be hoped that this world-war will level up the masses and kill and forever crush out of our midst this hydra-headed microbe, the greatest danger of which is that on the surface it is invisible.

Members of the Secret Service knew all along that the War Office and the Admiralty were like oil and water, because they would not or could not mix.[1] If one required anything of importance from the War Office it might have blighted the hopes of success to have blurted out that one came from, or was a member of, the Admiralty, and *vice versâ*. These two mighty departments never seemed to work in harmonious unity. Hence, whenever Jim had business at the War Office he advisedly concealed that he had any interest in the Admiralty; and when-

---

1. "So far from co-operating, the army and the navy were rival purchasers of aircraft."—Mr. Ellis Griffith, House of Commons, February 16th, 1916. See also Air Defence Debate in House of Commons, March 22nd, 1916. At Hull, which was under military control, it was rumoured that a certain naval officer, in command of a small warship lying in the Humber at the time of one of the first of the Zeppelin raids, was court-martialled because he fired at and hit one of the Zeppelins whilst it was bombarding the town, without having first received an order from the military permitting him to do so. *Annals of Red-tapeism*, June, 1915.

ever he was at the Admiralty he denied all connection with the War Office. It saved so much friction and avoided so much unnecessary formality, trouble, and delay.

That this friction was bad for the country, detrimental to the shortening of the war, and most expensive to the taxpayer, goes without saying; but perhaps the fault lay with our system, which permits so many men over sixty years of age to remain in, or to be suddenly placed into positions of such terrible responsibility and such colossal and continual accumulation of work; men who hitherto had had a slack time and who perhaps had hardly ever been contradicted or denied in their lives; men who constantly demonstrated to those around them that their dignity and self-importance must be admitted and put before almost every other consideration; men who ought to have taken honorary positions and not for a single hour kept from the chair of office more efficient and younger officers; men who knew only the old routine, who were long past their prime, and who were consistent upholders of the greatest curse that ever cursed our island Kingdom— the red-tapeism of the Circumlocution Office.

Volumes could be filled with examples of the pernicious results arising because this country has not adopted modern and up-to-date methods. Volumes could be written to prove the reckless waste and extravagance that has been allowed to run wild and caused by our not providing for a department having a Minister of Conservation and Economy. Volumes could be written to prove that if jealousies could be stamped out, false dignity crushed, and red-tapeism abolished, our nation would rise far above the heads of all other nations in the world, and our taxpayers' burdens, both now and in the future, would be materially reduced.

Although thousands of examples could be given it is submitted that for a book of this description an example from two or three departments should be sufficient to illustrate the argument.

From the Admiralty

Sometime in the autumn of 1915, two fields were acquired by the Admiralty at Bacton, on the Norfolk coast, for use as an aviation ground. In order to give a sufficiently large unbroken and even surface for aeroplanes, it was deemed necessary to level a hedge-bank of considerable length, dividing the fields in question.

Within a few miles of these fields were stationed a thousand soldiers, who were chafing at and weary with the monotony of their daily routine, an unvaried one for over a year. The majority of these men would have welcomed the acceptance of such a task as this. But follow the events which happened, and it is proved convincingly that some silly, ridiculous reason prevented any approach, by those who sit in chairs at the Admiralty to those who sit in chairs at the War Office, to utilise this unemployed labour, or to save the nation's pocket in so simple a matter.

The expenditure of money seemed to be of no consideration whatsoever, although the House of Commons was at this particular period shrieking for economy in others, which they were quite unwilling to commence themselves; whilst the Prime Minister (Mr. Asquith) addressed a great economy speech to the massed delegates representing 4,000,000 organised workers at Westminster on December 1st, 1915. So a contract was offered and entered into with a civilian to do the work. Owing to Lord Derby's scare-scheme system of recruiting instead of National Service (which ought to have been enforced immediately after the Boer War, as pressed by Lord Roberts and others), the unlucky contractor lost most of his young men and was quite unable to get more than a very few old men who were past the age of strenuous labour. His job progressed so slowly that the Admiralty realised the work might not be finished for months and months to come if permitted to continue on the then present line.

What was it that prevented the Admiralty, on this second occasion of necessity, from approaching the War Office, or even one of the officers in command of the thousands and thousands of troops stationed in Norfolk, a few of whom could and would gladly have completed the work in a few hours without a penny extra expense to the country?

Instead of incurring any possible suspicion of an obligation from the War Office, an appeal was made to the newly-formed City of Norwich Volunteers for their men to put down their names for this work. That loyal, energetic, and patriotic body of Englishmen, which was drawn from all ranks of society, although working at their various vocations all the week, immediately acquiesced, without stopping to reason why, and agreed to go to Bacton the next ensuing Sunday.

The distance from Norwich to Bacton is twenty miles, but the nearest station is about three miles from the fields in question.

By reason of the War Office having taken over control of the railways, these men could, by a simple request from the Admiralty to the War Office, have been provided with free travelling passes. They had expressed their willingness to walk the remaining three miles of the journey, do the work gratuitously (although quite unaccustomed to any such rough manual labour), find their own rations, and walk the return three miles to the station afterwards. Such, however, was not acceptable, nor permitted.

At North Walsham, five miles from the aerodrome site, at least a thousand troops were stationed. They were provided with motor vehicles capable of travelling thirty miles per hour. A few of these vehicles could have carried the whole party from North Walsham station to the fields in under half an hour; or they could have fetched them from Norwich in about an hour. But no; such an arrangement might incur the obligation of a request and a compliance.

So the Admiralty arranged to send some of their own motor lorries from Portsmouth to Norwich in order to convey this small party of civilian volunteer-workers twenty-one miles to the job.

It was said that five lorries were ordered, but only three were sent. They were of the large size, extra heavy type, which cannot, with general convenience, travel at a speed beyond ten miles an hour—if so fast; whilst their petrol consumption might be estimated at about a gallon per hour. They arrived at Norwich on Sunday morning November 28th, 1915, apparently after several days on the road. They took part of the small party of enthusiasts to Bacton, who worked all through the Sabbath; whilst other Admiralty motorcars were ordered specially over from Newmarket which took the remainder of the party to and from the job.

The three lorries avoided London, thus the full journey of each must have approximated 500 miles.

Consider: the running expenses of a private two-ton motor-car would not be less than a shilling a mile; compare the petrol, oil consumption, and wear and tear. It is thus not difficult to estimate this absurdly unnecessary and recklessly extravagant waste of the taxpayers' money; and all because of some ridiculous personal prejudices, or of the sacred cause of red-tapeism; or the possible touching of some false sentiments of dignity or hollow pride, assumed by those who sit on chairs on one side or the other of Whitehall, and who direct the details of war expenditure.

FROM THE WAR OFFICE.

Every Englishman must deeply regret the memory of countless examples of reckless waste, incompetent management, and riotous extravagance which particularly marked the first two years of the war; and which, alas, appeared much more flagrantly in connection with the army than with the navy.

During the progress of the war groans arose in this strain from every county. The Yorkshire £10 to £15 tent-pegs case, as recorded in the Press, December 18th, 1915, was never denied.

A motor trolley accidentally smashed about half a score of tent-pegs at —— camp. Instead of replacing them at the cost of half a crown or less, the C.O. ruled that a report must be drawn up and submitted to the War Office requesting a new supply of pegs. In due course the answer arrived saying: "Loose pegs could not be sent, as they were only supplied with new tents, but a new tent would be sent, value £150, *with the usual quantity of pegs*." Which course in all seriousness was actually adopted.

★★★★★★

In June, 1916, a chimney at a Drill Hall in the town of Lowestoft on the east coast required sweeping, and an orderly suggested to the commanding officer that he should employ a local man residing a few doors away, who offered to undertake the job efficiently at the modest outlay of 1s. But the commanding officer was shackled body and soul in red-tape bonds. Following his duty he reported the matter to headquarters. Further particulars were required and given and in the course of a few days the army chimney-sweep arrived, did the work and departed. *He came from and returned to Birmingham*, and stated that his contract price was 10d. The third-class return fare from Birmingham is 26s. 7d. It probably meant two days occupied at an expense which could not have been much less than 30s. A total of £2 16s. 7d., plus payment, postages, paper and possible extras, to *save 2d*. and to do a local man out of a 1s. job in a town admittedly ruined by the unfortunate exigencies of the war!

FROM THE HOME OFFICE.

The Leicester correspondent of the *Shoe and Leather Record*, wrote on February 25th, 1916:

> The government have intimated, through the medium of the usual official document, that they are willing to receive tenders for twenty-four emery pads, the total value of which would be one shilling and four pence. The tender forms are marked 'very urgent' and firms tendering are warned that inability of the railway companies to carry the goods will not relieve contractors

of responsibility for non-delivery.

The goods are presumably intended for the Army boot-repairing depôts, but in view of the admitted 'urgency' it will, I think, strike most business men as strange that there is not an official connected with this branch of the service possessing sufficient authority to give the office boy sixteen pence with instructions to go and fetch the goods from the nearest grindery shop.

Up to the time of writing I have not heard which local firm has been fortunate enough to secure this 'contract.'

★★★★★★

After this gigantic tussle of titanic races is over and the bill of costs has to be met, perhaps the nation will realise the cry, that for some years past has been lost like a voice crying in the wilderness—*We want business men*: business men in all government departments which have to handle business matters. England's colossal financial liabilities, pyramided up during recent years, are practically all traceable to her lack of efficient business men in her business departments.

In the navy, in the army, in the transport, in the supplies, and throughout, let the head of each department be chosen from a member of its body, if believed best so to do; but let the business side thereof be presided over by an efficient and fully-qualified business man—a man who knows the purchasing power of a pound; more important still, who knows how hard it is to earn one. The men entrusted with such responsible positions should have full responsibility placed upon their shoulders; they should be highly paid and they should be free to act without being tied down by the fetters of "the book," by red-tape precedents, and by the counter-consents of so many others who in nine cases out of ten are men of no previous business training nor qualification concerning the majority of details which they are called upon to handle.

Recent army and naval administration, as the public have seen, requires little further comment here. The hundreds of thousands of pounds absolutely squandered in surplus rations, billeting, pay, and transport, etc., should have impressed the minds of observers in a manner that this generation is never likely to forget. A business man in each department, with a free hand to economise and arrange its details, in a business-like way, would have saved the country the salaries paid to them ten thousand times over, with a gigantic surplus to spare.

The British Intelligence Department probably suffered least of any in this respect. Its actual managing chief never wasted a shilling where he could personally see a way of saving it. To my knowledge he never overpaid anyone whilst he was not at all adverse to using the persuasive argument of patriotism, in order to get a mass of useful work done for nothing at all. To quote an instance. It was the case of a man who, at his country's call, had sacrificed an income of considerably over £1,000 *per annum*, together with all his home and business interests, and who in the chief's absence had accepted a thankless and a dangerous task on the active foreign executive at a remuneration less than he had been paying a confidential clerk.

The chief on his return to office did not hesitate to ask him to waive altogether his remuneration, and to pay out of his own pocket twenty-five *per cent.* of his personal travelling expenses in addition! Loyally he agreed, and for months he thus served, although those in authority above him showed no sign of appreciation or gratitude afterwards for the sacrifice.

If other government departments were half as careful over their expenditure as the Secret Service, the British public would not have much cause to find fault nor even to grumble. But what hampered its efficiency, and was neither fair, nor politic, nor economic, was the policy of the Foreign Office, which permitted others, in no way whatsoever connected with the Service, or with the Intelligence, to interfere (during 1914 and 1915) with its work and with members of its executive both at home and abroad. This was not the worst of it. Not only was the organisation of a whole and important branch of the department on two occasions brought to a complete standstill, owing to the interference of one vainly conceited incompetent who had collected a string of high-sounding qualifications behind his name, but he caused money to be scattered in thousands where hundreds, and probably tens, or a little judicious entertaining, would have been more than sufficient. If these monies were debited to the Secret Service Department, such a wrong ought to be righted.

In due course the colossal indiscretions of this interfering bungler involved matters in such a dangerous tangle that he apparently lost his head, and for a period of time was quite inaccessible for business. On recovery he coolly announced that he should wash his hands entirely of all Secret Service affairs. Imagine the feelings of the patient chiefs of the Foreign Secret Service Department. They had silently sat for months watching the efforts of their captured staff hampered at every turn whilst they were persistently building up a sound, practical, useful organisation, which a fool and his folly overturned, like a house of cards, in one day. They had been actually stopped from controlling the movements of their own men, yet they were responsible for their pay and their expenses; whilst possibly they had had a heavy load of extravagant outside expenditure heaped upon their department without any equivalent advantage. They had been compelled to endure this indignity, because, as service officers, they dared not, for the sake of their then present position and possibly their future, openly remonstrate or criticise, or even report the bare facts concerning the all-too-palpable incompetence of this somewhat powerful gentleman who had insisted on poking his officious and inefficacious nose into a department which did not concern him, and the existence of which it was his loyal duty to ignore.

Without a word of complaint (except to members of his executive, to whom his language was as emphatic as it was sultry), our good old managing chief set to work afresh. Within a couple of months he had straightened out the line, when, to the astonishment of all concerned, the old enemy appeared once more upon the scene. Moved either by jealousy, or by vindictive spite at the success which followed where he had failed, he again attacked the department by hitting at individual members of its actively working executive! Remember, England was at war at the time; thus a more unpatriotic action could hardly have been conceived. Yet the Foreign Office, although impressively advised of the wrong-doing and the probable consequences, either dared not or would not trouble itself to investigate the details of the matter.

Yes, verily, my friends, *suppressio veri* has much to answer for. It is well for some of those who sit in high offices that a rigid censorship and secrecy was maintained throughout the war; or the very walls of England might have arisen in fierce mutiny.

Mr. Le Queux touches the point in his book on *German Spies in England*:

> We want no more attempts to gag the Press, no evasive speeches in the House, no more pandering to the foreign financier, or bestowing upon him Birthday Honours: no more kid-gloved legislation for our monied enemies whose sons, in some cases, are fighting against us, but sturdy, honest, and deliberate action—the action with the iron hand of justice in the interests of our own beloved Empire.

Whilst Burnod—*Maxims de Guerre de Napoléon*—quotes:

It is the persons who would deceive the people and exploit them for their own profit that are keeping them in ignorance.

Napoleon's greatness was achieved by employing only the best men obtainable for positions of the highest responsibility. His most important officer in the Secret Service Department seems to have been a German, by name Karl Schulmiester, who drew the princely salary of £20,000 *per annum*. Proved efficiency was the little Corsican's only passport.

Germany has learnt well from this lesson. Soldiers, sailors, and business men waged her war. Not a lawyer or professional politician took part in it except in the trenches. Germany entrusted the administration of her affairs to experts. Blue blood, patronage, and reputation carried neither weight nor meaning. It was ruthless, but it was business—it was war. The magic of a great military name did not save Lieutenant-General Helmuth von Moltke from dismissal from the Head of the German staff when the *Kaiser* was convinced of his inefficiency. Vice-Admiral von Engenohl, Commander-in-Chief of the High Canal Fleet, had to retire in favour of Admiral von Pohl owing to failures; whilst the septuagenarian father of bureaucrats, Dr. Kuhn, had to vacate finance in order to make way for the professional banker, Dr. Helfferich, who although quite unknown to distinction was appointed Chancellor of the Imperial Exchequer.

From the very commencement, Germany appointed experts over each department of her colossal war machine—*expert business men*. Every solitary industry which has aught to do with war-making was linked up with the government. By way of example there was a Cotton Council, a Coal Advisory Board, a Motor and Rubber Committee, a Chemical Committee, etc., etc.

That able journalist, Mr. F. W. Wile, has proved again and again by his articles that war is and always has been a scientific business with Germany. He argues that there is nothing hyperphysical or mysterious about the successes she achieved. They were essentially material. German soldiers are not supermen, or as individual warriors the equal to those of many other nations. Their victories have been due to a chain of very obvious and systematic circumstances: to organisation, strict discipline, thoroughness, and far-sighted expert management; in other words, making a business of their business and employing therein only business men who know the business.

Apologising for this partial digression from the main subject matter, the French Secret Service of modern times has been principally conducted on the Dossier principle, which came to light in the Dreyfus affair. In the present war this system has seemingly been of little practical value, and France has had to depend almost entirely upon her Allies for foreign intelligence work. Eighteen months after the war commenced her foreign Secret Service department was said to have practically closed down for want of finances, so far as the north of Europe was concerned.

Harking back to before the South African War, we find that Paul Kruger, the late President of the South African Republic, was a great believer in an efficient up-to-date Secret Service department, and vast sums were expended by him with little, if any, inquiry or vouching. Messrs. D. Blackburn and Captain W. Waithman Caddell, in their book on *Secret Service in South Africa*, record how Tjaard Kruger, a son of the President of the Transvaal Republic, who was for a short time Chief of the Secret Service Bureau, paid £2,800 in one afternoon in 1906, out of the many thousands of pounds in gold coinage which he always kept in his office, to casual callers only, to men who came accredited by some person in authority as being able to supply valuable information.

Tjaard Kruger was succeeded in office by a most clever and interesting celebrity, Dr. Leyds, Secretary of State, who was the only man who made the department a success. He showed the unfailing tact of the born diplomat. He was a great reader of character and formed a pretty accurate estimate of a person in a surprisingly short time. He conducted his affairs so delicately and diplomatically that he won universal esteem and the staunchest and most loyal adherents. He would hand over disagreeable work to a subordinate so gracefully that it gave the impression that he was relegating the work, not because it irked him, but because he had found a man more capable than himself—the man whom he had long sought.

Dr. Leyds' letters of instructions to his agents were clear, precise, and exacting, and provided for every possible contingency; yet had they fallen into the hands of the unauthorised they would have conveyed little. These letters bespoke the diplomat. They would have come safely out of an investigation by a committee of suspicious spy-hunters.

When he required to "draw" any person he would instruct his agents to ascertain carefully that person's tastes, habits, prejudices, and amusements. These he would study to the minutest trifle, and by skilful play upon a weakness, or by the evidence of a similar taste, he would successfully penetrate to the most exclusive and jealously guarded *sanctum sanctorum*.

Mr. Hamil Grant is an author who may be congratulated upon his carefully-compiled work, entitled, *Spies and Secret Service*, which contains the history of espionage from earliest times to the present day. He shows how the practice was used by Joshua, David, Absalom, and the mighty warriors whose deeds of valour are recorded in the Old Testament. He quotes Alexander Mithridates, the King of Pontus, who made himself the master of twenty-five languages and spent seven years wandering through countries he subsequently fought and vanquished. He traces developments from Alexander the Great, who lived 300 years before Christ and was the first known to start secret post censorship; from Hannibal, who could never have crossed from Andalusia over the Pyrenees and the Alps into the plains of Piedmont to fight the Battle of Trebia (218 B.C.) without the assistance he received from the intelligence scouts who preceded him. He points out how Cæsar and the great generals who conquered Europe invariably used scouts and intelligence agents. He quotes Napoleon's admission of indebtedness to Polyænus for original strategic ideas of espionage; whilst he has much to say in proving that no war of either ancient or modern times was successful without it.

His most interesting chapters are those dealing with the rise of the Prussian empire, which he claims to have been built almost entirely upon such an unenviable foundation. The author has taken the liberty of quoting somewhat numerous extracts as follows:

> The Modern System of espionage seems to have been originally conceived by Frederick the Great of Prussia and subsequently elaborated into a kind of National Philosophy by writers like Nietzsche, Treitschke and Bernhardi. But a nation which is ruled as if it were a country of convicts actual or potential cannot fail inevitably to develop in a pronounced degree those symptoms of character and predisposition which land its converts in the correction institutions where they are most commonly to be found.
>
> Baron Stein, a well-known statesman of the Napoleonic period, was responsible for the practical application of the theories in the philosophy of Frederick the Great. He was followed by the celebrated Dr. Stieber, who had the handling of millions of pounds at his discretion and whose character had all those ele-

ments which were associated with the criminal who operates along the higher lines. He was a barrister, born in Prussia in 1818, and he first curried favour with the officials by persuading his friends and relations to enter into illegal acts in order that he might betray them for his own advantage. The German word *stieber* seems appropriate; in our language it means sleuthhound. In appearance he represented an inquisitor of old. His eyes were almost white and colourless, whilst there were hard drawn lines about his mouth. With subordinates he adopted the loud airs of a master towards slaves. In the presence of high authorities he was self-abasing and subdued, with a smile of deferential oiliness and acquiescence, with much rubbing of hands.

He seemed to have commenced Secret Service work with a standing salary of £1,200 a year, in addition to which he received side emoluments. He organised an internal and external service with complete independence from all other official bodies, subsidised by full and adequate appropriations from Parliament. His system was thorough. He commenced by spying into the privacies of the Royal family and court and government officials, army and naval officers, and everybody of the slightest importance, down to the labourers' and the workmen's organisations. In a very few years his nominal salary had risen to £18,000, but about 1863, in spite of his having been honoured with every German decoration conceivable, he was for a couple of years suspended from office, during which period he organised the Russian Secret Police.

With Stieber's assistance, Bismarck struck down Denmark in 1864, Austria in 1866, and France in 1870. Even Moltke, the great Prussian organiser of victory, was astonished and astounded at the vast amount of valuable military information by which Stieber had facilitated the rapid advance of his armies.

As a preliminary journey into France in 1867, Stieber appointed 1,000 spies, within the invasion zone, with head centres at Brussels, Lausanne, and Geneva; and on his return he handed over to Bismarck some 1,650 reports which contained full military and original maps of the French frontiers and the invasion zone. Year by year this army of spies was increased, until in 1870 Stieber had between 30,000 and 40,000 on his pay-roll.

In 1867 an attempt was made on the life of Alexander the Second of Russia when on a visit to Paris in order to create a closer

Franco-Russian Alliance, which dastardly act was planned by Stieber in order to be frustrated by him. When the assassin was tried for his life the jury were bought by Prussian gold to acquit the accused in order that the two nations could be kept apart and the object of the journey thereby frustrated, but whether it was the fertile brain of Bismarck or Stieber who planned the scheme of the plot will never be known.

In 1870 Stieber boasted that he controlled the opinions of some eighty-five writers in the French daily and weekly newspapers, furthermore that he had paid sympathisers on the Austrian, Italian, and English Press in addition.

By 1880 Stieber and Prince Bismarck had extended their organised system materially as well as personally, which can be seen in the present day network of railway lines and stations controlled solely for militarist uses rather than for the development of the country; whilst the funds demanded yearly from the Reichstag for Secret Service work increased proportionately.

No one but a native of Prussia was allowed to hold any responsible position in Prussia, yet in 1884 there were 15,000 Germans or semi-foreigners serving on the French railways, all of them more or less in the employ of the German Espionage Bureau and prepared to destroy the plant, the lines, the buildings, and to paralyse French mobilisation at the word of command.

In addition to this, Stieber's plans embraced upheavals in all industrial classes.

It was German gold which instigated and carried through the Dreyfus agitation, also the Association Bill which brought about the disestablishment of the Church of France and the so-called Agadir incident in the spring of 1911, which coincided so remarkably with the devastating strikes in Great Britain.

"It is a cry of the Fatherland that every good citizen is required to pay taxes, build barracks, and shut his mouth.

The recent agitations in Ireland and practically all the strikes in England have been indirectly supported by German gold; to which the circulation of the extraordinary manifesto in August, 1914, was also directly traceable. £4,000 was used for the purposes of the French Railway Strike of 1893; in the same year a local subscription of £48 was raised for a bootmakers' strike at Amiens, whilst an alleged sympathetic £1,000 was sent from

Frankfort.

The English suffragettes are also said to have received thousands of pounds from unknown sources which in reality were German.

Stieber died in 1892, possessed of over £100,000.

As a part of his deep-rooted policy multitudes of Germans were sent to France, England, and elsewhere to establish small businesses, practically every one of which was subsidised by the German Secret Service Office; as also were German clerks and others who could obtain positions giving access to information of any value. Stieberism practically demoralised the entire German nation, whilst it inoculated its poison into other European countries in such a manner that their energies and sound judgment seem to have been paralysed in more ways than one.

Stieberists follow the same creed as Jesuits, 'All is justifiable in the interests of the future of the Fatherland.'

Major Steinhauer succeeded Stieber, and the present Secret Service Bureau of Berlin was in his hands when this war started. He also was a past master in the art of organisation. The entry into Brussels of 700,000 men without inconvenience or mishap was practically entirely due to his organisation. Over 8,000 spies had been placed on the various routes between Aix-la-Chapelle and Saint Quentin, whilst those in the Belgian capital had some two or three years previously actually worked out on paper the billets and lodgings for all those troops in advance.[2]

The ordinary German Secret Service agent started with a salary of £200 a year and 10s. a day expenses, with a bonus for each job to an unlimited amount. Whilst abroad or on any matter of delicacy, out-of-pocket allowances were increased to £2 a day, but 33% of all current monies owing was kept back as a safety-valve until he left the service.

Amongst the members were to be found princes, dukes, counts, barons, lawyers, clergymen, doctors, actresses, actors, mondaines, demi-mondaines, journalists, authors, money-lenders, jockeys, printers, waiters, porters; practically every class of society was represented.

"The remuneration cannot be considered high when compared with the dangers undertaken, and since no official countenance

---

2. This fact refutes the theoristic argument that Germany was forced at the eleventh hour to invade Belgium.

was ever given (nor indeed expected) on the part of the agents once one of them fell into the hands of the enemy, the game was far from being worth the worry and strain it entailed. The training and examination before efficiency was reached were far more difficult than our cadets would have to pass at Woolwich or Sandhurst, or even officers for a staff college appointment.

The head offices of the German Secret Service Department, which was presided over by the *Kaiser* himself, were situated in Berlin at Koenigergratzerstrasse No. 70. So far as callers were concerned the same routine was followed as at our War Office and Admiralty: the portals were guarded by commissionaires who kept records of every visitor, with such particulars as they could gather. Army or naval officers were in charge of all departments. They planned the work, but they never or very rarely executed it. The secretaries and general assistants were all civilians. No ambassadors, ministers, secretaries of legation, envoys, plenipotentiaries, consuls, or recognised officials were permitted to interfere in any way with the work of this department, although they undoubtedly gave it every material assistance whenever they could.

History has clearly proved this. No jealousies or acts of favouritism to relatives and the nominees of indirect influences were countenanced. For such an offence the very highest in office would at once be deposed and punished, whilst there was no appeal to a Parliament, Congress, Chamber of Deputies, or political newspapers, against the *Kaiser's* decision. He was not only the supreme head of what he himself described as "My army of spies scattered over Great Britain and France, as it is over North and South America, as well as the other parts of the world, where German interests may come to a clash with a foreign power," but he took a very keen interest in their individual work. Efficiency and obedience only counted in his estimation.

The persons selected for this work were specially trained in preparation for the prospective tasks ahead of them. For days, weeks, and months, as the case may be, they were grounded in topography, trigonometry, mechanics, army and naval work; with a mass of detail which might be of service, possibly when least expected. Their studies embraced visits to the big government construction works and yards; they were made familiar with all necessary knowledge concerning war-ships, submarines, torpedoes, aircraft, guns and fortifications; silhouettes of vessels; uniforms of officers; secret surveys of interesting districts; signals, codes, telegraphs and multitudinous other matters which the thorough-going German considered absolutely essential to the training of an efficient Secret Service agent.

Mr. Le Queux, to whom all honour is due for his persistent and patriotic efforts in unmasking German spies, their systems and organisations in this country, corroborates Mr. Hamil in recording that the German Secret Service dates back to about 1850, when an obscure Saxon named Stieber began the espionage of revolutionary socialists, from which original effort the present department originated. Also that the work was fostered under the royal patronage of Frederick William, the King of Prussia, which guarded it against anti-counter plotting from both militarism and police, and which permitted it to grow and flourish until it ultimately became the most powerful and feared department of the State. In August, 1914, with an income approximating £750,000 *per annum*, the agents of the German Secret Service extended all over the world, organised to perfection as are the veins and arteries perambulating the flesh and tissues of a man's body.

Herr Stieber's present-day successor, Herr Steinhauer, also seemed to enjoy the full confidence of His Majesty the *Kaiser*. He was then between forty and fifty years of age, charming in manners, excellent in education and of good presence. This officer of the Prussian Guard is well known throughout the capitals of Europe. He has collected information concerning every foreign land which is almost incredible. He had maps of the British Isles which in minute detail and accuracy surpass our own Ordnance Survey. The Norwegian fiords were better known to German navigation lieutenants than to the native pilots and fishermen who daily use them. These are facts which practical experts in many countries have seen put to successful tests since the world-war started.

For some years Mr. Le Queux made it his hobby to follow up the movements of German spies in England. He collected information of value and importance which he says he placed in the hands of our Government officials, but that our government departments were so hopelessly bound up and entangled by red-tapeism that for years his communications and warnings fell upon ears that would not listen, eyes that would not see, brains that would not believe, and hands that would not act.

The late Lord Roberts, who devoted his life to his country, referred to this in the House of Lords some ten years before the present war, but the Liberal and Radical politicians scoffed and laughed at him; as they did when he urged other reforms so sound, so urgent, and so necessary for our very existence. Now prayers are offered for the dead who never would have died had these warnings been accepted in time.

German espionage in England has been worked from Brussels, the chief bureau being situate in the Montagne de la Cœur; whilst Ostend and Boulogne were favoured rendezvous for those engaged in the work and the go-betweens.

Large English towns and counties were divided into groups or sections. In each were selected numerous acting agents who received small periodical payments for services rendered. Such sections acted under the supervision of a Secret Service agent, the whole system being visited from time to time by agents higher up in the service, who paid over all monies in cash, collected reports, and gave further instructions. The favourite cloak or guise to conceal identity was usually that of a commercial traveller.

It is a great pity that full reports of various trials of German spies captured in England have not been permitted to be made public in the Press, passing, of course, under a reasonable censorship which would have deleted only such parts as referred to matters affecting the safety of the realm. The scales would then perhaps have fallen from the eyes of our fatuous and blinded public. And many another secret enemy who was, or had been, working throughout the war, would have been reported and laid by the heels; as well as many a noble life spared which has fallen through such short-sighted folly.

If the public are under the impression that the great round-up of over 14,000 German, Austrian, and foreign spies so actively at work in England at the outbreak of war, and within a few weeks thereof, was due to our Secret Service Department, it is labouring under a great delusion. The credit for this exceedingly valuable work is due to the energy, zeal, and intelligence of Scotland Yard, backed up by thoroughly efficient police officers throughout the country, which force is without doubt the finest in the world.

Our censorships are also separate departments run on their own lines and quite apart from any direct control from the Secret Service.

On January 7th, 1916, Mr. J. L. Balderston, the special correspondent of the *Pittsburg Despatch*, U.S.A., published data he had collected in Europe showing that German propaganda had been carried on with feverish energy in eighteen neutral countries, two of which had been won over at a cost of £19,000,000, and one lost after a vain expenditure of £10,000,000. During the first eighteen months of war, Germany had spent no less than £72,600,000 to foster intimidation, persuasion, and bribery, in conjunction with her colossal Secret Service system.

The following extract gives the estimated expenditure in each country where German agents were at work:

United States	£15,000,000	Spain	£3,000,000
Turkey	£14,000,000	Holland	£2,000,000
Italy	£10,000,000	Norway	£1,600,000
Bulgaria	£5,000,000	Denmark	£1,000,000
Greece	£4,000,000	Argentine	£1,000,000
Roumania	£3,000,000	Chili	£600,000
Persia	£3,000,000	Peru	£400,000
			£72,600,00

The moderation of the estimate that only £15,000,000 has been spent in influencing the United States, a figure half or one-third of that often mentioned in America, is also characteristic of the other estimates, all of which are probably too low, since they deal only with expenditures which have been traced or have produced observable results, such as *harems* for Persian potentates, or palaces for Chinese mandarins, or motorcars for poor Greek lawyers who happen to be members of Parliament on the king's side.

It should also be noted that no attempt is made here to deal with the German system of espionage in hostile countries, or with the organised, but of course secret, attempt to sow sedition among the subjects of Great Britain, France, and Italy, in India, South Africa, Egypt, Tripoli, and Tunis.

To the German Government, the stirring up of trouble in the dependencies of her enemies is an aim of perhaps equal importance with that of winning over neutrals to be actively or passively pro-German.

Returning to the actual work of the English Secret Service agents, it is soon noted that any ordinary British Service officer of a few years' standing is a marked man in whatever society he may find himself. His bearing and mannerisms invariably give him away. There may be exceptions, in which he can disguise himself for a time, but that time will be found to be much too short. There are, of course, in the service many officers who are different from the ordinary standard, men whose veins tingle with the wanderlust of the explorer or adventurer, or who are of abnormal or eccentric temperament; men who generally hold themselves aloof from the fashionable society vanities, which in the past have been dangled too much and too closely round our stripe-bedecked uniforms to be good for efficiency. But even with these men, after they have been a few years in the service, they find that their greatest difficulty is to conceal that fact. It should be unnecessary to add that for the particular work which is under discussion it could hardly be considered an advantage for anyone to start out labelled with his profession and nationality. What ruled Rome so successfully in olden times should have taught the world its lesson; namely, a triumvirate.

In this particular venture, a naval man, a military man, and a civilian strike one as a good combination to be allotted to a given centre of importance. A paradoxical coalition abroad, in that it should ever be apart and yet together; each should know the other and yet be strangers; each should be in constant touch with the others' movements and yet be separated by every outward sign. The duties of service men should be limited to those of consulting experts, whilst specially selected and trained individuals should be employed to carry out active requirements. In some places and in some instances Service men can undertake executive work better perhaps than anyone else could do; but these opportunities are limited. Perhaps they may almost be classed as the exceptions which prove the rule.

There seems to be an unwritten rule in the British Secret Service that no one should be engaged for any position of any importance below the rank of captain. In the head office it was a saying: "We are all captains here." And it may be assumed that every officer so engaged in the Intelligence also ranked as a staff officer.

Most people have an idea that the pay in the British Secret Service is high, even princely. On this they may as well at once undeceive themselves; the pay is mean compared with the risks run, yet officers are keen on entering the B.S.S., as it is known to be a sure stepping-stone to promotion and soft fat future jobs.

Germany was said to vote about £750,000 *per annum* to cover direct Secret Service work, in addition to £250,000 for subsidising the foreign Press; £1,000,000 each year in all. Yet certain members of the House of Commons grudgingly and somewhat reluctantly gave their consent to the £50,000 originally asked for at the end of 1914 by the

English Secret Service Department.

The actual amounts voted and expended on English Secret Service work are shown hereunder.

Year Ending 31st March	Grant £	Expended £
1912	50,000	48,996
1913	50,000	48,109
1914	50,000	46,840
1915	110,000	107,596
1916	400,000	398,698
1917	620,000	593,917
1918	750,000	740,984
1919	1,150,000	1,207,697
1920	200,000	(not known)

How much of the money was actually available for direct Secret Service work, and how much may have been diverted into other or indirect channels (*exempli gratia*—the Liberal solatium of £1,200 *per annum* to Mr. Masterman for perusing foreign newspapers)[3] is not known; nor has the government allowed any explanation to be given.

Mr. Thomas Beach, of Colchester, Essex, whose identity was for so many years and so very successfully concealed under the pseudonym of Major Henri le Caron, and by whose energies the United Kingdom was saved the loss of many millions of money and many thousands of lives, proves, from so far back as the year 1867 and for the twenty-five years following, during which period he was employed in the Secret Service of the British Government and stultifying the popular fiction which associates with such work fabulous payments and frequent rewards, that "there is in this service only ever-present danger and constantly recurring difficulty; but of recompense a particularly scant supply."

At the conclusion of his somewhat interesting volume *The Recollections of a Spy*, he complains bitterly of the meanness and cheeseparing methods of the British Government:

On this question of Secret Service money I could say much. The miserable pittance doled out for the purpose of fighting such an enemy as the Clan-na-Gael becomes perfectly ludi-

---

3. Reports of House of Commons.

crous in the light of such facts as I have quoted in connection with the monetary side of the dynamite campaign.

After quoting the vast sums used by the enemy he adds:

How on earth can the English police and their assistants in the Secret Service hope to grapple with such heavily-financed plots as these on the miserable sums granted by Parliament for the purpose?. . . . Someday, however, a big thing will happen—and then the affrighted and indignant British citizen will turn. The fault will be the want of a perfect system of Secret Service, properly financed . . . . Imagine offering men in position a retainer of £20 a month with a very odd cheque for expenses thrown in! The idea is ridiculous. I have heard it urged that the thought of Secret Service is repugnant to the British heart, wherein are instilled the purest principles of freedom. The argument has sounded strange in my ears when I remembered that London, as somebody has said, is the cesspool of Europe, the shelter of the worst ruffians of every country and clime. America is called the Land of the Free, but she could give England points in the working of the Secret Service, for there there is no stinting of men or money.

What a contrast were the life and actions of this man to Nathan Hale, one of the heroes of the American War of Independence, who said:

Every kind of service necessary for the public good becomes honourable by being necessary. If one desires to be useful, if the exigencies of his country demand a peculiar service, its claims to the performance of that service are imperious.

When caught and sentenced to be shot he exclaimed:

I only regret that I have but one life to sacrifice for my country.

Throughout the period that I was connected with the B.S.S. there were constant difficulties about money. Had not my personal credit been good, which enabled me to raise large amounts almost everywhere I happened to travel, I, or my colleagues, might have been stranded again and again. It was nothing unusual for appeals to be made to me to act as banker and Good Samaritan until long-deferred payments eventually arrived.

In the early days most of the B.S.S. agents travelling abroad seemed to labour under the same difficulty: a shortage of funds and overdue accounts wanting payment. It may not have been any fault of, but merely an eccentricity of, our good old managing chief; be that as it may, impecuniosity never bothered me. Some of the others got very angry about it, whilst their irritation increased as their banking accounts became more heavily overdrawn.

So far as actual pay went, a B.S.S. man drew the equivalent to his ordinary army or naval pay, with nothing over for rations or extras. He, however, returned a list of his travelling expenses and hotel bills which were agreed to be refunded each month. If he were a married man, he had to pay his wife's and his family's expenses out of his own pocket, should it be necessary for any of them to accompany him, which often absorbed the whole of his pay and a good bit above it. If he entertained anyone with a view to drawing out some point of useful intelligence, it would be passed in general expenses, provided the outlay was exceedingly moderate. But the members of the executive with whom I came in contact were inclined to be of the parsimonious type, much too much afraid to spend a sovereign, either because they could not really afford it, or for fear they would never see it back again.

Their entertaining was conspicuous by its absence, which necessitated a rather heavier drain upon my pocket and upon my good nature. It had at times to be done, and someone had to do it; that someone was nearly always myself. The chief preached economy at all times and he religiously practised it. It was paradoxical in that if a big amount was wanted for some exceedingly doubtful purpose no limit seemed to be made; the wherewithal was almost certain to be forthcoming to meet the demand. But the loyal Britisher who came along to help the Service and his country in her hour of need, who freely and ungrudgingly offered to sacrifice everything he possessed in order to serve, who worked for nothing or practically nothing, and who perhaps paid a good part of his own expenses, received an absurdly small remuneration and little if any thanks; most certainly he never received a line in writing from anyone in high authority to express his country's gratitude.

Those who sit in chairs in Whitehall take their regular fat salaries and periodical distinctive honours as a matter of course. They are the men who watch the wheels revolving. They collect and hand over results, the fruit garnered in by others working in the twilight which shades their individuality. With the powers-that-be these men (the gentlemen who sit in chairs) are ever in the official limelight, whilst the reckless, devil-may-care workers over the horizon, the men who carry their life in their hands and who go right into the lion's den to collect facts and data which often mean success or defeat in battles raged elsewhere, or who manipulate and pull the strings on the spot, seem to be ignored and forgotten. The secrecy of the service is so absolute that no mention of the way their work is accomplished may be made.

The cloak of mystery is drawn so completely over the whole department that no matter what sacrifice a member may make for his country's sake, no matter what bravery he may have exhibited in almost every instance alone and unsupported, probably in an enemy's domain as one man facing a host of his country's enemies, his deeds are unrecorded, unhonoured and unsung. Whilst he is in the service he is merely a cipher, a unit, an atom. When he has left it he is hardly remembered as once a member. What of it? He only did his duty. Now he is out of the Service he is no longer interesting, he ceases to exist. The big wheel of life continues to revolve. The B.S.S. Department is but a very minute little wheel which cogs into the larger machinery of State in its own respective corner. As the rim of this very minor wheel comes up from the dark recesses of the working world and the separate cogs become revealed, those in authority who sit watching each and every cog, upon the stamina and reliability of which so much depends, from time to time find one that cannot stand the strain, because it is hurt or damaged, either in body, or in mind, or in fortune. It is at once removed. We are at war. Sentiment is dead and buried, except with the weak, who in life's battles are crushed and accordingly find themselves forced to the wall.

Any cog believed to show signs of weakness is instantly extracted, and those who sit and watch the wheels revolve seek another piece of tougher and believed to be better material which may come to hand, and which they force into the vacant space created. For a second perhaps the discarded hard-used cog is looked at with admiration for past and valued service when knowingly driven at highest pressure; or with regret at having to part with such a tried and trusted friend; then it is hurled into outer darkness, on to the scrap-heap of broken and forgotten humanity. The new cog is pushed in and hammered home, it is smeared with the grease of experience, and the wheel continues its monotonous revolution. Such is a good similitude of the short and exciting life of a Secret Service agent.

CHAPTER 3

Initiation to Active Work

The only open route to Northern Europe which members of belligerent nations could safely take was through Bergen in Norway. The Wilson Line from Hull to Christiania continued to run one weekly boat regularly, which carried mails, general cargo, and an occasional passenger. It was considered advisable by most people to avoid taking this boat.

From Newcastle a Norwegian Company ran a line of small steamers daily, which had not been molested by submarines or warships. They were mail-boats, and although their accommodation and fittings were far from up-to-date, and travellers had to look after themselves much more than they should have been called upon to do, they appeared to be crowded each trip. The neutral flag and the shortest direct passage was responsible for this.

There were many other available ways of crossing the North Sea open to me, and no restrictions as to route had been laid down. I had simply to visit a certain hotel in a certain town, in a certain country, at a certain hour, on a certain date—arranged well ahead. The margin of time allowed was ample for a crossing by sail if desired.

With a passport, a revolver, a bundle of English banknotes (of my own providing), and as little luggage as possible, I made my way towards Scotland to take ship for Norway and the beyond.

There were three vessels which sailed from the port of embarkation I selected, two Norwegians and a Swede. One of the former was fortunately taken. It was certainly fortunate, because the latter was blown up and sunk by a mine within a few hours of her departure. Such is the luck of war.

The voyage across the North Sea was uneventful. It was rough, as it generally is. The passengers were few. They were almost entirely

Russian Poles; I was the only Englishman on board, and there was one Japanese. All were ill with sea-sickness, which was perhaps accentuated by a deadly fear of mines and torpedoes. Few slept, less ate, and as they were charged for the meals they did not consume the owners must have made money, more particularly so when it is remembered that fifty *per cent.* extra was charged in addition to the ordinary fares, to cover war risks.

The sea seemed to be utterly devoid of life. Not a sail, not a column of smoke, nor even a bird was sighted until the ship emerged from a fog-bank, wherein she had rolled for many hours broadside on, within a few miles of the outer island-barrier of the Norwegian coast.

To the ultimate intense relief of everybody the fog lifted, and a few hours afterwards a small fishing-town on the south-west of Norway was reached. Cargo was discharged, more cargo was taken on board, and again the chains rattled in the hawser pipes; the engines throbbed and the siren aroused echoes from the rocks around as the voyage was renewed northwards.

Later in the day other towns were reached, and similar scenes repeated, until near midnight the lights of the historic port of Bergen danced in the distance.

Securing the services of a friendly native, one of the numerous hangers-on who flit round the quays of seaport towns in every land in the hope of picking up money with the least possible exertion expended to earn it, I made my way to a quiet hostelry in the quietest part of the pleasant old town and installed myself as comfortably as circumstances permitted.

At the appointed place and hour, I strolled casually into the entrance hall of a certain hotel and stood apparently puzzling over the railway and steamboat time-tables which were hanging on the wall. Several people were in evidence, but no one seemed to be particularly interested in anyone else. I had been there quite a time, and was wondering how I could explain my presence in order to excuse and justify a prolonged lingering, when I observed a small-built, quiet inoffensive-looking young man cross the hall and stop near the hotel register. Absent-mindedly he tapped his teeth with his *pince-nez*, and muttered to himself and half aloud, "I wonder if Mr. Jim has called for that letter."

Now "Mr. Jim" was the password I had been instructed to listen for. The unknown was to give me certain orders. Without them I would have been like a ship in a gale minus the rudder.

The little man never looked at me nor even my way. He had stepped near enough so that I could overhear his *sotto voce*, also within range of two or three others who were congregated in the hall. His utterance was low, but it was as clear as a bell, and he spoke in Norwegian.

No one took any notice of him or his remark. This, however, appeared to trouble him not a bit. Adjusting his glasses he pulled a newspaper out of his coat pocket and proceeded to make himself comfortable on a settee in a remote corner, where he could observe all that passed and all who came or went; provided he wished so to interest himself should the contents of his paper fail to hold his attention.

Having marked down the man there was no need to hasten matters. Caution at one's initiation is generally advantageous. Ten minutes later I seated myself on the same settee as the stranger and also became absorbed in a newspaper. Assuring myself that no one was within earshot except the little gentleman before referred to, I murmured soft and low, whilst I still appeared to be reading the paper: "I know Mr. Jim. Can I give him the letter for you?"

"Who sent you to ask for it?" the stranger queried. I named a name which was a countersign. "For whom does Mr. Jim require it?" I gave the third and final word which proved beyond doubt my title to the precious document in question.

During this short conversation both of us had been studying our news-sheets, and unless an observer had been stationed within a few feet of us, nothing transpired that could have given the smallest clue to the fact that any communication had passed.

With no sign of recognition the little man got up to go. He left his paper on the seat, and in passing me he whispered: "You will find the letter in my *Evening News*. Good luck to you."

In the privacy of a bedroom the letter was opened. It was typewritten, with no address and no signature. It contained instructions to proceed to another hotel two full days' journey away, where I was to look out for, and make the acquaintance of, a certain English staff officer to whom I had to deliver my dispatches.

It was fortunate I had provided myself with plenty of money. The ten pounds for preliminary expenses, which was all I had been given, was already over-exhausted, and travelling in those days of war scares, high freights, and shortage of accommodation, was far more expensive than the gentlemen who sit in easy-chairs at home would believe.

I was the only passenger on a semi-cargo boat which sailed next day for the port desired. The weather was awful. Severe frost coated the deck and rigging with ice, in places inches thick. Heavy snow-storms impeded navigation, whilst again and again the vessel had to lay to for hours at a stretch before her captain dare make any attempt at headway. Wrecks were continually passed, not cheery encouragement to one's spirits; whilst, generally speaking, that two days' voyage was about as severe a shaking up as anyone could possibly expect to receive at any time, or anywhere, during a year or more at sea.

During the night, about 2.0 a.m., the engines suddenly ceased running. Feet pattered up and down the deck and everyone on board instinctively became aware that something unusual had happened. Slipping on a thick overcoat and a small Norwegian forage cap, I cautiously negotiated the companion-way. I suspected a German war-vessel had held up the ship. If so, I had no desire to meet any members of a boarding party until I had destroyed the sealed dispatch entrusted to me. After turning over possibilities in my mind I had decided to make use of the exhaust pipe of the lavatory. It was therefore essential that one's lines of retreat should be kept open without fear of being cut off.

It transpired, however, that my fears were groundless. The captain had suddenly been taken ill, and an immediate operation seemed to the first mate necessary as the only chance of saving his life. The ship had, therefore, run to the neighbourhood of an island whereon a doctor was known to reside, and the unfortunate captain was about to be conveyed ashore.

Poor chap! It subsequently transpired that he died the following day in spite of every effort to save him.

During the voyage the ship touched at various small stations to deliver and receive cargo. Sometimes a few passengers would come aboard, generally for short trips. At one place a couple of Danes rushed over the gangway as it was being dropped preparatory to departure. They had made a record journey across the mountains, and exhibited intense anxiety for expedition. They wanted to reach rail-head in order that they could get back to their own country as soon as it was possible.

Why? That one little word gave something to concentrate one's thoughts upon during the long hours at sea.

Danes, generally speaking, are heavy drinkers. They have a fondness for spirits, particularly with their coffee. It was advisable to wait until after the midday meal, when it was customary to repair to the smoke-room, if further curiosity was to be satisfied. Securing a corner seat I cocked up both my legs on to the settee and buried myself in a book—the Sagas of the North. After ostentatiously appearing to drink a number of small glasses of spirits, signs of somnolescence followed. Soon the book dropped with a bang on the floor and intermittent snoring became almost a nuisance to the only two other occupants of the saloon, the Danish travellers.

The confined space of the apartment caused them by compulsion to sit within a few feet of where I was lying. They had been whispering in so low a tone that not a word could be heard. As the snoring increased they raised their voices. Under the impression that the sleep was probably alcoholic, they were soon discussing their affairs in distinctly audible tones. And very interesting business it turned out to be.

Shortly, it concerned the purchase, transport, and delivery of some hundreds of horses which they had been buying for and on behalf of, or for resale to, the German Government. This business had apparently been going on for some time. Denmark and Sweden had been early denuded of all available horseflesh at enormous prices. Norway was now being swept clean.

The two travellers were discussing the probabilities of any action being taken by the British minister at —— to attempt to veto or put what obstacles he was capable of in the way of this traffic.

One of the twain was a fat, good-natured man whom nothing seemed to trouble. The other was thin and dyspeptic looking, who seemed suspicious of his own shadow.

"He'll never be fool enough to sit quiet under the thousands we are sending over," the latter remarked.

"Oh, he'll never trouble. Look at Consul —— at ——. Ever since the war broke out he has been sending hundreds of thousands of barrels of herrings to Germany. He is shipping them off now, as fast as he can get them. And, the devil burn me, he's the English Consul. The minister has never stopped him. Why should he trouble us?"

"But has he not power to remove him?" asked the thin man.

"Of course he has," replied fatty. "Ministers appoint and remove consuls as they please. And when an English consul is allowed to rake in a fortune in a few months, supplying the Germans with food, how can you argue he will stop us dealing in horses *to go to Denmark*?"

"Anyhow, the sooner we can get ours through the more relieved I shall be," grunted the other. "It will take them two days to reach ——, and once they are shipped it's all right."

Their conversation drifted to other topics, and although I waited patiently on the sofa for another hour nothing further of importance was divulged. Sometime after this an exceptionally heavy sea struck the vessel, causing her to roll so heavily that everything on the tables was spilt, whilst I was pitched, *nolens volens*, amongst the spittoons on the floor. This foretaste of further rocking to come sent all three of us to our respective berths.

On landing at the port of —— I lost no time in searching for my unknown commanding officer. The hotel which had been named to me was a good one, its guests included many nationalities. At dinner I spotted three men of military aspect, each of whom might well be the gentleman in question. Coffee and a cigar in the lounge failed to procure any sign of the expectant one; I therefore strolled out into the town to make a few small purchases.

An hour later I returned. Only three people now occupied the lounge. One of them undoubtedly was an army officer belonging to a smart regiment, but it would have been difficult to guess to what country he belonged. A first venture would probably have elicited German as the answer. All the more reason for double caution, thought I to myself.

In nonchalant fashion I overhauled the mass of periodicals upon the tables, and having selected a local one, settled myself down at ease in a long deck-chair under a potted palm to watch and wait for possible developments.

In half an hour's time two of the visitors departed, whereupon my *vis-à-vis* looked hard at me over the top of his newspaper and elevated both eyebrows. I nodded. He smiled, and with a slight indication of the head, implying that he wished to be followed, slowly left the room and proceeded up the grand stairway. Waiting perhaps a quarter of an hour I also took the same route. The first and second landings were devoid of life. On the third I noticed a half-open door, which I entered as though the room were my own; whilst I was quite prepared to apologise if a mistake was made in my so doing.

Here, however, I found my friend of the elevating eyebrows, who received me cordially, and I was introduced to his wife as an Englishman recently arrived. I gave the name in which I had booked on arrival; my newly-found friend did the same. This, of course, was not sufficient. For some little time we talked of trivialities and verbally fenced, and thrust, and parried, the while certain secret passwords were casually introduced and exchanged in a somewhat similar manner as has before been narrated in connection with the little gentleman at Bergen. When assurance had become doubly sure, the door was locked and bolted, the dispatch handed over, and the story of the horses told.

Thus it came to pass that I was first "blooded" in the Foreign Secret Service of His Britannic Majesty's Government.

CHAPTER 4

Intercommunicating With Temporary Codes and Incidents

No reader must expect or anticipate a disclosure of the direct methods which the British Secret Service uses for communicating with headquarters. That is a carefully-guarded secret which no one in or out of the service would dream of referring to. Suffice it therefore to say that it is difficult to conceive anything more clever or effective than it is, both as to its efficiency and its celerity in use.

On the other hand, when Secret Service agents are working abroad they must perforce rely upon codes of sorts, for means of intercommunication between themselves, their friends and supporters. These codes are invented by them entirely at their discretion. If they are wise in their generation they never keep the same code too long in use, but change it, at frequent intervals, for another entirely different in every respect. Such codes cannot be too carefully prepared; whilst every user knows that if his deception is discovered the consequences to himself might be serious indeed. Simplicity is invariably the safest and most effective rule to follow. In order to give the reader a good idea of how the work was accomplished a couple of these codes are roughly outlined, with examples of their working in each case.

One was used for sea work. It was a grammatical code, which, although simple enough in its patent aspect, was not easy to memorise with that strict accuracy which is so essential to future use. Shortly, this code ran somewhat on the following lines, although English names are therein substituted in order to give better illustration. Needless to add, these messages were worded in the language of the country in which they were despatched, and signed with an assumed name which would be in common use in that country.

Example 1.

1. Communications signed with *Christian Name* refer to *War Ships.*
Communications signed with *Surname* refer to *Merchant Ships.*

2. *Please send a copy of The Times to* . . . . .means "a base is being formed at . . . . ."

3. I received a letter from . . . . . *on* . . . . .means (German auxiliary cruiser(s) in port at . . . . or (German battleship(s) hanging about near . . . . .

4. I received a message from . . . . . .*on* . . . . . means (German large merchant ship in port at . . . . . . .or (German cruiser hanging about near . . . . .

5. I am hoping to hear from . . . . . . *on* . . . . . .means (German small merchant ship in port at . . . . .or (German torpedo-boat(s) hanging about near . . . . . .

6. I am expecting a message from . . . . *on* . . . . . . .means (German collier(s) in port at . . . . . .or (German submarine(s) hanging about near . . . . . .

7. The *first blank* in the sentence is to be filled in with the *name of the place* at which the base is being formed, or at which the ships have been seen.

8. The *second blank* in the sentence, after the word "on" is to be filled in with a *day of the week* indicating the number of ships seen (*see* 9).

9. 1 is Monday   6 is Saturday
    2 is Tuesday   7 is Sunday
    3 is Wednesday   8 is Monday-week
    4 is Thursday   9 is Tuesday-week, and so on.
    5 is Friday   15 is Monday-fortnight, and so on.

10. If, *instead of the singular person* "I am (had)," the *plural* "We are (had)" is written, it means that the ships in question, if merchantmen, have left port and are *going South.*

11. If neither the first person singular nor plural is written and the communication begins, for instance, "Letter from . . . *on* . ." it means that the ships in question, if merchantmen, have left port and are *gone North.*

12. Any mention of *illness* means that the ships are *disabled.*

13. *I am expecting a letter from ... on ...* means that several German warships (or merchantmen) of different classes (or sizes) have been seen.

14. *Specimen message*:
We are hoping to hear from Newcastle on Sunday.
(*signed*) Charles.
Decoded, means 7 German warships have been observed outside Newcastle, proceeding South.

The week after my arrival, this code had been completed and put into use. I was one evening sitting in the best and most popular restaurant in a certain town. The place was crowded with customers and business was brisk. The walls were decorated with magnificent frescoes by a celebrated German artist. Hundreds of electric lamps added warmth and attractiveness, whilst dreamy *valse* music from Wald Teufel, given by a German orchestra, seemed to help the digestion. Between bites and sips of German lager I was absorbed in the perusal of an evening news-sheet wherein every belligerent army was reported to be making marvellous forward movements, which, if half true, would have carried them respectively quite through Europe and back again in the course of a few weeks. Whenever my eye shifted from the newspaper to my plate an opportunity offered to note casually my surroundings, as well as my immediate neighbours.

Two seats only were vacant. They were located next my own and in due course were occupied by a young naval lieutenant accompanied by an outwardly appearing charming *demi-mondaine*. The champagne of sunny France soon loosened their tongues. But the more their voices became raised the more absorbed I became in my reading. Presently snatches of conversation drifted my way. The lady was complimenting her gallant upon his patriotism and prowess. He, as the Americans say, was blowing hot air. A listener's difficulty was to sift the substance from the imaginary boasting. Subject matters dealt with were mostly of a frivolous nature, but ever and *anon* the lieutenant would return to his sea trips and the results from their patrolling. *Inter alia* he related the number of drifting mines taken up, vessels sighted and submarine visitation, which matters only were of interest to me.

Presently he paused, then, sinking his voice almost to a whisper, informed his enchantress that just before his ship entered port, that very afternoon, a German cruiser had been sighted going full steam north and close in shore. He proceeded by giving at length his personal opinions and suppositions as to her destination and objective. Now I happened to be aware of several objectives which would be very attractive to such an enemy vessel. For some weeks I had been over-anxious regarding the safety of a line of steamers, the uninterrupted running of which was a matter of some importance to England. And although I entertained considerable doubts regarding the truth of the latter part of the young lieutenant's statement, yet I felt that I should send the information along to headquarters for what it was worth. So I despatched the following telegram:

> Received letter from B . . . . on Monday about you from a chic lady although do not believe what she says.—Christian.

Which on being decoded would run:

> One enemy battleship is stated to be hanging around B . . . . . going North. Information obtained through female source and doubtful.

It had been previously arranged that all local wires should be sent to a certain individual at his private residence, who conveyed them to another who had his fingers on the reins of management.

If the news contained was sufficiently important it would be trans-mitted home, which would mean a duplicate communication and ensure a double chance of safe arrival.

The first recipient at local headquarters was a man of gentle dispo-sition, a domesticated and homely parent, whose many years of con-nubial bliss had never been marred by a single cloud of unhappiness. He was one of those lovable personages who is generally captured by a lady who may have enjoyed numerous innocent flirtations before marriage, and consequently might perhaps be of a suspicious and jeal-ous disposition, who, knowing the goodness of heart of her spouse, might imagine that every woman showing an amiable or friendly spirit towards him was trying to wean his affections from herself; and who might accordingly be always on the watch for all possible emer-gencies.

Never having seen, nor met, the good lady, I had no accurate data on these points, but the fact is recorded that when the telegraph of-ficial, who happened to be a personal friend of the addressee, received the aforesaid message, he warned the telegraph delivery boy to give it only to the addressee.

Unfortunately the addressee did not happen to be at home when the message arrived, and his faithful wife answered the door. Having been advised to a certain extent regarding these matters, and recognising the boy who brought the message, she naturally pressed him upon the nature of his errand and soon persuaded the reluctant youth to hand over the missive, which she at once opened and read. Not knowing its hidden meaning she jumped to wrong conclusions.

From the scraps of news which reached me afterwards relating to the domestic tragedy which followed, I pieced together that the believed-to-be wronged wife immediately donned her outdoor apparel in order to seek out her Judas in lamb's-skin. Before she ran him to earth, she had imagined the worst, and had worked herself up into a veritable furore of unnecessary excitement.

What really happened when they met, what was said, or done, were details which I never knew. But the unfortunate message-receiver implored me to invent another code at my earliest convenience; one, for choice, which was not quite so open to dual construction.

Most local codes, when and where possible, were worked out on domestic lines. By way of example, familiar and commonplace names were selected which could be found in an ordinary directory. To each was attached a definite meaning, and the message would be worded so that anyone seeing it would think it related to an ordinary everyday event. Christian names might be coded to mean definite objects; to wit—Bertha, a battleship; Dora, a torpedo boat destroyer; Sarah, a submarine; Tiny, a torpedo boat; Mary, a merchantman; Connie, a collier; Trina, a trawler; Louisa, an airship; and so on.

Surnames were useful to designate numerals; to wit—Oldman, one; Turner, two; Truman, three; Smith, four; Jones, five; Robinson, six; and so on.

Knowing that every telegram was stamped with the name of the place it was handed in at, the points of the compass, north, south, east, and west were conveyed by including the name of some place which could be found on any ordinary map within a reasonable radius of the place of dispatch.

Time spoke for itself.

Thus, a telegram handed in at Lowestoft worded as follows:

Sent your housemaid Sarah Jones to Felixstowe 4 o'clock this afternoon,

On being coded would read:

Five submarines passed Lowestoft at 4 o'clock this afternoon steaming south.

Any reference to an illness meant that damage had been done, or that a vessel had been adversely affected to some extent. Any reference to a marriage or engagement meant that a combat or battle had taken place. "In bed" conveyed the news that a ship or ships had been sunk. "Put to bed" meant sunk, annihilation, or defeat, according to the context; mention of "delirium or head sickness" conveyed suspicions, or suspicious circumstances; "doctor called in" that the enemy (or others, as the context might convey) had retired, or been put to flight, whilst any direct, or indirect, reference to "remaining here, or at some named place," that the object or objects in question were still there or likely to remain.

The above-mentioned outline should be sufficient to convey to the reader an idea of how the stunt worked out in practice.

That these messages were often tapped and became the subject of racking headaches to the code decipherers who attempted to unravel them, was quite probable. When we could we tried on the same thing ourselves; such was considered only fair in love as well as in war. Lady telegraph and telephone operators are sometimes amenable to flattery and judiciously administered attentions. It is also within the bounds of possibility that an occasional one might be met with who might not object to test a communication with a semblance of reason; whilst one of the most interesting enemy codes we managed to intercept during our rambles was confined to the limits of a postage-stamp. It meant not only intercepting the letter or postcard but having to unstick the stamp and test it before the message could be copied.

It is not at all necessary, however, to pursue this subject further, but once upon a time during the continuance of this war a certain message was handed in at a certain telegraph office in Holland to cable to a certain address in the U.S.A., which ran as follows:

Father dead.

The telegraph operator, for some reason which we need not trouble to inquire into, altered the wording to "Father deceased," and then despatched the message in the usual manner.

Immediately came back the reply:

Is father really dead *or only deceased*?

The following up of that simple message cost one government a considerable sum of money, but it was well worth the outlay.

To those who seek the sunny side of life, humour can be found in all things. Once at a funeral, when the author was broken in body and soul with the painful agony of dry tears, kind Providence sent relief from an unexpected quarter. In the pew immediately in front were seated two mourners, one a tiny man, the other about 350 lbs. in weight, whose head was nearly as big as the puny man's whole body. On leaving the church for the graveside each took the other's hat by mistake and they got separated in the crowd. At the close of the service they unconsciously and solemnly put on the hats they respectively held. That of the tiny man did not find resting-place until it had covered his head, ears, and face, and settled on his shoulders. That of the enormously fat man looked like a pea on a drum.

Likewise it was with our local code messages. Their use in practice was often the innocent cause of much trouble; more often, perhaps, the source of some humour. The gentle cherub who had undertaken the collection of messages and who has recently been hereinbefore referred to, maybe received another shock to his domestic bliss; and that only a week after the one before related. It is much to be feared that he did not fully appreciate the humorous side. However, as it gives an excellent illustration of the practical and simple working of the last-mentioned code, it is narrated.

The facts are as follows:

I one day received this request.

I shall be exceedingly obliged if you will undertake to deliver this package to —— personally. If you could start at once it would be very good of you; but please understand, no living soul may see the contents of this packet except —— himself.

I bowed my acceptance of the mission, murmuring how honoured I felt at an opportunity to render service to the illustrious personage soliciting my assistance. Then I hastened to my hotel to prepare for immediate departure.

The midnight express to —— was crowded. On the platform a few minutes before the scheduled time of leaving, representatives from almost every country in Europe could have been picked out. Detectives and Secret Servant agents glided through the crowd, observing, watching and noting the many strange and familiar faces. Their work meant an added consumption of current on the wires. The vacant stare, the side glance, or the wooden far-away expression of countenance, conveyed much to these men. To them it was always interesting to try and read the working of the brain behind. But I was a traveller and the doings of these night-hawks interested me but little, beyond such casual observation as could be made during a quick passage to the train.

In the corridor of the car to which I was allotted were several Germans. Two in particular I instinctively feared. Their faces were familiar. One of them had secured a berth in my compartment, and addressing me in excellent Danish, showed a desire to be affable. It was unsought, but it would perhaps be dangerous not to reciprocate.

Soon after the train had started on its journey I politely offered to share some refreshment with this fellow-traveller, which, however, that astute gentleman politely but firmly declined. It was an easy matter to guess the suspicious working in his mind. He meant to pass a sleepless night. So did I.

In due course I retired to rest, and the German secured the door of the cubicle before climbing to his berth, which was above mine. As soon as he was comfortably settled I opened the door he had closed. The German waited a while, and then, very stealthily, shut it again. I waited about a like period and reopened it. So the game proceeded, until about four o'clock in the morning the German complained of the draught. In the most polite language that could be commanded I replied by commenting upon the extreme heat and the unhygienic practice of curtailing fresh air.

At 6 a.m. the German decided to seek another car, at which I inwardly rejoiced exceedingly. No sooner had he departed than I secured the door and enjoyed a refreshing sleep of several hours.

Later that morning the door-closing German was observed in close consultation with his companion. On a ferry which had to be crossed both of them watched my every movement, and I began to congratulate myself in that I had taken precautions before departure in order to guard against contingencies.

Forearmed is forewarned. Before leaving I had prepared another packet in exact duplicate of the original I had been entrusted with. The dummy contained only an old newspaper, and it was placed in an inside banknote pocket of my waistcoat. Its outline could have been detected by anyone on the look-out for it. The original packet was elsewhere concealed, in a secure hiding-place, where it was least likely to be sought or found.

On leaving the ferry a rush was made at the gangway and I found myself involuntarily pushed forward and wedged in between the two over-night observers. I could feel their hands run over my chest, so I took some interest in the proceedings. I had not been on numerous race-courses, nor participated in football, boat-race night, and other big crowds in England, without learning something of the ropes. Every time a hand entered the inside of my coat it encountered small steel obstacles which lacerated and hurt. True I lost a few buttons, and my clothes were damaged, but the dummy packet remained intact, and I noticed with some satisfaction afterwards that one of the two gentlemen before mentioned had a hand bound up in a pocket handkerchief when they boarded the waiting train.

On arrival at ——— my taxi-cab was followed. Having been a constant visitor to the town in question for many years I redirected my driver to a public building which had a bolt hole at its back, by the use of which my pursuers were baffled successfully, and the package was safely delivered without further trouble or anxiety. After which I despatched the following cablegram:

Child delivered safely this morning mother doing well.

Whether this message was also intercepted by the jealous wife of our temporary receiving agent, history does not relate, but I tremble to think of the volcanic domestic eruption which must have ensued if it were so.

When war was declared, cables were cut, a most rigid censorship installed, and no printed matter was allowed to leave England. Yet news, most important news, continued to leak through to Germany, and most of it went through neutral countries.

Before the war, Germany used ciphers, but these were soon dropped. It is common knowledge that every government keeps a copy of all cipher and code messages sent over the cables from every embassy or consulate, whether the countries are at peace or war. The great cleverness of certain men at unravelling any code, however complicated, is also openly acknowledged.

Yet, in spite of every precaution and all science and knowledge the country could bring to bear, news continued to leak through and to fly across the North Sea. Scotland Yard, to which admirable institution the whole world owes so much, was put upon its mettle. It proceeded to watch with still closer scrutiny certain suspected persons who still claimed the privilege of freedom. One of these was a small London tradesman whose premises were situated in a remote and quiet back street. He appeared to have rather more corresponding friends than his position or his business justified. His correspondence, in and out, was intercepted, copied, and sent along in a manner not likely to arouse his suspicions. Nothing, however, occurred which could be looked upon as even suspicious, until one day a telegram arrived which had been handed in at a certain naval base of some importance in the U.K. It simply said "Been ill three days—John," or words to that effect.

Now the sender had also been watched, an attention which had been evenly divided amongst every one of this tradesman's correspondents. The police knew that the sender of the message, "John," had been in perfect health for quite a long time past, which fact was, of course, communicated to headquarters.

The information caused a flutter in the official dovecots.

Copies of the message, with comments, were forwarded to the War Office, to the Admiralty, and to other Government Departments likely to be interested.

To shorten the story, certain gentlemen in the Admiralty were amazed when they remembered vividly that secret orders had been issued by them which commanded a squadron of warships to leave the port at which the message had been handed in, and join up with the High Seas Fleet *exactly three days* from the date of the aforesaid message.

Needless to add that the further activities of both the sender and the receiver of the telegram were forthwith promptly crushed, once and for all future time.

Scotland Yard also discovered, probably with considerable assistance from the Censorship Department, that the Germans were successfully getting out information useful to them through open business letters addressed to residents in neutral countries, particularly Norway, Sweden, Denmark, and Holland, which were decoded by adding certain geometrical figures. For example, where the sides of an added triangle or triangles intersected one another, or cut the rim of a circle, there would be found the words used in the secret messages.

Several of these ingenious codes were described in a most interesting article which was published in *Pearson's Magazine*, October, 1918, with illustrations which more clearly demonstrated their latent meaning. Two of the most brilliant of them were the knot alphabet and the chess problem.

In the former case a parcel sent to a supposed prisoner in a German internment camp was found to contain, amongst other things, a woollen sweater, or knitted sports vest. It was apparently so badly knitted, and the wool was seen to be so full of knots, that the censor's suspicions were aroused. Subsequent searches revealed that no such person as the addressee of the parcel in question was known to exist. His name certainly did not appear in any army list. The aforesaid garment was most carefully unravelled. The wool was found to be whole, with a multitude of simple knots tied at irregular intervals. Alphabets were written on a board, each letter being placed at given distances apart, and very soon a most interesting message was read off.

The chess problem was deeper in its cunning and its intricacy. During 1917, a young and fascinating actress appeared in Paris. She was suspected and closely watched. In due course she captivated one of the junior secretaries of a neutral embassy. His integrity was absolutely beyond all doubt, but naturally he also was watched and shadowed in order to learn what was passing, or might be passing, between them or otherwise.

The watchers' notes, on being compared, revealed certain facts which when carefully pieced together laid bare the whole plot. The actress professed to be deeply interested in the serious game of chess. She inspired a similar passion in the breast of the young and inexperienced *attaché*. One day she produced to him a rough illustration of an alleged chess problem which she had cut from a local newspaper; in all probability she herself had indirectly caused its publication. She worried her admirer unduly to help her solve what had been, or were, the opening moves in the game which had caused the pieces to be left on the board as shown in the sketch. No one in Paris could be found who could enlighten or help her; at least, so she represented.

Gentle interrogation of the *attaché* by his *inamorata* caused him to admit the existence of a chess club of some renown in the capital of the country his embassy represented. It was a neutral country which bordered on Germany.

The actress then persuaded him to send this simple problem to the club mentioned with an urgent request to unravel the problem, if possible, and to let her know, through him, the result.

She knew, as does everyone who has had any close relationship with an embassy, that every embassy has its own private letter-bag, which is inviolate, and is passed over all frontiers uncensored and unopened, and is generally carried personally by some trusted messenger of the government interested.

The actress undoubtedly relied on the almost certain chance of her admirer sending his letters, this one in particular enclosing the problem illustration, in the embassy letter-bag. Which indeed he did. But the very astute members of the French Secret Service were wide awake to all her carefully-thought-out plans. They took measures accordingly, and the letter in question never reached its destination.

The watchers had reported that this actress had shown strong outward charitable dispositions, particularly towards the wounded soldiers from the war; that she frequently visited them in the various hospitals, sung to them, entertained them, and took them lavish presents of fruit and flowers. On one of these most praiseworthy visits she had been observed to linger unduly at the bedside of a young German aviation officer who had been shot down well behind the French lines.

The French Secret Service knew that prior to the war Germans had made many secret surveys of France, particularly of the northern territories and provinces. Greatly to the credit of the French, and unknown to the Germans, copies of most of these surveys had been obtained and filed away for possible future use or reference. Probably it was remembered that one of these survey maps had been ruled up with diagonal, lateral and parallel lines dividing the country into squares, precisely as is shown on a chess-board.

It was not therefore much of a surprise when it was ascertained on comparing the sketch of the chess problem, which had been brought back to Paris, with the copy survey plan of the Germans which had been ruled up as before mentioned, to find that the one exactly corresponded with the other. But the French War Office was certainly surprised to see before it, set out on the sketch of the chess-board, an accurate portrayal of all their reserve forces behind their front lines, posted in the exact positions which they then held. It required little perspicuity to understand that pawns on the board, or rather map, represented infantry; kings, heavy artillery; queens, field artillery; knights, cavalry; bishops, air divisions; and a castle, the military headquarters.

CHAPTER 5

Locating German Mine-Layers

The first work which was entrusted to me after having been granted a rating in the Foreign Secret Service was to hunt out the hiding-places of the large German auxiliary cruisers which had been specially fitted out for the important service of laying special minefields off remoter parts of the coastline of the British Isles.

Early in October, 1914, I landed at the south of Norway, and I zigzagged my way northwards on all kinds of craft that cruised about the thousands of fjords and islands, inquiring as unobservantly and disinterestedly as circumstances would admit in the hope of picking up some information which might lead me to the object of my search.

It was believed that these pests of the seas were using unknown fjords as hiding-places, and taking advantage of the double neutral routes of the inner and outer passage of the west coast of Norway to cover their coming and their going from Germany to the Icelandic coast, whence they dropped down upon the British Isles suddenly and unexpectedly, laid their dangerous batches of eggs, and returned the same way as they came.

I had travelled almost 750 miles northward, and I was quite convinced that no German mine-layer was concealed anywhere in that distance. Many reports I gathered of German war and other vessels of various rig and shape taking advantage of the neutral waterways; but they had all been under steam.

I had nearly reached the Arctic Circle, and I meant going north to Hammerfest, and even beyond, if the smallest clue showed itself. I was stopped in the town of T——, because there was a German vessel of some mystery which had been lying there quite a while. I wanted to learn more about her, so I lingered. She was a steamer of several thousand tons burden and loaded with coal. In spite of her disguised condition, she had been chased into neutral waters by English war-ships. Having remained over her allotted interval of time she became interned; but she was under suspicion and watched night and day by interested parties. This suspicion was accentuated by the fact that a strong head of steam was always kept up in her engine-room. Why?

Her name was s.s. *Brandenberg*, and it was openly whispered that she probably had on board supplies for submarines concealed under her coal.

The second night after my arrival, the proprietor of my hotel ex-hibited much friendliness towards me. Beside volunteering a consid-erable amount of interesting information about the war, Germany, and the Germans, he commented on "the great scandal," as he referred to it, that an English Consul at S—— was allowed to pocket hundreds of thousands of *kroner* by supplying the Germans with herrings whilst they were at war with the country he actually represented. He added, "It is no secret, the whole country is talking about it, and every man, woman, and child considers it disgraceful." Continuing a running fire of generalities, he went on to state that he had several German spies stopping at his hotel, and one who was English. He said he was quite sure about this, because they all seemed to try to watch each other, whilst the police and the military watched them. He said, as we stood in a secluded part of the *salle à manger:*

> That gentleman over there with the sandy moustache, sitting at a table in the corner by himself, is the English spy. He goes out every night about 8 o'clock and does not return until breakfast-time. He sits in railway trucks and woodstacks on the quays and other queer places, watching the *Brandenberg*. He thinks no one knows, but we all know. When he comes back in the morning, hints are dropped about amorous wanderings, and what 'won-derful dogs with the ladies some men are to be sure.' You see, he feels flattered in two ways, whilst we '*laugh in the trouser,*' as you English sometimes say. That man at the other end of the hall, with the military bearing, is a German spy, and so are the two at the middle table. Some of my servants draw money from all sides. They report to me a great deal. Perhaps a great deal more they keep to themselves. However, it seems to be good business for all of us, in spite of added and extra war burdens and taxes. It's a peculiar game on the whole, yet it's interesting.

I wondered why the proprietor should be so open with his confidences. It was probably the old, old feint—a luring to draw to attract, or extract, reciprocal advances. It was the proprietor's policy to sympathise and tender make-believe unanimity and agreement with all his guests; to humour all their troubles, whims, or fancies, so that all believed him to be their particular friend and supporter. It was the backbone of his business, which, needless to add, was a thriving and lucrative one.

Within twenty-four hours of arrival I instinctively felt and knew that I, too, had been labelled as a suspect. I was being watched and followed.

Immediate action to checkmate this was perhaps advisable. I knew personally the individual heads of some of the large business firms in the town and its neighbourhood. I had acted legally for or against several of them in England, in matters concerning the expenditure of thousands of pounds. It would be simple to raise imaginary or other business issues. I mentally determined that it should be done without delay.

When next I left the hotel a couple of the wealthiest local traders called shortly afterwards to inquire for me. They expressed annoyance at my absence and sought the proprietor. That gentleman, at their request, sent out the hotel porter and a page to visit the main streets, the barbers' shops, the post-office, and other possible places wherein I might be met with. Whilst they were chafing outwardly in their impatience, they casually mentioned to the proprietor that I was one of the best-known Continental lawyers in London, from Gibraltar to Hammerfest; that I had come over specially to transact some important business with which they were indirectly connected and which might detain me in the country some considerable period, and that I was a guest worthy of consideration.

An hour later I returned. I was all apologies for my absence. I had called at the respective offices of my visitors and I had found them out. The proprietor bustled away with the news, by which he probably ingratiated himself a little further into the confidence of other guests of different nationality.

Subsequent events proved that my ruse had for the time being worked successfully against my opponents, although the local authorities, who had known me and of me for many years past, may have entertained their own surmises concerning my advent at that particular place and at that particular period of the world's history.

Next day was blustering and stormy. Snowflakes fell thick in large globules in the streets, making them almost impassable to traffic; yet a silent and unobtrusive man ploughed his way to the hotel soon after daylight, carrying interesting news.

The German auxiliary fast cruiser *Berlin* had been seen entering the fjord.

This was indeed important. The news must at any cost be transmitted home, and at the earliest possible moment.

It appeared that the cruiser, a vessel of some 18,000 tons, armed with eight to a dozen quick-firing guns and other equipment, had, under her enormously powerful engines, and after disposing of her cargo of mines, laid a course northwards well into the region of floating ice, thus outwitting the vigilance of the English patrol boats. Taking the fullest advantage of the awful weather and frequent snowstorms, she had slipped unobserved through the tortuous entrances and difficult channels of the Norwegian coast; past the guard fortresses at ———; past the guardships; and finally dropped her anchor unchallenged and unhindered under the windows of the town of ———, which half encircles one of the most coveted harbours in all Europe.

It was a marvellous feat of navigation, but then it is an open secret that members of the German Navy know the ins and outs of the Norwegian fjords even better than Norwegians do themselves. They have also much better charts; both of which facts they proved in a startling manner in their manoeuvres before the war.

It is another open secret that at the German War Office, in the Wilhelmstrasse, Berlin, was kept a complete series of the Ordnance Maps of England, brought fully up-to-date by secret surveys, which gave detail and information that our maps do not show and which our War Office is probably quite unacquainted with. I was never more astonished in my life, although I had the sense to conceal it, than when an alleged German commercial traveller with whom I had been travelling somewhere in Finland sketched, in order to illustrate an argument, a correct plan of a remote part of the East Coast of England with which I was very well acquainted. On this sketch the aforesaid traveller proceeded to delineate fords to streams and hidden roadways, the existence of which most of those even who had dwelt all their lives in the parishes affected had either forgotten or never knew about.

To return to the subject. The long-lost *Berlin* had been run to ground. The burning question of the moment was whether she would face the music and make a bolt for the Fatherland or whether she would remain where she was and become interned. A collection of

British cruisers outside probably caused her to elect the latter course. So it was up to me, somehow or other, to try and ferret out all I could relating to her recent voyage. But how?

The chief of the British Secret Service is never interested in detail. To him the most interesting particulars, showing how an objective is attained, are irritating and merely so much waste of time. His requirements and mind centre only round concrete results, congealed into the fewest possible number of words. Whilst interviews in his office are limited almost to grudgingly-given minutes.

It is undoubtedly prudent and wise to draw a bough over my innumerable snow-trails in order to obliterate the footprints of my tortuous wanderings during the days that followed. Suffice to say that, night and day, awake or dreaming, the subject never left my thoughts, whilst I schemed and invented possible and impossible plans, until at last one day chance supplied the missing link.

Meanwhile side issues were not wanting. German agents had traced the hotel proprietor's show-English-spy to his nightly lair in the woodstacks. They naturally attached an unknown importance to what they believed to be his anxiety concerning the safety of these piles of innocent timber. They appeared to assume that this particular wood—worth possibly somewhere about £20,000—was considered of great value to the English Government. Accordingly they planned, by contra espionage, to lure the nightly watcher in another direction. As soon as his presence was thus temporarily removed they promptly fired the pile, which job was so thoroughly well done that hardly a plank could be salved from the flames.

Having been confidentially told that I was suspected of being an English S.S. agent, I promptly called up on the telephone the head of the department which controlled these matters, and invited him to lunch. Fortunately I knew him well and could do so. It was humorous that whilst I was doing this the gentleman in question happened to be attending a small committee meeting which was, at the moment, discussing my *bona fides*, and the somewhat important personage called for raised unavailing protests at being compelled to answer my insistent call, only to learn of the unimportant invitation to himself from the actual suspect whose presence was then under discussion and whom it was part of his duty to be accountable for.

I could not help subsequently smiling when I was privately informed by another member of the committee that the old colonel had returned from the telephone, very red in the face, and swearing audibly about that "d—d impudent mad-brained Englishman who was chasing him about, instead of waiting to be properly chased," or its equivalent in words in his own language.

In a snug creek, away from the busy waterways and the ever-moving industry of the heavily overloaded quays, was securely moored and laid up for the winter a palatial pleasure yacht, belonging to a well-known Russian sugar queen of reputed fabulous wealth. Her captain and crew were objects of interest to all. I considered it politic to ingratiate myself with the crew with a view to future possibilities.

In course of time, certain ladies of unknown origin appeared at various hotels in the town and its environs. They possessed youth, beauty, vivacity of spirit, charm of manner, and apparently plenty of ready money to add to their attraction and graces. They had friends who soon called, or met them at or away from their hotels. From information received and from personal observation, I deemed it expedient to push myself forward into this small but somewhat exclusive circle, although it required the utmost ingenuity to mix with the members of these various circles whilst in constant touch with the chief residents of the town without permitting one group to gain knowledge of my intimacy with other groups.

By judicious expenditure in hospitality and a free hand with small gifts, I was able to draw into my confidences half a dozen acquaintances whom I could trust to render any assistance I might perhaps at some time require. Meanwhile I was ostensibly engaged in legal matters. Clients called with masses of papers and remained closeted with me for hours. Often they remained for meals, and then the choicest of wines were ordered, and the last doubts the proprietor of the hotel might have entertained vanished.

Within a week or ten days an accurate report was secretly handed to me of the exact number, nationality, and rating of every man on board the enemy vessel. It also contained addenda giving the name and business of every visitor thereto, and the duration of each visit; this afforded matter for cogitation, reflection, and thought.

My next requirement was a roughly summed-up estimate of the characteristics of each person I designated, with all possible information and detail concerning their believed weaknesses, whims, fancies, hobbies, ambitions, or failings, which I persisted in procuring concerning every person I could on the before-mentioned list. This was a long and more difficult task. Pride, conceit, alcohol, women, and money figured against one or the other. The two former would seem the easiest to work upon, but in the end it was the latter which affected the *débàcle*.

Having laid well my plans, which promised almost certain successful results, it was advisable for me to depart from the town and district in order that matters might be permitted to operate successfully without any possible chance of failure through some remote suspicion being hatched and developed from my presence. It was far better for me to watch from a distance, to observe the effects of palm-oil penetrate deeper and yet deeper, until that which I was most anxious to get hold of, namely, material extracts from the log of the recent voyage of this important vessel, had been brought ashore and communicated; and, what was most important of all, the exact number of mines she had laid in British waters, with precise latitude and longitude of such laying.

It was expensive, but it was worth the outlay many times over. It would have been undoubtedly a very great surprise indeed to the *kultured* Hun sea-pirates, had they only known how their most jealously-guarded secrets were thus so easily opened up.

When in England some months after this information had been communicated, I had an opportunity of interviewing some officers and members of the crews on board various minesweeping vessels which had been employed to remove these pests from navigable waters. They were men engaged to harvest what the *Berlin* was alleged to have sown near Tory Island, which lies off the north-west coast of Ireland, and not far from the all-important Loch Swilly. The first and second fleet sent there to act upon the information which had been collected in the manner hereinbefore described seem to have returned to their respective bases and reported there were no mines to be found. But whilst those in authority were debating or doubting the accuracy of the original information collected abroad, proof positive soon convinced them.

Vessel after vessel was reported sunk by mine contact, including the new leviathan, H.M.S. *Audacious*, which awful disaster was religiously hushed up and kept away from the ken of the English nation. American papers, however, exhibited photos of the wreck and rescues which were freely copied by international journals, whilst Germany knew all about it from the first. The third fleet of mine-sweepers, eventually sent to Tory Island with instructions to sweep the same area as at first directed but at a greater depth, gathered in about 120 to 130 large mines out of the 150 said to have been sown there. But this was after far too many casualties had been reported, and much shipping, with valuable lives, had been lost to Great Britain.

Although at times I am notoriously loquacious, I can also be a deep thinker. Sometimes when alone during those dark days in the solitude of deep forests, or perched upon some bleak promontory jutting out into northern seas and watching over the angry waters beneath me, I would sit for hours lost in meditation turning over in my mind again and again passing events, weighing the possibilities, probabilities, alleged diplomatic mistakes and indiscretions; social upheavals, labour strikes, absurd optimism of a section of the Press; false security created by too rigid censorship; political dangers from continued vote-angling and pandering to obvious German agitation amongst workmen and miners; continued short-sighted political revenge upon English landowners for the suppression rather than encouragement of any increased user of the land towards food production; contradictions which were irreconcilable; on the one hand enormous and useless expenditures, on the other unparalleled meanness and littleness; the clinging to fatal fallacies by refusing conscription; the insistence with which old and admittedly absolutely incompetent officials were kept in office; refusals to find places—even honorary ones—for admittedly first-class younger volunteers from our colonies; muddle upon muddle; waste upon waste; mistake upon mistake; yet the glorious gallantry and irrepressible loyalty and patriotism of Britisher units and her allies on land and sea seemed to be pulling everything through.

Having regard to the thirty years' preparation of Germany and the utter unpreparedness of England, a miracle seemed in the process of evolution. Would the nations involved cease their strife owing to absolute exhaustion and attrition? Would the Entente eventually achieve full consummation of its hopes, so devoutly to be wished? Or was the sequel foreshadowed by the late Lord Tennyson:

Chaos, Cosmos! Cosmos, Chaos! who can tell how all will end?
Read the wide world's annals, you, and take their wisdom for your friend;
Hope the best, but hold the Present fatal daughter of the Past,
Shape your heart to front the hour, but dream not that the hour will last.

CHAPTER 6

Deposing a Rival

After a *coup* of importance has been successfully accomplished, it is sometimes advisable for a Secret Service agent to betake himself to a quiet, secluded place where his identity and his activities are least likely to be known, or even suspected.

Towards Christmas, in the first year of the war, I found myself in such a position; my work for some weeks past had been not only exceedingly strenuous, but, it was gratifying to remember, it had also been successful. Perhaps luck had unduly favoured me. Anyway, I knew quite enough of the enemy to be only too well assured that he would stop at nothing to get, or to attempt to get, even with me if he possibly could. I also thoroughly understood it was advisable for more reasons than one that I should take a well-earned rest, a few days breathing-space until further demands were made upon my individual efforts.

Thus it was I turned my face towards a lonely, secluded little haven snugly concealed in an inner fjord of the Norwegian coast where I intended to sleep and dream and sink all traces of my existence on earth for a few brief days at least.

December, 1914, in northern seas was a month of record storms and multitudinous wrecks. The daily life of those unfortunates whose duties took them there, or compelled them to navigate, was unenviable in the extreme. Ice, which accumulated and increased in its envelopment hourly, not only made decks doubly dangerous, but, unless removed from rails, ropes, deckhouses, and other parts of a ship at periodical intervals might possibly threaten worse disaster than the wrecks and sunken rocks around.

Fogs, snowstorms, floating mines, mountainous seas, submerged hulks and treacherous shoals, coupled with the long, long winter nights, were enemies more to be feared than the cruel Hun. A few weeks of this work would try any man; it had been more than enough for me, a landsman whose soul never yearned for the life of a sailor.

The relief at hearing the cranky, ought-to-have-been-long-ago-condemned old packet, rejoicing in the high-sounding name of some forgotten heathen god, bump and scrape and groan against the piling of the quay at my quiet sleepy little Scandinavian seaport, was a joy not to be expressed in words. To me who had roughed it, under strenuous conditions, the coarse fare and the still coarser bed-linen on even a flea-smothered couch seemed Valhalla adorned.

It was rest. It was peace. It was contentment. It naturally followed that it was supreme happiness for the immediate moment.

No shack, cottage, or villa in these northern parts runs to window curtains. Darkness comes early in the afternoon. Daylight follows late in the morning, varying in time in accordance with latitude. Sleep, the greatest blessing on earth, after such fatigues and endurance would be long and profound. There was no reason to arise early. To trust to Nature's call with the sun would probably mean somewhere about 10 a.m. or later.

It was, of course, necessary for me to convey to headquarters the information of my whereabouts, which duty performed, the luxuries and enjoyments at hand were embraced by me with limitless indulgence.

It was late next day when a frowsy-haired fishwife brought my *café au lait*, also news that I was wanted. I was not surprised. A Secret Service agent is never allowed to rest. Holidays, quietude, peace, or enjoyment are words not known in his vocabulary. Anyone envying those in the service should first contemplate that its units are looked upon as mere chattels of little worth, easily to be replaced should accident or machination cause them to fall by the way or to be removed to a better land. Such patriots must sink all home-ties, business relationships, pleasures, pains, and personal thoughts for the one and only object—to achieve the seemingly impossible.

Outside it was snowing in big, massive flakes, which added many inches in a few hours to the deep covering already settled on the solidly-frozen earth. It was biting cold, but I had to face it. Struggling along as best I could against the unkind elements, I made three doubles and a walk back to test whether any possible observer took interest in my movements, such a precaution being always advisable after advent on fresh ground. Then, slipping up an unfrequented pathway, I gained the shelter of another fisherman's hut, where an enthusiastic welcome from numerous chubby-faced bairns awaited me.

It's a good rule in life to remember the little ones. Every decent-minded parent worships his or her children. If a home possess none, then affections are often centred on some four-footed animal. Make a fuss over these and a weakness in the hardest heart is at once touched. My annual chocolate bill averaged many pounds, whilst it has returned to me tenfold its value in the pleasure created. Not a penny of such outlay could be grudged.

A good friend was awaiting my arrival. He had a small package, which had come to hand shortly before. He was one of those open-hearted, unsuspecting innocents who led the simple life and believed ill of no man. I wished him to continue to hold his good opinions, particularly regarding myself. In murmuring my thanks for the parcel, I hazarded the supposition that it probably contained some long-sought smokes. On opening it before his eyes, so to speak, there was disclosed a tin of pipe tobacco and a bundle of cigars, which were at once sampled.

Sherlock Holmes would probably have noticed that one, and one cigar only, had had its smoking-end bitten off. Further, that that particular cigar was not selected by me, owing perhaps—perhaps not—to the possibility of its having already been tested in a stranger's mouth. Be that as it may, after an hour's small talk (one must never be at all impatient in Scandinavia), I took my departure and carried the precious tobacco away with me.

A careful dissection of the bitten cigar, in the seclusion of my own quarters, brought to light a scrap of paper. A pocket glass helped me to decipher the mystic signs, the interpretation whereof read as follows:

Karl Von S——, a German Artillery officer, married to a native of Scandinavia, is posing as a convalescent consumptive and has been some time in a private villa on the Island of ——. He is much too friendly with the wireless operator there, also the garrison officers. Advisable that he be removed at once. You must do it. Act promptly.

Now I was a matter of 300 miles' travel from the *locus in quo*. It was in the immediate neighbourhood of large army reserves and was also much frequented by warships and naval men. Three times I reread the message in order to memorise it, then I burnt it to ashes. "He must be removed at once. You must do it."

Now it is very easy to sit in an office and give commands, right and left, for this and for that, or for anything which strikes the fancy. But it's altogether a different proposition to find oneself in the shoes of the commanded one. I soon began to feel worried. The thought of the seeming impossibility of the carrying out of the order was annoying. I lit cigar after cigar, as I lay on the couch with closed eyes; I smoked, and thought, and scratched for an indefinite period; until my all too lively stable companions effectually did for me what I was so vainly racking my brains to find some way of bringing about with regard to another.

Two hours' brisk walk in the open air did not solve the problem. So I despatched a message to a colleague, N. P., who was then on the Russian frontier, informing him that we must meet immediately, each coming half-way towards the other.

N. P. knew that I should never trouble him over trifles, and, good fellow that he was, he answered the call without delay. We met at a frontier town, within a day or so of the receipt of original instructions. When I explained the problem and how the more I had thought it over the further its solution seemed to fade away, N. P. naturally wanted to know why I had summoned him to meet me.

"That is easy, my dear Nixie," I exclaimed; "you are without doubt the cleverest man in the Service. You speak many tongues. You are a garrison artillery staff officer. What better material could anyone wish for to help unravel a proposition like this? He must be removed at once. You must do it."

"Not me, my boy. That won't come off. It's your job, and I would not deprive you of the honour and glory of it for worlds."

"Ah, Nixie, my dear fellow, we may get the jobs, but all the honour and glory is appropriated by the gentlemen who remain at home. I think we both appreciate that point; but what I want to debate with you are possibilities, actualities, and probabilities. If either of us, for example, were on a small island and we received a warning that a German had had orders to shift us—what would you fear most?"

"I should fear nothing."

"I don't mean it that way. What I mean is, wherein would you be most careful, or most on your guard?"

"He would not get a dog's chance with me, anyway," snapped N. P. Then he added in a petulant tone, "I want some more whiskey and another cigar. It helps one to think better."

"How about your line of communications?" I queried.

"No living soul would ever get hold of mine," Nixie replied.

"Of course not; but don't you see it's a danger, it's a weak spot that can be shot at."

"No, I don't," said Nixie, stretching himself at full length on the sofa until it creaked again and again.

I was lying on a bed, and the room was in darkness. One can think better in the dark. There is no counter-attraction for the sense of sight to divert any stray thought from the objective in being. The brain becomes more active and more concentrative accordingly.

"If you flatter yourself you can touch his lines of communication—after he has been established some time, as the message says, you are apt to get your fingers burnt in the trying. Won't do, Jim, my boy. Try and think of something else."

"Bide a wee. Don't you see where we are drifting to? My idea is that we don't try to touch him at all, but that *we make a line of communication in order to be able to break it. Twiggez vous?*"

A short silence ensued, which Nixie broke, in an emphasised drawling tone: "You diabolical devil! You mean you will send a note to him which you will take good care is intercepted before he gets it, and in such a manner that the local authorities will do the rest to complete the *coup de grâce.*"

"That's my suggestion," I exclaimed in a deliberate tone. "Also that's where you come in. You, being a garrison expert, will weave the strands and splice the knot of rope that will eventually hang him. Think it out. Ponder over how it will work."

For a long time we both smoked in silence, and we smoked in the dark, which somehow seems entirely different from smoking when one can see the blue clouds drifting. How long the interval lasted neither of us could tell. It seemed an age. Then Nixie Pixie demanded lights up. He wanted to get on with the business. He was keenly interested. His instincts foretold success, and, what was far sweeter to both of us, we imagined one more dictatorial militarist would shortly be driven back to stew in the *kultured* juice of Teutonic concentrated cruelties, in the Fatherland.

With lights burning and pens and papers before us, we soon filled in necessary details of the plan of campaign; chuckling the while in anticipatory satisfaction at the debacle to come.

Before dawn broke on the day following we had drifted apart; as silent shadows of the night we flitted to and from our respective destinations, whilst the world slept, and no watchman had observed our coming or our going. Nixie was away to the westward by train, whilst

I followed the currents of the ever-restless sea.

★★★★★★

Night and day I travelled, in desperate haste. I journeyed to the northern frontier of Germany, to a small, uninviting place on the map, where I had a colleague working, who for many years had lived in Germany and who had only crossed the frontier a short time prior to the declaration of war.

This English gentleman was perfectly acquainted with both High and Low Prussian. In a matter of this kind, where straws had to be grasped at and relied upon, it was essential to any hope of success to carry out every minute detail with the greatest accuracy.

I was anxious to have a certain message which I had drafted *en route* translated into accurate and perfect High German. I did not feel confident to do this myself, hence my present mission.

I hunted up my colleague, who entered enthusiastically upon the work, and immediately after its completion I journeyed away again to a small sleepy hamlet not far removed from the nearest point on the mainland contiguous to the island in question. I covered several hundreds of miles during the four days these journeys occupied my attention.

To carry out the plan which I had devolved I secured the necessary materials at places where no suspicion was likely to be aroused. They were simple in themselves: an etching pen, some fine, thin foreign correspondence paper, some oil-silk and a small tin phial. The message, which will be disclosed later, was most carefully written in German characters under a magnifying glass, which latter I always carry.

It was then rolled up, carefully protected by an outer covering of oil-silk and inserted into a tin phial.

The next steps in the plot to remove this obnoxious German officer from the security of his stronghold, which certain high officials were convinced he was using to contravene the laws of hospitality, trust, and friendship, were carried out by another.

The reason for this should be obvious. The risk was nothing in itself, but it was a matter of importance that I should not be implicated, either directly or indirectly, with such a matter, so that my own chances for further activity in the cause of my country might not be endangered. I remember the old adage, "*Sauce for the goose is equally good sauce for the gander.*"

I therefore arranged matters down to the smallest details, impressing every point upon my only too willing assistant, and then I quickly took my departure to a place many, many miles away from the locality in question, there to await with impatient interest the report I was promised, which should tell me whether the scheme attempted had succeeded or proved a disappointing fiasco.

I had not long to wait. Within three days a message was flashed to me. I visualise events as I believe they happened.

On the never-to-be-forgotten day a certain sentry was pacing a rocky promontory on a lonely island overlooking lonely waters. In spite of its uninviting outward appearance this island was a place of the utmost importance, because it guarded the watergate to many a European capital.

The sentry was impatient. It was growing dark. He was cold and hungry, and none too pleased at his job; besides, he imagined the relief guard was late. Perhaps it was.

Whilst in this uneasy frame of mind a small sailing-boat hove into sight. She was hugging the shore, or rather the rocky cliffs of which the shore consisted. When within a few hundred yards of the sentry's position, the mast and sail were taken down and stowed, and the boat-man proceeded to row.

The sentry was interested.

As the boat approached nearer to his position it disappeared into a small alcove, formed by overhanging cliffs, and he saw it no more.

Perhaps it was a coincidence that this happened just a quarter of an hour before the sentry should be relieved. But in that fifteen minutes he had ample time to work himself into a high pitch of excitement.

The gloaming had increased. He was straining his eyes into the coming night when the sergeant with the relief arrived.

A quick whispered report caused double guards to be mounted, men to be sent to cover possible lines of retreat, and a messenger to be despatched for assistance on the water. These precautions were efficient and effective. The mysterious boatman was captured.

It was not known whether he was too frightened, or too unintelligent, or too intoxicated to give a satisfactory account of his movements, but in a parcel concealed under odd bits of rope and sailcloth was a dead codfish addressed to Herr K.V.S.

Whilst the captured one was meditating under lock and key, the boat and its contents were minutely examined. Nothing unusual had been found on the prisoner, nothing else had been found in the boat. The codfish was ordered to be dissected, when, lo and behold! a small metal tube was extracted from the gullet. Inside this, tightly rolled and wrapped in oil-silk, was a small piece of thin foreign correspondence paper, which, on being held up to the light, revealed hieroglyphics in the smallest of German characters imaginable.

Subsequent investigation and examination elicited that the boatman had agreed to deliver the parcel personally to Herr K. von S—— at a certain place, and at a certain hour in the evening, for which he had received a generous sum of money. The advisability of remaining in the alcove until dark to prevent the military from holding him up, or prying into his parcel, had been suggested to him by his employer, who was quite a stranger to him. He had never seen him until two hours before he had arranged to bring the parcel along; he had assured him it was all right. It was only an act of kindness to a sick man. There could be no harm done by it.

A thin story indeed, but the fishermen of northern seas are a confiding, unsuspecting, innocent race.

The letter proved to be written in Prussian or High German. It required a good magnifying glass to decipher it. It was highly technical in its terms, and was evidently composed by a thoroughly expert *garrison artillery officer.* It ran somewhat as follows:

1. You say we can now communicate with you through more open channels but we doubt this and fear taking any avoidable risk.

2. On the plans you sent us you omitted to mark the ranges of the guns numbered 1, 5, and 7.

3. The exact location of the magazine was not clearly defined.

4. What are the reliefs? Give exact detail.

5. Ascertain exact amounts of ammunition at present stored, with full capacity for added reserves.

6. Advise estimated sum to cover wireless operators' requirements for a year.

7. . . . .

8. . . . .

9. . . . .

10. Next time cut a larger portion off the dorsal fin, as your last message was nearly missed through difficulty in identification.

The boatman, who was a local man and innocent enough, was lectured and frightened half out of his wits, and finally permitted to go.

Captain Karl von S—— with his wife and family were given twelve short hours to clear the country, once and for all, with peremptory orders never to set foot in it again. Probably he is wondering to this day what earthly reason could have instigated such a decisive and unmistakably severe command.

The inhabitants on the island cannot yet understand why no live fish of any description, nor dead fish which had not been split open from head to tail, were permitted to be imported or exported, whether destined for private consumption or for other uses.

Many miles away from the island in question a telegraph official a few days later in a small town carefully scrutinised an innocently worded message which was handed in at his office shortly after these stirring events had occurred. It was, however, permitted to pass and in due course its recipient, my headquarters department, interpreted its hidden meaning. It ran:

The shoddy article submitted and marked K. V. S. has been returned as not up to sample and unworthy of retention. Next please!—Jim.

CHAPTER 7

Fighting German Agents With Faked Weapons

The sudden transportation and exile of an alleged invalid German officer back to the home of his fathers had been a distinct secret score for the British Foreign Secret Service Intelligence Department, although probably no one was aware of this except those in the innermost circles of the Service of the two countries directly concerned.

As a necessary precaution for my own safety I had very discreetly removed myself some hundreds of miles in another direction as soon as it was certain that my trap had been properly sprung. With my mind concentrated on other matters I had almost forgotten the episode, when a whisper echoed and re-echoed from the south that the full fury of the Northern German espionage bureau had been invoked upon my fortunate or unfortunate head, and that I must beware of a certain Baron Nordenpligt,[1] which irate Teuton had started hot on my trail, vowing the direst vengeance imaginable. "*Nordenpligt*" in English means "the North duty or obligation," and I was at no loss to comprehend the full force of the hinted warning thus so auspiciously conveyed to me.

Whilst musing over events under the benign influence of my usual black cigar, some stir became apparent in the entrance hall of the hotel at which I was then stopping. Several newcomers had arrived. One very fat lady appeared over-concerned regarding the handling of her many belongings. A wheezy, consumptive-looking weakling of humanity was trying to assist her. Most probably he would have been crushed under an iron-bound trunk which a porter was lowering from the roof of the hotel bus had not another traveller, seeing the

---

1. A fictitious name, but near enough to give the desired clue.

danger, rushed forward to his assistance. As he did so he involuntarily ejaculated the short exclamation, "*Mein Gott!*" My ears tingled at once. The Teutonic oath had given away the nationality of this individual, at all events. It became my immediate business to ascertain who he was, and what his business might be. Without a moment's hesitation I also sprang to the rescue.

The result of too many persons concerning themselves with the matters of one led to a natural tangle and considerable jostling in which the German gentleman lost his *pince-nez*. In stopping to recover them a leather case fell from his inside breast pocket. But before he could reach it I had anticipated his desire, picked up the article in question, and handed it to its owner. In so doing I observed that on one corner was an embossed gold coronet and monogram, in which the letter "N" was prominent.

My room was on the first floor. I had registered my occupation as that of a fish merchant of Scandinavian origin, which, on a strict investigation, might have been held not too remote. The German baron, for such he undoubtedly was, had registered as a commercial traveller from an inland town in Denmark, whilst he obviously knew the language of that country as well as he did his own. It was ominous that he subsequently contrived to secure a bedroom adjoining mine, whilst the fat lady sandwiched herself into possession of another apartment which was situated on the other side.

After supper I placed three hair tests on my belongings, and lighting the inevitable weed strolled out to give matters a chance to develop.

At the back of the hotel was a large heap of moss-bedecked boulders, behind which was a rocky hill, in the crevasses and hollows of which some scant vegetation had collected and a few scraggy fir-trees formed an arboreal retreat where in the summer months loiterers could sit and enjoy the view with the added pleasure of light refreshments from the hotel.

This arbour commanded a full view of the windows of the back rooms, the centre one of which was for the time being in my occupation.

The hair test is a useful expedient for gauging the inquisitiveness or prying proclivities of one's immediate neighbours. It is affixed by tension from two notches, or with the aid of a little wax. Either method will be found equally efficacious. Human hairs a few inches in length are easily procurable; a single one is practically invisible to the naked eye, and a slight strain will snap it. If cunningly placed across the two covers of a box, on the lid of a box, over an unlocked bag, trunk, suitcase or elsewhere, few Paul Prys would ever dream of suspecting its presence, and the precaution inevitably tells its own tale.

A very clever investigator would probably be on the lookout for anything of this kind, but an equally clever actor would so place at least one of his precaution signals that it would be impossible to touch the object it protected without a break or disturbance sufficient to notice.

When night fell it was dark, cold, and raw, with a nasty wind blowing, and I found the draughty arbour none too cosy for my liking, but I stayed there for upwards of an hour in the belief that something was going to turn up. Meanwhile half a gale whistled through leafless branches and howled round the crevasses and protuberances of the rocky background. Just as I was on the point of quitting I observed a faint flicker of light upon the blind of my room, and I knew that evil agents were abroad.

An attempt to ascend the stairway behind a couple of other visitors whereby I could gain my apartment unobserved was frustrated by the stout lady before mentioned. She, by an extraordinary coincidence, started to come downstairs just as my foot had gained the last step of the ascent. In her haste she jostled first one and then the other of the gentlemen meeting her, for which she apologised most profusely and in a loud, jovial, bantering manner.

I leaned against the wall and laughed. It was my custom to take everything as it came, never to meet trouble halfway by worrying, and even to attempt the credit of gaining happiness under almost impossible conditions.

In the present instance the fortune of war favoured me, although conditions were adverse. A large mirror hung upon the landing, the reflection field of which embraced wide angles. I, happening to glance upwards and beyond the little pleasantries going on above, observed a shadow darken the surface of the glass, but the noise made by the merry-makers on the stairhead prevented any slighter sounds from being heard.

Later on, when I had entered and was alone within the privacy of my own apartment, examining the test traps at my leisure, all possible doubt of an interest having been taken in my belongings was removed.

What would happen next?

The veiled secret warning that had been given me portended mischief. It was hardly reasonable to suppose one's natural enemy would take a knock-down blow without reprisals. They were more than hinted at in the urgent message I had received. I was not deceived for one moment. I felt myself within the claws of the pincers and it was up to me to wriggle out before they could be closed. There must be no hesitation, no delay, and no "wait and see" about my decisions. I must quit, and that at once, or the worst might befall.

Having supped in the restaurant common to all guests of the hostelry, I retired early, but instead of undressing I lay upon the outside of the bed and smoked and read until the early hours of the morning, between whiles turning over many matters of more or less moment in my mind.

I remembered that the latest ejected one from that hospitable country was by no means the only one who had unceremoniously been pushed out by reason of information which had reached the authorities in a roundabout untraceable way. The origin had never come to light, but the inmates of Koenigergratzerstrasse No. 70 probably had a shrewd suspicion whom they could credit for the attention. S—— was another very active German agent who had recently been expelled the country; he returned almost immediately under another name and disguise. He successfully crossed the frontier and would in all probability have escaped identification had not certain strings been pulled whereby he was located and ejected again, within forty-eight hours of his arrival. Most annoying to him, of course, but then these small matters had of necessity to be attended to.

It was unpleasant to remember that the number of wrecks along the coast was abnormal. The majority of these unfortunate vessels were or had been cargo carriers to Germany. Perhaps it was a just retribution that they should sink or encounter disaster preventing their further assistance to direct acts of barbarism by the mad dogs of Europe. Be that as it may, Germans in that particular neighbourhood would hardly have agreed with any such sentiments; nor were they sympathetic towards the invective which was raised by the local police and others interested—although breathed *sub rosa*—against fellow-countrymen of theirs who were suspected of having fired several vast timber-stacks supposed to have been sold to England.

Taking one consideration with another no love was lost between travellers from England and Germany.

At 2 a.m., as the silent corridors of the hotel were awakened by the cuckoos from a Swiss-made clock on the landing, I stealthily emerged from my apartment. Tiptoeing along past several of the adjoining bedrooms, I changed the boots standing outside their respective doors, placing large for small and *vice versâ*. But one pair I selected from the extreme end of the corridor as being as nearly as I could judge a fair match in size to my own. These I brought along, and not being an obstinate, blind-to-all-home-principle-Free-Trade Britisher, I dumped them down outside my own door. It should have become obvious to the reader that I was contemplating my departure. There had been former occasions when I had been compelled to leave my own boots behind me, whereby thoughtful hotel attendants and others had been deceived into believing me to be a very late riser, and I had been thereby enabled to cover many a league before the simple deception had been exposed.

But on the occasion in question, in the course of my calm, contemplative meditations upon the bed, I had evolved the comforting conclusion that it would be better far to borrow the foot-gear of some other traveller in order to carry into effect my playful little deception, rather than sacrifice any more boots of my own. The ruse would assuredly work equally as well, whilst past experiences had taught me that it was a much easier matter to remove a pair of boots from a neighbouring doorway than to leave my own behind, necessitating the trouble and expense of their subsequent replacement.

"Shooting the moon" in this manner is a pastime which I may add is not usual with me, but there are occasions in the career of everyone when discretion and retirement are undoubtedly the better part of valour.

Next morning I was chuckling to myself at about 10 o'clock, and picturing the confusion and the language likely to be used by the parties mostly concerned, at the small hotel I had quitted so suddenly overnight.

What a sell it would be to His Excellency the Baron to find that his bird had once more flown, and what a head-aching task he would have of it if he tried to trail his quarry Indian fashion instead of relying upon the surer and less worrying methods known to the Secret Service agents of all nations.

At least I knew I was safe for another week certain, and much could be done in that time. So I journeyed away in an exulting frame of mind to a colleague who I knew had some very interesting investigations which he was following up in the neighbourhood of one of the largest and most important docks on the Baltic Sea.

Within a couple of hours of my arrival I was in harness again. Some important particulars from the manifest and bills of lading of a big steamer were wanted. The captain was a convivial soul with a great weakness for sport of all kinds; and it was suggested that I, being a sportsman myself, might be able to succeed in drawing him, although so far no one else had been able to do so.

A bottle of whiskey and a bundle of cigars were calculated to be sufficient to move the information required. But they failed. Patience and perseverance rarely fail. On this occasion both seemed useless.

From 2 p.m. until 2 a.m., twelve solid hours, I sat listening, talking, complimenting, criticising, flattering, cajoling, and arguing in such manner that at first I entirely disagreed, then allowed myself to be talked round to absolute approval. In short, no artifice that calculated cunning could suggest was omitted, yet results proved fruitless. Thus at 2 a.m. I was forced to abandon my objective of the day, and I agreed it was time to turn in.

Perhaps the disappointment of failing to achieve a purpose influenced my judgment. Perhaps it was the weather. Perhaps it was the mellowing effects of some decent whiskey which made me feel devil-may-care and careless. Anyhow, I was foolish in the extreme not to have accepted the proffered and pressed invitation of a berth on board the ship I was then visiting in preference to the more or less dangerous passage of the docks which was my only alternative.

That there was any real danger never entered my head. Had it done so it would probably have made little difference, excepting that I might have borrowed a stick, or some weapon of defence. It was not until I was actually cornered that I remembered I had left my revolver at home. The incident was so sudden there was no time to think. Spontaneous action alone was capable of saving what might have proved a remarkably awkward position.

Hanging on to a rope guide I slid down the gangway which was covered some inches thick with a coating of ice. Groping a pathway as best I could across the quay in the dark, amongst innumerable stacks of freighted goods and merchandise of every description, was no easy matter. Nor were my difficulties lessened by a snowstorm which raged at the time. Passing between some sheds, and stack after stack of cotton bales, destined for the land of barbaric "*kultur*," I made my way towards the only faint glimmering light which flickered its bilious rays from the one solitary lamp-post in that immediate neighbourhood.

Just as I reached it I heard a voice. At the same time I observed two shadows which seemed to appear and disappear somewhere near the piles of cotton. No complete sentence reached my ears, only two words, "*Das vas,*" uttered in a high-pitched key and with startling suddenness. The remaining words were lost in the lowered tone. Those words, however, were quite enough. I had been privately informed, only that morning, by an interesting conveyer of intelligence newly arrived, from Berlin, that some rather important German officials were taking a kindly interest in my welfare; certainly to the extent that they had offered quite a substantial sum of cash (not paper or cheques) for my delivery in their country, condition no object. The sum named was far and away beyond what I would ever have imagined my uninteresting carcase was worth. In a flash the situation became clear to me. It was a plant to kidnap. Great, blundering, self-satisfied, careless, conceited ass that I undoubtedly was, I had walked right into the spider's web without so much as a toothpick on me with which to put up a fight.

Immediately in front of where I was standing was an open space, some forty yards across. The ground was covered a foot deep or more with snow. Concealed thereby and beneath it were railway lines, points, uneven places, bits of wood, parts of packing-cases, hoops, and innumerable obstacles of all kinds, which I knew of too well, having been frequently tripped by them on former occasions. To attempt to rush it would be courting disaster.

The shadows, hardly discernible in the feeble light, seemed to flicker nearer and nearer. Then I observed a third, and silently I wondered how many in all I should have to contend with. Only one thing was absolutely definite in my mind, that was, come what might, I had not the slightest intention of having my liberty curtailed without a fight to a finish.

As before stated, I had reached the only lamp-post anywhere around. My movements were observable, whereas those who were hunting me were concealed by the shadows. Involuntarily I dived my hands deep into the pockets of the thick overcoat I was wearing. I felt a pipe and tobacco pouch—common enough objects, but the former was never more welcome.

Somewhere in the dim and distant past I had heard or read of highway robbers, or burglars, or other rough people, having been tricked by the use of a wooden tobacco pipe as a make-believe for a revolver. Why not try it now?

There was just a chance the bluff might come off. Anything was better than to be caught and ill-treated by Germans.

The thought was mother to the action. Backing a few yards to a veritable rampart of cotton, I half bobbed down and suddenly whipped out the pipe in my hand from the right coat pocket. It was of ordinary briar-wood, having a silver band, and holding it close to the pit of my stomach I slowly moved it round à la American up-to-date methods. Probably the small silver mounting showed some glint from the straggling rays of the solitary lamp. Anyhow, I saw the shadows, which had appeared well separated before, fading away and concentrating in the rear. This gave me a chance which I was not slow to avail myself of. Moving as rapidly as I conveniently could I crossed the open space towards the warehouses beyond. I had covered half the distance when I saw that I was being pursued in force. Risking all possibilities of a trip and a fall, I raced for my life to the first street turning into the town proper. I had obtained a bit of a start and had the great advantage of thoroughly knowing the ground. The leading German fell. I heard him swear. The language was distinctly Teutonic.

When I reached the corner of the street I was not more than twenty yards ahead of those behind me. Here again a practical knowledge of the tricks and ways of sportsmen of the Western States of America stood me in good stead. In fact, it saved the situation and pulled me through. Instead of dashing at full speed up the street after I had negotiated the corner, when I should for certain have been caught and pulled down within about fifty yards, I stopped short and peeped round, exhibiting my nose, one eye, and part of my hat; also the hand holding the spoof pipe-revolver. The effect was electrical, not to say humorous. The two Prussian sleuth-hounds who were racing full pelt after me pulled up dead in their tracks: so suddenly, in fact, that the third, who was rapidly making up lost way behind, bumped into them, and all three sprawled in the snow.

As soon as they could pick themselves up they cautiously opened-out the corner, fearing that their quarry was waiting behind it to pot them off one at a time as they came round. Imagine their disgust when they discovered the ruse and saw me in the distance scooting far away up the deserted street with a good long lead. As I turned the next corner leading into a diverging street I bumped into a crowd of merry-makers which poured out from some large, brilliantly-illuminated building. Every one of them was very exuberant and seemed to be embracing everyone else. Every one of them appeared to be supremely happy and good-natured, whilst every one of them was without doubt most gloriously drunk.

What a haven of refuge to a hunted being almost at his last gasp, fleeing from unknown terrors, from capture, torture, imprisonment, or possible death! Before they realised my presence I was in the very heart of the crowd, where I was at once embraced. Needless to add that I returned the endearments with a vigour and sincerity that I had never before equalled in all my life. Nor did I attempt to go further until I had linked up with a convoy of homeward-bound convivial souls, far too intoxicated to know whether I was myself or one of them, or some other person.

CHAPTER 8

Escaping From The Clutches of a Very Clever Lady

So many people imagine that anyone and everyone who is engaged in detective or Secret Service work carries about with him a large assortment of wigs, false hair, and other disguises. When any of this work is reproduced on the stage or in moving pictures, or in the pages of works of fiction, disguises of various kinds are generally well to the fore. But, gentle reader, take it from me, who have been through the real thing, and rest assured that any kind of disguise is always attended with danger. To wear false hair or wigs, or even to have them found in your possession, would mean death instantaneously, or at best next dawn, in an enemy country; probable imprisonment in a fortress for many years in a neutral one. The cleverest men I have met in the service rarely assume any artificial disguise, although I admit that there are exceptional and urgent occasions when its aid must be sought of necessity.

In fiction you will perhaps have observed the universal rule seems to ordain that the assumer of disguises invariably endeavours to change his outward appearance from juvenility to old age. That, to my way of thinking, is merely adding to one's difficulties. In real life it will be found far easier to play the part of a person much younger than you really are than it is to play the part of one who is much older.

On such rare occasions as I had to make it part of my business to disguise myself I selected for choice the transfiguration of my outward appearance to a younger rather than an older person whenever the circumstances so permitted. For example, I would enter a building to all outward appearances a man of sixty years of age or upwards, and within a very short space of time reappear as a man of not more than thirty. These tricks may be attempted at night in artificial lights, but by daylight the risks of discovery are not worth the small gain or advantage that may be believed to be attained by their aid.

The common sailor, or working-man who is badly dressed, very dirty in appearance and who has not shaved for many days, is generally an object which most men avoid and few women find the smallest interest in; whilst he can roam at pleasure in most public places, and if he has the price of a drink in his pocket he invariably gathers around him a multitude of friends ready to tell him anything they may know or to believe any cock-and-bull story as to his own antecedents which force of circumstances or a very vivid imagination may suggest.

All disguises and concealments of identity are of little avail unless very thoroughly attempted and carried out.

Sir Robert Baden Powell, in his book *My Adventures as a Spy*, speaks of the importance of remembering the back view. He writes:

> The matter of disguise is not so much one of a theatrical make-up—although this is undoubtedly a useful art—as of being able to assume a totally different character, change of voice and mannerisms, especially of gait in walking, and appearance from behind.

A service officer, whether of the army or navy, would have far greater difficulties to contend with in this respect than would any ordinary civilian—which is probably one of the main reasons why service men are avoided when possible by the German Intelligence Department for active executive work.

The face and body are easy to disguise, but the hands are not. For a rough character rough hands are essential. Remember that it is a sure test, when questioning a tramp or hobo before probably wasting one's sympathies as well as one's substance in trying to help him, to demand an examination of his hands. They tell at a glance whether he is a genuine trier, or merely a chronic waster. Therefore, before undertaking to appear as a unit of the working-classes, it is advisable to take on a job which will put one's hands into the condition that would appear compatible to one's outward appearance.

Unloading or loading bricks into a vessel, or a truck, is the quickest and surest way of accomplishing this purpose. In a few hours, hands which are unaccustomed to this work will crack up and blister beyond recognition. Its continuance for a couple of days will pull the nails out of shape and give the full, true, horny, hardened grip of a genuine son of toil. Want of soap and water will complete a supreme finish to the seeming ideal.

Once upon a time there arose an occasion when I had to ship as deck-hand and general knockabout on a small Baltic coasting craft of no classified definition. It was rough work, rougher living, and roughest weather. But one soon accustoms oneself to one's surroundings in life; and it really is marvellous what a satisfactory clean-up one can make with the assistance of a little grease and a tiny piece of cotton waste.

The cruise had been completed and the vessel was returning to a friendly port when her skipper undertook to ferry a party of ladies and gentlemen across from one small island to another. The deck hand—need I explain that I acted in that capacity?—was indisposed. He sought his bunk below, only to be sworn at and cursed, and ordered out again in a manner which unfortunately brought him under observation, exactly the opposite to that which his modest, retiring nature desired; more particularly so on the occasion in question.

One lady, a bright-eyed, vivacious, sweet-faced woman of between twenty and thirty years of age, remonstrated on behalf of this seemingly ill-used and unfortunate mortal, and she pleaded with the skipper that the poor man looked frightened and ill. Alas, poor me!

"D——d idle, dirty, good-for-nothing scamp," is the nearest equivalent in English to a translation of his retort. I had been playing up for a discharge, and plead guilty to the indictment.

★★★★★★

A few days later a fashionable gathering took place. It was held in a beautifully situated house, having extensive grounds, fine gardens, and magnificent views of the surrounding seaboard. Everyone of any local importance was there. Amongst the guests was an Englishman. Five minutes' intercourse with him would have been amply sufficient to have based the conclusion that he was one of those effeminate, lisping, soft, silly slackers, who hang round tea-tables and curates' meetings, and who have a horror of all things manly.

He was dressed in a neat suit of blue serge. Every speck of dust coming to it was at once flicked off with a silk handkerchief. His trousers were of the permanent turned-up cut, carefully pressed and creased. He sported bright yellow wash-leather gloves and spent most of his time toying with a rimmed eyeglass. That he was shy, reticent, and retiring was at once obvious, but in spite of a vacuous, far-away look, his eyes seemed to travel over most of the company, and whenever any serious conversation took place he appeared to be wandering aimlessly about, but well within earshot.

One lady in the crowd seemed to take a more than ordinary interest in this personage. She was a bright-eyed, vivacious, sweet-faced woman of between twenty and thirty years of age. She was also a clever and far-seeing individual—one who watches, listens, and observes to advantage. The stranger's face attracted her. She felt somehow that it was familiar. She was sure that she had seen it before; but when, or where, puzzled her.

An introduction was an easy matter. Soon she was sipping tea and exchanging views on every-day frivolities with the object which for the moment so attracted her curiosity. I can assure those who read these lines that the object in question wished himself anywhere but where he was.

"It is most unusual to meet an Englishman who speaks our language, even badly. How is it that you seem to know it so well?" she suddenly asked; experience having apparently taught her that questions leading up to the point desired merely forewarned the interrogated.

"No, no. You flatter me. I'm positively wrotten on the grammar. I only know a number of words. You see, I had to learn those because I come to your delightful country so much on business, also for sport," I replied.

"Business? What kind of business?" she asked.

"Well, you see, I'm rather interwested in wood and in herwings."

"Oh yes! And sport?"

"Well, you see, I come here every year for fishing."

For some moments the lady maintained an ominous silence, whilst her eyes focussed the horizon of some distant islands lying far out upon the smooth and sunlit sea. She smiled to herself, as though she had caught a delusive object of great worth; then, turning her fair head—and she really was pretty—so that she could look me full in the eyes, she asked:

"Is it your business or your sport which gives you so much fascination for the sea?"

"Fascination for the sea?" I exclaimed doubtingly. "Now, weally you are quite wrong. I never go on the sea unless I'm weally forced to do so. In fact, I hate it. It's so beastly wrestless when it might be quiet and let everybody else be quiet too." I lisped painfully.

"I think you said it was herrings that interested you," she replied, following up a point she seemed determined to push home. "Are you sure it's not a larger species of fish?"

"Yes, quite sure," I hastened to add. "I have no interwests in your extensive cod fisherwies; nor in the oil which I am told is such good business."

"I did not mean codfish," she said. "I meant a much larger sort of fish—a big fish closely related to the whale family!" Whilst as she uttered the sentence her bright eyes looked laughingly at me with a keen glance that seemed to wish it could penetrate my very soul.

"Whales! Whales! I've never touched a whaling share in my life, and I'm quite certain I don't mean to in these times," I muttered.

Again the lady favoured silence, but her eyes never left my face a second. She studied every line, every flicker of the eyelid or twitch of the mouth, to try and read what thoughts were passing through my brain; but fortunately for me an assumed innocent expression of countenance successfully concealed the tumult within.

I dared not attempt to change the conversation. I merely followed whatever topic my enchanting *vis-à-vis* chose to select. I answered her questions quietly and without hesitation, but still she persisted.

"I mean those large whales which have been so frequently seen along our coast ever since the first week of August, 1914. Those great big whales *with iron skins.*"

It was a sudden, bold, frontal attack, which, however, failed entirely. In spite of her many self-satisfied smiles, gentle head-noddings and knowing side-glances, it elicited nothing but a hearty peal of laughter. This was repeated twice, and the diplomatic lady joined in to hide the chagrin she undoubtedly felt.

"My dear good lady, if you take me for a spy, you flatter me. You do indeed. I'm neither clever enough nor bold enough, nor energetic enough, ever to be selected for such a business. Even if I had the chance offered me I should never know what I ought to do, or how I could or ought to do it; and if I met a clever person—like yourself, for instance—you would be able to twist me wound your little finger and I could not help myself. Spy, indeed! You are funny! You know you are. Yes, you know you weally are." And I continued to laugh softly, as though the idea suggested was the most humorous thing I had ever heard, although I admit I was perspiring all over.

"Then what were you doing on board that trading boat in which we crossed from —— to —— last Monday? And why were you disguised as a common sailorman, all dirt and grease?"

"Me?"

"Yes, you. I recognised you the moment I saw you here today. So it is useless to deny it. Besides, I wish to be your friend." And sinking her voice to a whisper she added, "I can be of great assistance to you if I like. I am related to several members of the government. They will tell me anything I want to wheedle out of them—anything it may interest you to know. I love England; I hate the Germans and I adore the English. I think you are very clever indeed, but you are not clever enough to deceive me; so it's utterly useless trying to do so any longer. Am I not right, sir?" Saying which she tapped me playfully on the arm, accompanied by many languishing smiles.

It was a mighty awkward moment, a very trying situation. My only hope was boldness.

At the first words of her last sentence I had raised my face to hers, looking her full in the eyes until its conclusion, and assuming to the best of my ability an amazed expression of absolute astonishment. Then, after a long pause, suitable to the part I was enforced to play, I blurted out: "My dear madam! What on earth are you driving at? Last Monday I was in Copenhagen, miles away from here! Disguised as a common sailor-man! All dirt and grease! What can you mean? Is it another joke, like the whales *with iron skins, or the spy*? Or has someone been telling you fairy tales?"

In vain she continued to pound me with straight, searching, direct questions. In vain she coaxed and cooed to me to confide in her and make her a friend and an ally. In vain she cast amorous glances, full of deep meaning, with those wondrous eyes of hers, which she knew so well how to use; glances which were calculated to move a heart of stone, and, I could not help thinking at the time, would have been sufficient to tempt St. Anthony himself from his lonely cell.

I, however, merely continued to stare at her with an insipid, in-credulous, vacant look, until at last she petulantly stamped her tiny foot. Her patience was evidently quite exhausted.

"You must be an imbecile, a bigger fool than I would have believed it possible to find anywhere. My favours are not lightly distributed, nor have they ever before been refused."

As a woman scorned she hissed this sentence into my ear, and toss-ing her pretty head like an alarmed deer in the wilds of a great forest she trotted away and left me gazing silently after her.

What would be her next step? I wondered. Did she really take me for a blithering idiot, or did she entertain doubts on the matter?

Would she remain silent, or would she make further inquiry? To what lengths would she be likely to go if she so decided?

It sent a cold stream of collected perspiration trickling down my back to think of what trouble that pretty creature could create if she really did make up her mind to follow up my trail.

It was terribly bad luck to happen just at that particular time, because I had wanted so much to remain at least a week or ten days in that particular locality; now I had to debate with myself whether I dare risk a stay over, and what it might lead to if I so decided and acted on that decision. Then I remembered my hands. Good heavens! If she had not got so angry, if she had only kept cool, and had challenged me to remove my gloves. What a give-away it would have been! Whew!

I was finding the atmosphere much too warm for my liking. I began to imagine that bright-eyed, vivacious, sweet-faced lady sitting in her *boudoir* at home in a dainty *kimono*, with a winsome handmaiden brushing the silken tresses of her crowning glory; whilst she surveyed her captivating features in the mirror and contracted her pretty forehead into ugly wrinkles as she mentally reviewed the day's proceedings.

★★★★★★

That night at an hotel in the town not so many *kilomètres* away from my lady's chamber a very wide-awake Englishman lay stretched at full length upon a very short bed. His legs protruded some two feet over the backboard. He was partly undressed, and he sucked vigorously at a strong black cigar. He also frowned in serious disapproval at the mental review of the day's proceedings, at an irrepressible, annoying thought which would repeat itself again and again, a conviction that if he did not clear out of that immediate neighbourhood at once that "confounded demnition woman" was certain to make trouble somewhere. Quit he must and quit he would.

That man was myself.

CHAPTER 9

Wild-Fowling Extraordinary and Trawling for Submarines in Neutral Waters

A few years previous to the declaration of war several Englishmen took rather an unusual interest in the western coast of Germany, particularly in the islands lying near to Heligoland.

Some of these Englishmen were watched and arrested on the grounds of espionage. Some were tried and imprisoned for varying terms of years in German fortresses. Some were never caught, although they were closely chased, and were very much wanted indeed.

Maybe I was one of them. Maybe the Germans took little, if any, interest whatever in so insignificant a mortal. But the fact remains that for many years prior to 1914 I had annually visited the Danish and Schleswig-Holstein coasts on wild-fowling expeditions and for wild-goose shooting.

To those who are ignorant of the nature of the western coast of Germany and would learn concerning it, a perusal of that most interesting little volume, *The Riddle of the Sands*, is recommended. No cliffs are to be found there, with the exception of some upon the islands of Heligoland and the hillsides which adorn the northern side of the Elbe on the way up to Hamburg. A low sandy shore running in places far out into the North Sea stretches the entire length of coastline from Holland to Denmark. The changes, additions, and developments along this forbidden strip of land, which during past years has been so jealously guarded by the Germans, have always been a source of deep interest to John Bull's Watchdogs who have the welfare of the British Empire at heart. At no time has this interest been deeper or more

112

absorbing than since August 4th, 1914.

I knew them well. One of my wild-fowling companions had been a Frenchman, about my own age, who lived in Copenhagen. He spoke half a dozen languages, and was a very keen sportsman, and wild geese were his speciality.

Cruising in the depths of winter along the vast extent of mud-flats, oozes, shallows, and islands, which guard the west coast of Schleswig-Holstein, is no child's play. It requires bold and hardy navigators; men who are not frightened at the horrors of ice-floes, or of breakers on the bar; who can stand a temperature below zero; who can live on the coarsest of rations; and who can sleep anyhow and anywhere.

The *Nordfriesische Inseln* tract, lying south of the island of Fano, the natural buffer to the Esbjerg fjord, was a favourite hunting-ground, but it had its drawbacks. Many a fine shot into big flocks of geese and ducks was, to the sportsman's annoyance, spoilt by the unwelcome interference of German sentries or soldiers stationed at all kinds of unexpected and outlandish points among the islands. Sometimes those interlopers would put out in boats and give chase, but we knew within a little where they were generally stationed and by taking advantage of the ground managed to avoid being captured. More than once we had been hailed and warned and ordered to keep within Danish waters or we would be shot—which, however, was nothing out of the common. There are many good fishermen residing at Nordby and Ribe (in Denmark) who have netted flat fish in these waters for years; also intermittently throughout the war, in spite of rifle bullets perpetually being fired at them.

Soon after the date particularly referred to above, the Germans mined the area fairly heavily and no channel was safe. But a local fisherman located the mines and started marking their positions, much to the annoyance of the Huns. One man in particular would insist on fishing wherever the mines were thickest. His argument was that, although the work was dangerous, the mines kept others away, to the protection of the fish, therefore the fishing must be the better for it. The Germans warned him often enough, whilst they shot at him so frequently that he became heedless of their threats and he appeared to entirely disregard their rifle fire.

One day he was caught and taken before an officer, who impressed upon him that if he came there any more they would use him as a practice target for small cannon. Nevertheless he returned, and found them as good as their word. Luckily he escaped being hit, but after the experience he sold his boat, nets, and belongings, and emigrated to America.

I happened to arrive at Ribe just too late. I had travelled far to meet this man, as I was anxious for a *little more wild-fowling*; and no one knew the creeks, the channels, and the local geography of that shifting, dangerous coast more thoroughly than this bold and careless fisherman. He was, however, by no means the only pebble on the beach. I found others.

My arrival on the frontier between the two countries coincided with certain marked events—the collapse of an airship at Sonderho, and the escape of some Russian and English prisoners of war from the compound outside Hamburg. The airship became a total wreck, and the prisoners of war succeeded in reaching Danish territory. Thence they travelled to Copenhagen, where they were well and humanely looked after.

During the autumn of 1914, and the spring of 1915, the west coast of Denmark and the extensive mileage of flats running south therefrom was not the happy hunting-ground it had been in the past. There seemed to be too many *Landstürmer* aimlessly wandering around carrying guns loaded with ball ammunition, which they were nothing loath to use at any target within sight that might appear above the horizon. Ducks and geese were scarce and very, very wild. They seemed to object to rifle shots even more than wild-fowlers. They were kept constantly on the move.

It is true there was a regular "flight" of Zeppelins and aircraft of various shapes and make along the coast every twilight; yet these only appeared in fine weather, when it is known to all wild-fowlers that flighting birds fly too high to encourage heavy bags; whilst it must not be forgotten that so far as the country of Denmark was concerned, these foul (this pun is surely permissible) were not then lawfully in season. Their close time, or period of protection, still remained covered. To violate it would have created much too serious an offence to be treated lightly. But to observe the movements and habits of *these unfeathered birds* with as much secrecy and security as possible was another matter. In due course I moved camp to the Kleiner Belt and sought sport and entertainment among the islands of the Southern Baltic, where, in the air above and in the waters beneath, there was much activity.

For sometimes a fisherman's hut sheltered a supposed-to-be Norwegian skipper, whose ship held cargo of a contraband nature which was caught by the war and thus temporarily detained. He was taking a little shooting trip by way of diversion from the monotony of waiting an opportunity to get away. That man was myself. It was a thin story, but it lasted out with local natives for the necessary time required. In harbours or bays nearby were about a thousand vessels laid up in consequence of the dangers of navigation; whilst round neighbouring islands, on the Danish side, fleets of ships of varied nationality could be seen at anchor in many sheltered nooks, all too frightened to venture further on the high seas.

The natives of Northern Europe are extraordinarily inquisitive, and unless one is willing to divulge family secrets it is necessary to draw vividly upon the imagination when interrogated as to antecedents, home, and calling. It would have been dangerous in the instance in question not to have humoured this characteristic peculiarity, or to have declined to satisfy such searching curiosity. The only thing to do to ensure some degree of safety was to blow "hot air" in volumes around; to answer all questions; and, above all, to remember every detail of the untruths thus unfolded. It is a true adage that "*a good liar must possess a good memory.*"

This seemingly annoying inconvenience had, however, its redeeming feature. The almost daily bombardment of leading questions opened up excellent opportunities for return sallies of a reciprocating nature. It was an easy step to lead from home and domestic particulars to the all-absorbing topic of the hour—the mighty overshadowing cloud of national troubles. I therefore encouraged rather than narrowed any disposition to talk, whilst I was never backward in attending any meetings of the natives in the confined and fuggy dwellings in which they congregated and resided, despite the most objectionable atmosphere.

A free hand with tobacco and a few drops (sweets) to the children added to one's popularity; and "the captain," as I was familiarly called, soon ingratiated himself far beyond all doubt or suspicion. This was as it should be.

Now the Kiel *fjord* was within an easy sail. Its entrance was an object of interest; whilst the Kiela Bay was used as a patrolling or exercising ground for various designs of aircraft and warships. Amongst the crowd of men out of a job was one, a mate, whose life had been passed sailing in foreign seas. He was a devil-may-care, happy-go-lucky individual, ready to join any venture that came along. Of course he drank when he was ashore; at sea he was a total abstainer—by compulsion.

Whiskey was his weakness, wild-fowling his hobby.

He knew the haunts and habits of both short and long-winged fowl, which, in his company, I often sought, and it is a wonder we came back alive.

Every channel that was navigable round those northern islands seemed to hold German or Danish mines. Every storm broke quantities of these mines from their moorings; and every day floating mines could be seen, washed up somewhere, or reported. Many vessels were lost by unfortunate contact with them, and the sea was dotted with the mastheads of the sunken craft. Christian—that was the venturesome mate's name—thought little of this. One danger was quite equal to another with him. He argued that if fate had ordained he should be blown up by a mine, instead of being drowned, what did it matter? Call-day must come sooner or later, and after all, perhaps a quick blow-up was preferable to the prolonged suffocation of drowning. The former at least would not be a cold or a lingering death, but all over in a second, with no trouble about funerals and that kind of thing. The latter caused a shudder to think about.

At first one was inclined to believe Christian was boastful in his talk, but the following venturesome exploits prove that such was not the case.

Indented into a certain island in the Southern Baltic is a certain bay, which has always been a favourite haunt of wild geese. They visit it in thousands during the spring and autumn migrations, whilst a sprinkling of them seems to be ever present. A low promontory of sand and sand-dunes circles part of this bay, which is so washed by the sea that it is difficult to tell where the low-water mark really begins. From one point of the promontory a long spit of sand and mud projects far out into the sea. It is a peculiar formation and is much sought by waterfowl for resting and toilet purposes. During the opening months of 1915 geese made a habit of congregating here in unusual numbers.

Out at sea, in the fairway, was moored an ugly, evil-looking craft, with huge uprising bows. She was fitted with wireless, and although she had been anchored there since the outbreak of war, a head of steam was always kept up. Her official name and number was G. No. 53. She was supposed and alleged to be lying outside the Danish seaboard limit. That, however, to the casual observer looked to be open to grave doubt. She flew no flag and showed no outward sign of life on board, but she was known to be a German vessel, well crewed, victualled and provided. Those on board could command the sand-spit before mentioned with their binoculars, as well as with other human inventions. Apparently they did not neglect to make full use of what they had to hand.

On two occasions, within a period of ten days, a couple of ardent wild-fowlers might have been observed (history seems to point to the fact that they were observed) at early dawn, crawling along the said sand-spit, close to the water's edge, on its lee-side. Very slowly indeed they worked their way along until they were within range of a small gaggle of geese which habitually rested there. On each occasion a successful shot had been recorded. Fable tells us that the pitcher can go too often to the well. These intrepid sportsmen attempted to repeat their previous successes.

It was in the gloaming of eventide. About a dozen or fifteen black (brent) geese were preening their feathers at the end of the sand-spit, apparently well satisfied with their lot and the world in general. Just under the uneven line of washed-up seaweed and other refuse two dark forms crawled along. They seemed to be hours covering the space intervening between themselves and the birds—their evident quarry. Between decks on the gloomy vessel this minor tragedy in life and death was probably an object of equal interest. The crew could watch and observe without themselves being seen. They could gloat over the spilling of blood, and the death-dealing power of well-placed explosives, without the outside world ever knowing that they had any knowledge of such events happening. How keenly they must have anticipated.

As the sun sank deeper and deeper in the west, and the shades of night crept up from the east, the two wild-fowl hunters drew nearer and nearer to their objective. At least they began to think it time to prepare for a serenade. They were in the act of unlocking their guns when suddenly the ground immediately in front of them rose, like an active volcano, into the air and a mighty explosion shook the earth. What a shock! It raised their caps and, as Christian remarked, so singed the hair on his head and face that he would not be likely to want the attentions of a barber for a fortnight. His companion was glad enough to escape whole in body and limb, whilst he cursed the cowardly Huns under his breath for their death-dealing intentions. Christian seemed to emulate the immortal Mark Tapley. He was infernally happy and grateful to somebody to think they had helped him kill geese, which he would probably never have bagged without such assistance; and he joyfully rushed forward to pick up the dead and wounded before they could recover from the concussion consequent upon the shock of the explosion.

Natives who heard the report put it down to a floating mine which had been washed up on the beach and exploded when brought into contact with the shore. Had one of them visited the place where the upheaval occurred he could have seen at a glance that the depth of water was such that a mine could not have floated within half a mile.

How disappointed must have been the crew of G. No. 53.

Christian was a born sportsman. He was one of those who would have willingly exchanged a year's earnings for a red-letter day at sport. If the sport was such that danger was coupled with it, the greater the danger, the greater the excitement, and the greater his consequent enjoyment. For one reason only he was constantly lamenting that his country had not been brought into the struggle, so that he could have seized the opportunity to join actively in the fray. At heart, of course, he did not really desire that his country or his countrymen should have inflicted upon them all the horrors of war; but when a scrap was in progress he longed with his whole soul to be in the thick of it.

Now it so happened that certain people had declared that the Germans were violating the neutrality of Denmark, or at least jeopardising her position and welfare, by certain nocturnal submarine visitations in certain waters—not so very far from the Great Belt. German officialdom replied that these complaints and protests were mythical and without foundation. Christian thought otherwise.

It was a strange coincidence that at this particular time Christian should take a violent fancy for trawling. It was perhaps strange that his particular friend should argue that the best and heaviest fish always frequented the deepest channels which ran between the islands. Christian agreed, and supported the contention by quoting his experiences of fishing in far-off foreign seas.

He was not interrogated as to where, and when, and how, and for how long he had abandoned the forecastle for the trawl-net; nor did he give much opening for any such questions. He knew. Others might think they knew, but he knew he was right; that, according to him, was incontrovertible.

Christian's enthusiasm carried all and everything with it. A small vessel suitable for trawling purposes was secured and fitted out with the necessary gear and equipment. A chosen crew was selected. Fish were very scarce and consequently were very dear; the fortunes of all were to be made in a miraculously short space of time. The skipper was a heavy-bearded individual who knew his job, but nothing beyond it. He was easily persuaded, whilst his crew followed the lead blindly, thinking only of easily-earned *shekels* to come. In due course the party put to sea, with Christian & Co. acting in the capacity of spare hands.

For several nights results were precarious. The mighty draughts of promised fishes did not come along, and Christian had to use all his persuasive powers, backed up with innumerable excuses and explanations, to prove why it was his theories had not produced practical solid results.

The spirits of the once optimistic crew had sunk to zero, but they were over-persuaded to venture forth yet again. It was a dark night, but the moon was due to rise at 11.30. The sails of the little vessel had been trimmed, and the trawl dropped in a well-known channel, picked off from the chart by the ever enthusiastic Christian. For a few hours nothing out of the common occurred. Towards midnight the wind freshened slightly and the moon, peeping out from occasional obscuring clouds, cast pale, fitful lights over the cold, dark waters.

Presently the watch on deck became alarmed. An extraordinary phenomenon appeared to take place. The fishing-boat gradually began to go backwards—actually into the eye of the wind, although her sails were properly set and full. The watchman rubbed his eyes and pinched himself to see whether he was properly awake, or dreaming. He looked at the trawl warp to see whether it was slackening, as he reasoned that if some current sufficiently strong to counteract the force of the wind was flowing there, however unusual or from whatsoever unknown but possible cause it might have originated, then surely the trawl warp would show it.

No. The trawl warp was tight. It was strained to its utmost. He looked at the far-off land and took bearings. He was not mistaken. *The boat was going backwards.* Her speed was easily perceptible.

He rushed to the hatchway and yelled at the top of his voice to the sleeping crew to come on deck; to which alarming summons it responded quickly enough.

Wildly gesticulating and with much waving of arms the thoroughly frightened and superstitious fisherman explained matters as best he could. Others sprang to various positions in the boat to investigate for themselves. The story was indeed too true, and consternation at the unknown plainly showed itself on the countenances of all—except perhaps the imperturbable Christian and the other spare hand. Whilst the crew was debating with its skipper what was best to be done under the circumstances, another phase of the phenomenon developed. A huge, unwieldy shape gradually rose from the sea abaft the taffrail. It had a smooth, polished skin, which shone and glistened in the moonlight like the back of a whale. But on looking farther along to gauge as accurately as could be the whole length of this mysterious leviathan of the deep, a break in the smoothness of its form was apparent, together with an excrescence which the skipper of the trawler was not long in recognising as the conning tower of a submarine.

Ye gods above! How frightened they all were. How the skipper swore, and raved, and shrieked for a hatchet to cut away. How he sawed at the trawl rope with his belt knife before it arrived, and how he hacked the warp in two when he did get it. What a commotion there was to pack on sail in order to get clear before the Germans could get out of their steel shell and make things unpleasant for them. How everyone flew about and gave orders to everyone else. Yes! All seemed to lose their heads entirely, except the two spare hands whose whole attention seemed attracted aft. They gazed, with looks which might have been mistaken for gleams of triumph, at that huge, ugly monster, now bumping the stern of the little fishing-boat. They noted every detail open to visional observation, while their unusual coolness was not noticed in the general alarm of the crew, who thought only of their individual escape and safety.

A close, impartial observer might almost have been led to the belief that the expression on the countenance of Christian betrayed the realisation of an all-too-long delayed event which had at last crystallised and fully justified his anticipations.

In due course it was reported that the propellers of a believed-to-be German submarine, which, it could be said, had got out of her course in the dark, had fouled the fishing-nets belonging to some unknown boat. The local press was furious. Officialdom was stirred from its lethargy, much red tape and sealing-wax were expended, many politely worded notes passed between two governments, and the event was soon forgotten by the Powers-that-be. But the fishermen concerned remembered all too vividly every detail and the horrible scare they had had, whilst they loudly lamented their lost gear. However, a Danish gunboat appeared a little more frequently round that particular part of the coast; mines, and yet more mines, were laid out; whilst the waters in question, which had so many times rippled round the boat of mystery, knew the activities of the conscienceless Hun no more. Meanwhile the Golden Argosy of unlimited profits from deep-channel trawling by night, as exploited by Messrs. Christian & Co., proved a ghastly financial failure.

CHAPTER 10

The Mysterious Harbour

Whilst prowling along the northern frontier of Germany in the early spring of 1915, with a companion whom I would have trusted with my life, we quite unwittingly got caught in a manner least expected.

I had been over the frontier more than once, but never far into the interior. I had neither occasion nor object in so doing. I was at the time on the lookout for some Danish workmen who I knew had been employed on some of the important and secret war material of Germany. If I could meet them on German soil, so much the better; they would then be much more likely to open out and talk more freely than they would do if met elsewhere. I had had experience of this and was at the time most anxious to get corroborative evidence of some rather startling rumours which I had recently heard regarding the (later on called) Paris Big Gun.

Whilst so prowling, as before mentioned, we heard speak of a certain harbour. The mysterious harbour, it was called, which no one might visit, which was jealously guarded, and which the Germans had every intention of occupying at an early date. Wild, speculative talk, perhaps, but it was enough to determine me to go and see for myself and so learn the truth and judge the possibilities from the facts gathered.

Not so many miles from the Island of Femern, where the German warship *Gazelle* was torpedoed by an English submarine in the spring of 1915, although the fact was never communicated to the English Press, it was said to be situated. A small, exceedingly convenient harbour, with at least eighteen feet depth of water at all tides, and it was said to be capable of great developments.

Its existence was not chronicled in ordinary guide-books nor on the maps in general circulation. Visitors were not welcomed and the local inhabitants were fearful lest their neighbourhood should be seized and overrun by undesirable foreigners.

During the period with which we are concerned frost at night was intense. All open marshland was frozen as solidly as if encased in iron, whilst the ice-bound ditches, canals, and drains were levelled to the headland with drifted snow. Storms, of varying magnitude, were of daily occurrence. Cruel winds swept the bleak area visited, cutting through the thickest of garments till the marrow in one's very bones seemed congealed. No one at the time, acting from his own free will, would have appreciated either a business or a pleasure trip to the harbour in question.

Yet early one eventful morning, when the weather was at its worst and everyone else had sought shelter, we braved the elements and attempted to lay a course through the maze of marshland roads, dams and banks, which would not have been an easy task to many of the natives. Our struggle to win through these and other unseen difficulties seemed hopeless. But our minds were made up. We were both determined, obstinate, persistent. Many times we were blown flat by the violence of the storm. Many times we fell, sunk to our necks, in a snowdrift. Many times we lost our way and had to retrace our steps or correct our course. But all the while we proceeded forward, with lips compressed and faces set in grim determination, to accomplish the task we had in hand; to view, to inspect, and to survey roughly the harbour and its works.

Not a soul was observable upon all that vast flat area stretching away uninterruptedly to the horizon as far as the eye could command on either hand. The distant, dull, booming, angry roar of the sea upon the breakwaters and the shrieking wind made conversation impossible. No cover was available until the great embankment was attained. It guarded some tens of thousands of acres of reclaimed land. What a relief it was to us poor wayfarers to reach this comparative haven of peace, an oasis in the desert of howling storm! We had traversed many, many weary miles of most awful walking, under most exhausting circumstances, and a long rest was indeed welcome. Having reached the embankment unobserved, the remainder of the venture was, comparatively speaking, an easy matter.

With such a gale in progress no vessel was likely to brave the mines laid out under the Admiralty administration of several nations and to attempt a passage from the sea. On the land side, the temporary railway and all roads concentrated upon a point where a cluster of new houses had sprung up, which at the moment in question were full of individuals—refugees from the storm and others. The windows of these houses commanded every road within miles. Was it likely, the sentries undoubtedly argued within themselves, or to be suspected for a moment, that anyone in sane senses would attempt to avoid these solid paths and risk an approach to the harbour through the swamps (although they were frozen) and by way of the embankments thus reached, to the east and west? If there were such rash and foolish people about then they ran a good chance of being lost and frozen to death.

So it was that even the sentries were under cover, making life as pleasant as could be, drinking coffee heavily strengthened with brandy, and playing cards for small stakes.

Having rested and eaten and drunk from a thermos flask, we proceeded along the sea side of the embankment with as much caution as though travelling in an enemy's country. Somewhat to our surprise we encountered not a living being, not even a stray dog to exercise his lungs at strangers. On arrival at the harbour, which was concealed from view of the houses by the height of the embankment before mentioned, we quickly and dexterously got to work, free from observation or interruption. My companion kept watch on the main entrances whilst I overran the works, mapped and thoroughly investigated them, sounded and checked water depths, accommodation calculated, and the quay head-room, and roughly surveyed and noted to the minutest detail all the surroundings, in a very short space of time.

As soon as this work was accomplished we left the danger zone. It was unwise to linger a moment longer than was necessary in such a situation. Retracing our steps until we were quite convinced there was no chance of trouble from possible prying followers, we paused on the outskirts of a small wood. It was the first rest since our objective had been left, it was the first opportunity we had had to exchange a sentence.

"Why not look in and see old Pedersen, the smuggler? He may know something."

"Good; let us go then." This was all I had to say.

In a lonely hut, in still more lonely and uninviting surroundings, resided the interesting individual sought. He was a friend of long standing with my companion, whom he received with every outward sign of cordiality and pleasure. But how deceptive can be the ways of men time will show. Coffee was at once put on the hob to boil, and a liberal supply of potato-brandy and eatables forthcoming. The glow of the fire and warm food after long exposure caused my blood to tingle in my veins, down to toe- and finger-tips. The sensation was glorious, and a quiet smoke crowned the extreme bliss of the moment.

In due course ordinary generalities of conversation broadened further afield. The grey-haired, bright-eyed old deluder of Revenue officers dilated upon the war pickings and opportunities which seemed to be bringing him a rich harvest. It appeared he had many relations living and working in Germany. They helped him not a little. Custom officials on that side also knew him well. They winked at most things now which before the war would have been suppressed with an iron hand. His goings and comings were of more frequent occurrence. His business proceeded almost openly, and he was accumulating money as he had never done in his life before.

No, he did not fear the mines. It was true there were plenty of them. Danish, German, Russian, and English. He knew exactly where each group was laid; thus he avoided them.

Yes, he believed the English had laid out some mines. He could not say for certain, but he had seen English submarines in the Femern Belt. He had spoken them and he knew English when he heard it. Of course they must have laid out some mines.

Everyone knew of the existence and whereabouts of the Danish and of the German mines. Fishermen who were daily at sea, fishing or cruising around after one thing and another, had seen and heard quite enough about them; but the Russian mines were another proposition. He believed most of the Russian mines were floating ones, either from design or accident. Anyway, there were plenty of them about. The more the merrier so far as he was concerned. They kept a lot of people away and they did not frighten him. It was all good for business.

For some time the old man ran on with the utmost freedom of speech, which tended to disarm any suspicions we might have entertained against him. We, however, gave no hint of our doings. We preferred to pose as good listeners.

When he turned his conversation to the building of new submarines and airships, and events and happenings in the interior of Germany, I drew into deeper reticence and avoided asking questions which might have raised possible suspicions of the deep absorbing interest such knowledge carried. The veteran smuggler apparently had two brothers working on war machines in German territory, and they had told him——

Here he broke off in the middle of a sentence to ask his long-lost friend who I was, where I came from, and all about me.

It appeared that overcome by the strong wind, coupled with perhaps the stronger alcoholic libations, I had fallen asleep.

"Oh, you need not trouble about him. He's a Norwegian ship's captain, whose ship is stranded up at Marstal. He is visiting a few friends hereabouts and doing a little duck-shooting with me. He's a real good sort and quite all right."

"Of course," replied the smuggler, "I knew if he was with you he must be all right. But in these times you never know, so you'll have to excuse my asking;" and he continued to describe all he had heard and knew concerning the building of the new improved German submarines, which were claimed to be able to run at great speed on the surface and to traverse a distance of some thousands of miles independent of base reliance for resupplies.

When the subject had been exhausted he switched off to the 1915 Zeppelins, upon which another brother had been for some time employed. These engines of destruction, he stated, would be a wonderful improvement on all former known airships of their kind. They would be very much larger; have their cars covered in; there would be more of them; their speed would be materially increased and their capacity for weight-carrying considerably augmented. There were many other minor yet important details which the old man, in his enthusiasm, enlarged upon in garrulous volubility.

At last there seemed nothing more to tell and a renewal of the journey was suggested, but so soundly did the pseudo Norwegian captain sleep that it took the combined efforts of both of them, with much prodding and shaking, before he could be aroused from his lethargy. When apparently I was only half awake we left the hut, cursing the belligerents generally for upsetting everybody's livelihood, instead of thanking our late host for the friendly shelter and hospitality; nor did I offer any apology for having slept throughout his most interesting discourse upon these unknown things.

The old smuggler audibly expressed an unsought opinion that the liquor had got the better of my senses. I was gratified by that.

Later in the afternoon we found ourselves in the neighbourhood of a small township. We made our way to an inn in the main street, where we ordered something substantial to eat.

To specially prepare a meal anywhere on the Continent takes time. At a remote country inn where nothing is kept in readiness it takes much more time than elsewhere. An hour is the minimum. I sought my bedroom with an excuse for forty winks, giving orders to be awakened as soon as the soup was on the table.

Every hostelry bedroom in the north of Europe is provided with a table, pens, ink and writing materials. A few minutes after the door had been locked I might have been seen seated at table preparing a despatch and puzzling deeply over certain sprawled hieroglyphics which had apparently been made on rough paper, *possibly inside my pocket with a pencil stump when perhaps reclining in an awkward position and unable or unwilling to see to guide the fingers which gripped the active stump of lead.* Be that as it may, the writing was awfully bad and very difficult indeed to make out. I studied it with the greatest of care all ways, upside down, and at every angle; whilst the smiles on my face may have portrayed evident satisfaction at the result.

Suddenly a heavy tread caused the solid stairs to creak, and loud knocking, equivalent to peremptory demands, upon the door of my room caused me to jump in my chair as though a guilty conscience plagued my peace of mind. Quick as lightning I removed and concealed certain precious belongings, doubled up the sheet of paper upon which I was working, and started to scribble silly messages upon some picture postcards I had purchased at the village store to people of no importance who lived at no great distance away.

Again the knocking was repeated, this time louder and more emphatic than before. "All right, my friend, no hurry. Take all things quietly and all things will be well." But the impatient visitor would not and did not wait. He placed so much force behind the lock that it yielded, and he nearly fell on to his nose as the door gave way.

Recovering himself he came quickly forward, and I rose to meet him half way.

"You know who we are?" he said to me.

"My dear sir, I exceedingly regret to say that I have not that pleasure," I replied.

"We are police officers." As he spoke, another burly individual appeared in the opening of the doorway, who, without sign of interest in the preliminary conversation, proceeded to prop up the broken door to some semblance of its former state. "You have just landed from Femern and we arrest you as a German spy."

At these words my eyes glittered, I clenched my hands in a way which did not augur well for the visitors.

"My good sir," I muttered through compressed lips, "you may do what you please, and you may assign me to any nationality in the wide, wide world, except that one. I am not in any way related to the barbarians, nor will I permit you to take me for one. If you repeat such an insulting accusation again I shall throw you out."

"You forget, sir, you are under arrest," he snapped.

"I do not forget that, if I am anything at all, I am an Englishman, and that I am in a private apartment. If the door is guarded, the window is not; you will observe that it is an unpleasant height from the ground to fall."

"Anyway, you pass yourself off as a Norwegian, now you say you are English, but we know you are German. Search his belongings, sergeant, and search thoroughly." Saying which the senior officer coolly proceeded to take up and to read the postcards on the table.

It was not a pleasant position to be in, and well I knew it. The new law was very elastic. It made it an offence to use the telegraph, the telephone or the postal facilities, or to enlist directly or indirectly any assistance from any native for the purpose of conveying any information which could be considered likely to be of use to any belligerent power; whilst the only literature which had recently found favour in the eyes of the reading public seemed to relate to spies and espionage, whether in fact or in fiction. Hence every local junior or senior police or other officer seemed to imagine himself a born Sherlock Holmes. In vain I indignantly protested against the intrusion. It merely seemed to whet their appetite for investigation. Every belonging I had with me was turned inside out, even to the lining of my raiment. Hats and boots were separately and collectively opened up, whilst the marks on my linen, off and on, were compared and commented upon.

"Perhaps a cigar would cool you down a bit?" I remarked somewhat sarcastically, but the suggestion was refused with an indignant snort.

"Well, I presume there is no objection to my smoking, even if *you* don't care about it," I added, as I bit the end off a big black cigar and hunted round for matches. Blindly ignoring a box on the table, I eventually extracted some from the pocket of my greatcoat, which was hanging on a peg. In doing so I pulled out a glove which fell to the floor.

Of course my every action was watched. But I did not appear to notice this until I had twice paced the floor smoking. Then, seeing the glove lying there, I picked it up and sarcastically offered it for examination, after which I placed it in my side pocket. Quite a natural thing to do.

Meanwhile, it should have been recorded that I had purposely left the folded piece of paper containing the partly-written message lying on the table and in sight during the whole interview. When the officer had advanced to read the postcards I had taken care to be there first. I had carelessly picked up the aforesaid paper and played with it; twisting it round my fingers as though it were a piece of string. When the officer was out of reach of the table I threw it down again. If he came closer I annexed it and played with it as before.

After the glove incident, the officer, evidently in command, made a dash to secure it. I reached and picked it up just a second before him and proceeded to twist it with even greater vehemence than before round my fingers, as though my nerves were somewhat strained.

The officer held out his hand for it. Instead of giving it to him direct I first passed the paper from one hand to the other. A very simple thing indeed in itself to the uninitiated, but that little act covered an operation which if bungled might have provided me with solitary confinement for a period of many years. As the officer unrolled the twisted paper I had handed over it proved to be utterly devoid of interest or utility; it was, in fact, a piece of blank paper, in size about the thickness of a man's thumb. By way of explanation to the reader I must add that in years gone by I had been an adept in the art of legerdemain, thus it was easy for me to deceive him and also to dexterously convey the original document into the thumb of the glove which lay conveniently for such purpose in my right-hand coat pocket.

After an hour and a half of search and interrogation the two officers engaged in whispered conversation and the venue was changed.

In due course I was arraigned before the head magistrate of the district, a stern but just man who appeared to carry much weight and influence in local affairs. He was the equivalent to our lord lieutenant of a county in England, and probably to a State governor in the U.S.A.

His first step embraced a bodily search to the skin in which I, the prisoner, helped by turning out my pockets and opening up my clothes, and giving all seemingly possible assistance.

After three and a half hours' interrogation I was dismissed, but informed I must not leave the inn without a permit. Meanwhile my travelling companion was also thoroughly overhauled and examined apart from me and *in camera.*

Whilst this second act of the drama was in progress I was chuckling in my room. With most satisfactory smiles I extracted my various treasures. From the roll of my collar I drew forth a document of value. It looked uncommonly like a rough sketch plan, as indeed it was— quite a good map of the mysterious harbour which had so suddenly sprung into existence. My handkerchief was not without a crumpled paper within its folds; whilst my glove was sought and relieved of its twisted draft despatch. But what amused me most of all was a book entitled *King Alcohol,* a discourse on the curse of drink. I had called special attention to this book, a Danish edition of Jack London, and it had been indignantly cast upon the table both by the magistrate and the officers.[1] It had lain there with my glove, pocket-handkerchief, pipe and tobacco-pouch as uninteresting and neglected throughout the proceedings. This book was bound in a paper cover, but even an ordinary paper cover can hide more than some people would give credence to. In this it concealed blocked-out silhouettes on very thin paper of every fighting vessel in the German Navy. I had been using them—oh, so recently!

Laughing softly to myself, I reflected on the deception; the very openness of which was its greatest safety. The repacking of my disturbed belongings was necessary, and then I wondered how my companion was faring at the hands of the authorities, whose exasperation and disappointment at not finding any of the evidence they had expected with such seeming certainty upon me was badly concealed.

One reflection led to another. How, when, and where had the local police or the military been led to suspect us, to hit our trail? Who had given information and what did they really know? The more I turned the matter over in my mind the more puzzled I became. Could the old smuggler have communicated possible suspicions? Could we have been seen at work on the harbour? Was my companion everything I believed him to be? It was one of those riddles which Secret Service agents are constantly being called upon to face, but if they seriously trouble themselves trying to solve them they are apt to fall early victims of brain fever.

The examinations had been severe as to past movements, intentions, motives, and present occupation or pastime. The mention of wild-fowling had been received with ridicule until an argument con-

---

1. The Danes being a race of notoriously hard drinkers resent any literature savouring of Prohibition.

vinced the magistrate that I knew far more about that sport than he did; whilst addresses of certain local fowlers, which had been given him with seeming reluctance, were at once tested by telephone with results not unfavourable to his temporary prisoners.

Our interrogators either knew, or had assumed a knowledge, that the harbour had been visited; whilst they had searched diligently and persistently for any trace of a plan or particulars relating to it.

When the magistrate returned from his second search he announced his final decision to send us both as prisoners under an escort to Copenhagen to be tried by the higher tribunal which handled these affairs. This sentence would have been acted upon forthwith had I not questioned the authority and the wisdom of carrying any further so delicate a matter as interference with our personal liberty when there was no evidence whatever for him to go upon. My criticisms were pleasantly and playfully worded, but they were also concise and crushing in their logic; besides which they carried throughout a quiet threatening undertone that portended possible international trouble, with severe punishment upon unauthorised officials who tampered unlawfully with the freedom of a loyal subject of His Gracious Majesty, King George the Fifth of England.

Thus it came about that the informal court adjourned until the morrow, and our long-deferred meal was the more appreciated.

Discussing an after-dinner smoke, my companion unanimously agreed with me that wild-fowling in that particular neighbourhood hardly augured well, nor did it hold out promise or comfortable prospects; that although the suspicions which had been aroused had been checkmated for the moment, there seemed every probability that further trouble was likely to develop. Perhaps it would be better far to solve the difficulty and ease the minds of all parties concerned if a rapid, mysterious departure, which left no traceable trail behind, was taken.

★★★★★★

Later in the day, as the twilight darkened into night, two shadows might have been seen for a moment as they angled the corner of the inn in that southernmost Danish township and disappeared in the surrounding gloom; travellers once more amidst the flotsam and jetsam of life's highway; travelling they knew not whither, with but one mind and one paradoxical thought—to seek for, and at the same time to avoid, the unknown.

CHAPTER 11

Mad Gambling and a Big Bribe

The life of a Foreign Secret Service agent in wartime is one of kaleidoscopic changes. He never knows where he is likely to be from one day to another, nor the class of company it may be his lot in life to associate with.

One day it may elevate him to be a guest of royalty, the next may find him in company with the very scum of the earth. *Pro Bono Patriæ* is his motto. His life and everything he possesses on earth is thrown for the time being into the melting-pot. His sole aim, object, and ambition is to make good. To shoulder successfully and carry through his little bit whereby something may be accomplished, something done, for the furtherance of his country's cause.

All through that hard-fought fight the British played the game. They conducted themselves as gentlemen and they never forgot that they were sportsmen as well. We in the Secret Service prided ourselves that we never knowingly abused the hospitality of the neutral nations whose land we were compelled *nolens volens* to operate in, we never interfered in any way with their politics or their national affairs. Our work lay with the Hun, the enemy; we strictly confined our attentions to him, and to him alone.

Yet we were constantly being tempted to be drawn into side issues which it was at times really difficult to avoid.

In the early spring of 1915, whilst I was cruising in the Baltic, amidst ice-floes and storms frequent enough to chill the ardour of any patriot, I received an innocent and simple-worded note, the interpretation of which meant I must hasten to Christiania for orders.

On my arrival there I met my old friend N. P., who had been similarly recalled from Sweden, with others who have not figured in these pages. Days passed in listless idleness. No orders arrived. There seemed to be nothing doing. But it was heart-breaking to see the constant stream of the necessities of life—cotton, copper, foodstuffs and metals—going to Germany, which the feeble remonstrances of our ministers, both at home and abroad, seemed utterly powerless to stop or to diminish.

For some weeks all members of the Foreign Secret Service operating round the Baltic were kept at the Norwegian capital in daily anticipation of something important turning up. The expected, however, never happened, yet we were still kept there, in spite of repeated remonstrances and urgent appeals to be released in order that we might attend to our respective interests in other spheres.

One evening I had been dining with a friend at the Grand Hotel. Whilst I was in the vestibule about 2 a.m., putting on my snow-boots preparatory to the short walk home, a middle-aged man, with hands clenched, face as pale and clammy as a corpse, and teeth set hard, rushed up to me in such an alarming manner that I fondled the butt of a revolver lying in the outside pocket of my overcoat by way of precaution against possible contingencies.

"My God, sir, you are the one man I've been praying to find! I believe I should have committed suicide tonight or by tomorrow morning had it not have been for this chance meeting. I must see you, now, this moment. You must save me. I have millions, yet I am a ruined man. I dare not face it a second time. You must either come to my room, or I must visit yours. I have not slept for nights. It will take hours to explain matters. You must save me. Save me! Yes, only promise me you will save me!"

Thinking I had a madman to deal with, I humoured him. I promised any reasonable assistance that lay in my power, and fixed an appointment for the afternoon of the following day.

The twelve hours intervening made little improvement upon the nerves or excitement of the stranger. It was some time after my arrival before he could articulate a connected story; whilst it took considerable interlocution and some cross-examination before I could draw forth the main facts of his case.

Shortly, it was as follows:

He was a merchant from the West Coast. He had gambled in fish oil some years previously and lost his all. Financial difficulties had since embarrassed him. When the country was thrown into panic by the declaration of war he had seen his opportunity and plunged once again into an enormous speculation. By promising large sums of money for direct financial assistance, and by offering brokerage remuneration far in excess of what was either necessary or reasonable, he had become enabled to buy on credit practically every barrel of fish oil held in the country. It was a special kind of oil which could not be replaced until next season's harvest was gathered in. He was therefore in a position to control the market and to regulate prices, provided he could only finance the deal uninterruptedly and his movements were not hampered by new laws—particularly prohibition of export.

Terribly anxious on both these points, he had approached the British Minister and pressed upon him the acceptance of his whole purchase at a price more than double its initial cost. In addition he had hinted rather too strongly that Germany was a certain buyer should the English Government not care to accept his preferential offer.

It amounted in fact to a threat: "If you don't buy this oil at once, the whole lot goes off to your enemies."

The minister had promised his answer in five days. But when the merchant's financier heard what he had done, that gentleman was so irate he had threatened to cancel his credit, because, as he argued, he had tried to threaten England; which meant that the oil in question would promptly be made contraband, whilst the English Government would call upon the Norwegian Government to cause its export to be prohibited. There was admittedly no sale for such large quantities as he had bought in the home markets, hence he became quite convinced that he was a ruined man, although, according to market prices, he was a millionaire.

When recounting his folly in thus putting his head into the lion's mouth, to which he metaphorically likened his visit to the ministry, the poor unnerved merchant worked himself up into a tremendous pitch of excitement. He perspired so freely that all the starch was exuded from his linen. He drank bottle after bottle of lager beer in a vain endeavour to keep his lips moist, whilst his eyes at times assumed an unnatural appearance, rolling round in their sockets in a manner alarming to behold.

I knew simply nothing of the subject put so vehemently before me, but the idea of any goods of any value being permitted to go into Germany was so distasteful to me that I listened with the greatest patience and until my visitor could say no more. Then I inquired where and how I could be expected to be of assistance.

"Why, you're a newspaper man. You represent the best and most influential periodical in London, the greatest city of the world. I know what tremendous power and influence the English papers hold. Your minister would certainly listen to what you said, if you would only interview him on my behalf; if you would only intercede against any prohibition being put on my oil."

"Why should I interfere?" I said. "As an Englishman, I certainly object to your selling any goods to Germany. If I thought you intended sending a single barrel there I should do all I could to get the prohibition put on it, not to help you to keep it off."

"But that would bring Norway into the war."

"I don't agree," I snapped.

"Yes, it would. A prohibition on oil or fish would mean the throwing out of employment of many thousands upon thousands of Norwegian fishermen and workmen. They would revolt and march on the *Storthings-Bygning*" (House of Parliament) "and compel its members to take the prohibition off in spite of the British Government. Your minister might say that England had been slighted, which would lead to war. One of our own ministers himself told me this only yesterday, so I know I'm right in what I'm talking about."

In vain I poo-poohed the idea; the perspiring merchant was insistent.

Having delivered himself of these troubles, he walked up and down the confines of the room in a frenzy of nervous excitement. Banging his fists one into the other, alternately running his fingers through his hair, which was absolutely wringing wet from perspiration, he, literally speaking, groaned out his mental agony.

I watched him in silence. Suddenly he steadied himself somewhat, then stopped short, and, looking me straight in the face, he exclaimed: "I feel, I know, I am positively certain sure you can save this situation if you will. I am paying the man who is putting up my money 40,000 *kroner* as a private honorarium over and above the usual interest of five *per cent*. It's worth it. But neither he nor I shall see a cent in return if it's to be prohibition. Now, I'll make a square deal with you. I'll give you 100,000 *kroner*" (about £5,500) "if you'll interview your minister for me and you can successfully guarantee me no prohibition for six or even three months. If you can only stop it for three months, then I shall be safe, and I shall have more than enough to pay my late creditors and everybody else everything I owe, and to spare." At this point he positively gasped for breath and more beer, whilst he re-mopped his streaming neck and face.

During this scene my thoughts had not been idle. They had conceived, turned over, and evolved a scheme which I believed would work out to the advantage of all concerned, excepting only the Germans.

I would promise him the assistance he desired; to intercede and do my best to pacify the British Minister's wrath, which I was given to understand was burning at white heat against the unfortunate merchant for his presumption and impudence in daring to suggest a twist of the lion's tail for so large an amount as the £100,000 profit he had suggested. It was well known that the Legation had given out, and wished it to be understood, that England would not look favourably upon any business relationships whatsoever, directly or indirectly, with Germany. Furthermore, that such a flouting of England's goodwill would not be to the future advantage of any such transgressors. Some merchants made a joke of this, others expressed their feelings in withering scorn, a few took notice. The idea that their trade should be allowed to continue with England whilst its continuance with Germany was to be looked upon as an unpardonable offence seemed a top-heavy argument. They did not view the proposition through similarly tinted glasses. And as soon as the minister began to voice his objections, so soon did trouble begin.

The position of the merchant from the West Coast, however, was hardly on all fours with other traders in the country. He was particularly anxious to keep in the good graces of the British Minister. At the same time, the earning of money seemed dearer to him than most other worldly considerations.

I knew he held an appointment which he was desirous to retain—an appointment which the British Minister could influence considerably. He, the British Minister, could easily keep him in it or he could scorch him out of it, whichever he desired. I also knew that the British minister, generally speaking, was not too popular; whilst it was said that he was a man who would never understand the Norwegian race any more than it would ever understand him. I could read what had passed in the minds of both of these individuals of such opposite temperaments at that memorable interview. I could imagine the grim, determined, waiting watchfulness with which the one man weighed up the weaknesses, the failings, and the awful nerve-racking sensations of realised blunders, abandoned hopes and fears, and despair probably revealed on the face of the other.

It was all as plain to me as though the drama had been re-enacted in my presence. I felt a contempt I did not express at the sordid details of such vast credits being bought and risks run with other people's money, at bribery prices over and above the usual business rates; at the exorbitant brokerages which were being exacted from this rash and hazardous speculator; and more particularly at the heavy sum which was pressed upon me for a service that the eager donor had seemingly never seriously weighed or considered with an evenly-balanced mind. Thus I delivered myself:

"My good sir, you seem to have put your foot into it very badly indeed. It looks as though you, and all those involved with you, will crash through the very thin ice you are skating upon. It looks to me an odds-on chance that you will all be drowned in the financial vortex beneath. I don't for the life of me see how a poor insignificant journalist like myself can be of any real service to you. So you need not worry about your 100,000 *kroner* or any other sum. What fragment of weight do you suppose that so great a personage as our minister would attach to either my words or to my presence—to me, a stranger and an ordinary civilian?"

In a tense, hoarse voice he replied: "You forget you are English, an English journalist, representing the most powerful newspaper in London. Everyone is afraid of newspapers. They can uproot a throne. I know. I have lived in London. I have seen what a newspaper can do. You are cool. Your nerves are strong. You are a man of the world. You can state my case as it would be impossible for me to state it myself. Let the English Government buy my oil at its own price. I don't want an exorbitant profit. I will leave the negotiation to your absolute discretion. Prohibition would ruin me. You can save me if you will only try. I will willingly pay you any sum you like to name. If you stave off the threatened prohibition you will earn it ten times over. You may even save our country from war. I have not slept for nights. I cannot eat properly. Unless this strain on me is relieved I feel my brain will give way and I shall go mad, or I shall kill myself."

He sat down heavily upon a chair, and, burying his head in his hands, wept aloud.

Allowing a reasonable time for the unhappy merchant to settle down to a more even frame of mind, I placed my hand upon his shoulder, not unkindly, and said in a soft voice: "Well, I'm afraid I shall not carry much weight, and I don't want your money, but I will go and see him. One thing is quite certain. You can rest assured that England would never knowingly permit an injustice to be done; but if you're trading with the Germans, then of course you'll have to paddle your own canoe."

Further inquiries from the now subservient speculator elicited the existence of a contract made with German merchants by which a by-product of the oil passing through his hands in the ordinary course of business, amounting to about five *per cent.* of the whole, had to be delivered to them periodically for some few months to follow.

In due course I carried out the promise I had made, and as a result I conveyed certain proposals to the merchant, whereby that gentleman gave a written undertaking that not a barrel of his oil should be sold to Germany, directly or indirectly, excepting the by-product before referred to, which was considered a bagatelle, he receiving assurances that so long as his undertaking was faithfully carried out no steps would be taken without fair and reasonable notice to press for a prohibition of the particular oil in question.

To say that the gentleman most interested in this matter was effusive in his expressions of overwhelming gratitude would be a gross exaggeration of mild description. If permitted he would have fallen on my neck and almost drowned me in a flood of tears of relief and joy. He produced a pocket-book bulging with paper money and attempted to force a handful of notes for large amounts upon me, which I firmly and emphatically refused to accept. But I did agree to lunch with him, and the late dejected one ate what he described as his first decent meal for a prolonged period.

During the following week we occasionally met. The merchant was now all smiles and enjoying life consequent upon a successful venture and an undisturbed peace of mind. Prices continued to rise in his favour, and ten days later he declared himself a millionaire in Norwegian *kroner*. He vainly continued to press me every time we were alone to accept something substantial for the service rendered, whilst he was extravagant in his sentiments of eternal gratitude. He also proposed that I should abandon my journalistic career and accept a position as one of the foreign representatives of his firm, which offer I likewise politely declined. Then he hinted at the bestowal of a high Norwegian decoration, which made me smile still more.

Whether the unlimited ambitions of this wild speculator followed usual precedent and tumbled from the height of success to the abysmal depth of failure by reason of too oft-repeated temptations of Providence; whether, and if so, how the assurances given and the guarantee obtained were carried out, the ultimate turn of events, and how all these things developed, progressed and fructified, remain, as Rudyard Kipling says, another story.

CHAPTER 12

Shadowed by Police

Most people who interest themselves in the detailed working of Secret Service show greatest curiosity regarding the actual characters assumed by its members when in foreign countries.

A Secret Service agent should never assume a character he is not absolutely familiar with, both inside and out. It is possible to act up to a certain pitch, which will carry a certain distance, but artificiality is never safe. The stunt that is most in favour with the Intelligence Departments of all nations is journalism; thus it has been worked threadbare. Every foreign newspaper man on the Continent in recent years has been suspected, marked, and watched from the start, simply because he is what he is and for no other reason.

I was never warned of this, but it did not take me long to find it out. I fell into the *rôle* on my second trip out and adopted it naturally. I had been a free-lance journalist for upwards of twenty years, and I concluded that I could assume the character of special correspondent without any anxiety, and that I would be received for what I was. I had previously posed in many characters which were not so aptly fitted, and I believed I had carried them through successfully. This would be child's play to an old hand; besides, it had been part of my livelihood and was no assumed *rôle*, it was merely acting as one's self. One of the best, most influential and respected newspapers in London was therefore approached. I was no stranger to its editor, who received me with cordiality and gave me the necessary credentials.

In order to supplement my London references I sought for and easily obtained a further commission from the head editor of a series of country daily and weekly issues. A passport carried the announcement that I was a journalist, and everything appeared to be in order.

On arrival abroad, in the first country to which my work was allotted, as a special journalist I made application to the head Transmission Department to bespeak a legitimation card, which added an additional official stamp to my papers.

No one could have been more helpful or sympathetic than the Transmission Department officials, but in this particular instance it subsequently transpired they took copies of my credentials, which they handed over to the chief of the Criminal Investigation Department. Of course, I knew nothing of this at the time, although it would not in any way have disturbed my equanimity or peace of mind if I had.

A chief superintendent, whom I had to interview, was exceptionally kind. He strictly adhered to his duty to his country, but the leaning of his sympathies he appeared absolutely unable to restrain. "Your paper," he said, "is a power in Europe. It is always fair, impartial, and reliable. Many of my countrymen read it, and we know that it does not exaggerate the true facts. I respect it, my colleagues respect it, although they might not say so, and you may rely upon all the help I can give you. You must remember, however, the position we are placed in. You must be careful not to offend against our recently passed laws or you will not get your messages through. Also, you may be misunderstood." I thanked him and sought further enlightenment. I guessed what he was hinting at, but I wished to draw out of the man all he was willing to disclose.

"You know," the superintendent continued, "that you must not use our wires, either telephone or telegraph, to report movement of any ships of foreign nations which are at war. Our instructions are very strict upon this point. We must carry out our duties to the utmost. But these Germans! They are not men, they are mad dogs. Their idea of war seems to be extermination without regard to the law of nations. They murder women and children; they seem to have no feelings. They would overrun our small country tomorrow if they thought any advantage could be gained thereby. Alas, poor innocent, unoffending Belgium, whom they undertook by honourable treaty to protect and uphold!

"How they have ruined her, burned her towns, ravaged her entire country, raped her daughters, robbed her churches and treasures; and, on top of all, fined her inhabitants for not returning to be made slaves to oppressors and brutal taskmasters. '*Vengeance is mine*,' saith the Lord. If they do not suffer for all this, then there is no justice on earth or in heaven above." We were alone in his private office. Before speaking he had carefully closed the door, having first looked anxiously into the outer office. Now he turned to me and, extending both hands, added: "Reading these things, hearing of them from eye-witnesses, hearing even worse in detail which made my flesh creep, can you wonder that we, a peace-loving people, who never did like those overbearing Germans, pray for the day when they will find their level in the world and when they will be compelled to behave like decent-minded people?"

I cordially agreed, and inquired what my loquacious friend was leading up to.

"You have a Press Censor in your country, I presume?"

"Yes."

"If he saw in the course of his duties anything which he thought might be of advantage to your government, or to its naval administrators, to know, I suppose he would at once cause it to be sent along?"

"Really, my dear sir," I interjected, "I have no knowledge of what our censor does. I know he's an awful nuisance to us newspaper men; he holds up our copy for indefinite periods. But I, like yourself, assume he is an Englishman." And I looked him square in the face and wondered whether he would guess what I certainly had no intention of admitting.

"Good!" he exclaimed. "Now, in this country our newspaper men get round our regulations by using simple little codes, which in their wording refer to things domestic, but in reality can be translated into something very, very different. For example, 'Mrs. Jones of —— has just had twins; one is strong, the other very weak and not expected to live,' might easily be arranged to convey the interpretation that a couple of German submarines had entered the port of ——, one of which was a damaged condition. I expect your paper would like to have such items of news? Even if it were not allowed to publish it, your Censor might like to have the news to hand along. Such a message, worded as I suggest, would not offend against our rules and regulations. We should accept it, not knowing or caring for any possible hidden meaning. Do you understand, my dear sir, what I want to convey?"

Wondering at the back of my mind whether he was just sounding me, or whether he was so truly sympathetic with the Allies that he was really anxious to help stop the war as soon as possible, I followed the wise course of terminating the interview. After thanking the superintendent for his kind assistance and sympathy I left.

It is an unwritten rule of the Secret Service never to give anything away unless it is imperative so to do, or a more than commensurate advantage is gained thereby.

It is an unwritten rule of the same service to keep away from all government officials, irrespective of nationality, in so far as one reasonably can.

In spite of the deadly earnestness of the gentleman I had just left, I felt puzzled. I did not understand his voluntary and unnecessary outburst of outraged sentiment. Instinct told me that somewhere there was something moving which I must guard against. What it was, or from which quarter I was to expect it, I had no idea.

In the Secret Service one must paddle one's own canoe, alone and unassisted; always upstream; always through dangerous rapids, wherein at every yard are hidden rocks and snags ready to tear the frail craft asunder; always through countries overrun with enemies armed with poisonous arrows which are fired singly and in volleys whenever the smallest opportunity is given; always hunted and stalked both day and night by the most persevering, cunning, and desperate huntsmen in the world; always on the move, with never a sure, safe, or secure resting-place for one's weary limbs; and always on the *qui vive* against a thousand and one unseen, unknown, and unsuspected dangers. No wonder that members of this service so soon become fatalists.

A few days later I was closeted with a local journalist out of collar. He wanted a job. He spoke six languages, had had smooth and rough experiences in America, and was a man of great ability. His weak spot was alcohol. He had had chances innumerable. Friends had helped him until their patience had been exhausted. Now that his domestic ship was badly on the rocks, the whole family half-starved, and himself a total abstainer—by force of circumstances—another last chance seemed to his unfortunate wife to fall as the blessed manna from heaven in the wilderness. I treated him generously and trusted him—as far as I could have trusted any ordinary person—but he, an ordinary mortal of this proverbially ungrateful world, at once sold his benefactor to a higher bidder, in so far as it was possible for him so to do. It happened thus-wise.

Not satisfied with the liberal terms I had agreed to give him, which covered full travelling expenses, living expenses and remuneration separately assessed, he approached various carrying firms and tried to wheedle from them free passes. Meeting with no sympathy—probably they knew him by former experience—he visited the police and sold me over to them as an alleged spy. Naturally the police wanted evidence. This the man undertook to get. He made excuse after excuse to delay his departure on my business. He visited me daily with a long list of questions; he suggested the obtaining of information concerning local naval and military intelligence which did not interest me in the least; he pressed for written instructions, special codes, and complicated arrangements regulating the sending and receiving of correspondence—anything, in fact, which would gain him time and which might prove my undoing—all of which, however, I suggested he should prepare himself if he wanted them.

The man's testimonials were excellent upon all points excepting the one weakness before referred to, and I treated him quite unsuspectingly. Little did I know that when he made notes in shorthand they were in fact literal and verbatim reports of our entire conversation, made at the suggestion of the police and for their special benefit. I afterwards heard that detectives had helped to prepare the very code he brought to me and which he was so eager for me to substitute for one I had suggested.

Had I been indiscreet, and had I given anything at all away, or had I trusted this man with any facts relating to or concerning those connected with my real employment, I would have been arrested on the spot. As it was, the police learned nothing which did not appear to them legitimate, in order, and most flattering to their country, to their countrymen, and to themselves.

Remarkable as it may appear, it was, however, a fact that I was restless and uneasy. Instinct seemed to whisper in my ears, continually day and night, messages of warning that all was not well. The air seemed overcharged with electricity. It felt heavy, like an ominous calm preceding a violent storm. Yet, rack my brain as I would, I could not for the life of me fathom the depth of the mystery, nor could I trace its origin to any fountain-head.

Meanwhile my new assistant entered upon his undertaking. In a few days he sent to me by code a detailed description of a sea engagement between German and English warships. It was the fight off the Dogger Bank in the North Sea, in April, 1915.

In the course of the next six weeks, in addition to his proper work, arranging with outpost correspondent agents, he collected and forwarded at regular intervals a mass of interesting matter, all good newspaper copy, with many little tit-bits of special news which were most acceptable. But he would rub in items of local naval and military intelligence in spite of my repeated instructions to the contrary.

Not only was I a staunch fatalist, but I believed in a Divine Providence which directed one's actions and destinies, which shaped one's ends, rough-hew them how one might. In this instance it probably saved my liberty from being suddenly and inconveniently disturbed. Before I received any of these reports before mentioned they were all (I have since ascertained) intercepted and carefully studied by the Criminal Investigation Department. Naturally, my replies were anticipated by them with still greater pleasure. Dame Providence, however, directed the pen when I upbraided my assistant, reminding him he was engaged in journalism, not espionage; that he was representing a great newspaper and for the time being I was a guest in an hospitable, generous country; further, that I would at once dispense with his services if he offended against that country's laws; and that, when he sent information concerning German spies, such was wrongly addressed—he should have sent it direct to the local police, whom, I added, were *the most intelligent, fair-minded and smartest crowd of their kind anywhere in Europe.*

I cannot help smiling to myself now when I think of this. It seems so ridiculous to think that I should have penned such flattering words regarding those who were attempting to catch me, *flagrante delicto*, as the law puts it! It probably puzzled them not a little, whilst it must have caused them to suspect their wily journalistic friend as running with the hare and at the same time hunting with the hounds.

About this period something else occurred which added to my uneasiness. Naturally my most closely-guarded secret was my main line of communication with London. No one held the secret of this but the most trusted in the service. One day an intercepted message was brought to me. It contained a sign by which one of my messages could be identified. I tested this message by a dozen different ways; the result was rubbish in each instance. I knew by this that nothing of any importance was known; but why should the message have been floated into channels wherein it seemed to be known that I had nets? Who had floated it? How had the sign even come to be used? I puzzled for hours in a dark room smoking my customary strong black cigars furiously all the time, and I left off more puzzled than when I began. I put on an agent to follow and to watch myself from a distance, to try and see if anyone, and if so whom, were then amusing themselves with that interesting pastime.

I put on another agent to "smear," or to attempt to, a volunteer agent whom I relied upon to a certain extent for local correspondence. I had long entertained strong suspicions concerning the latter, but I could never find any tangible proof against him. I wrote spoof letters to myself and I caused other similar missives to be sent to myself from various quarters, upon which I was sure my interceptor would take action, and his movement would probably be thereby detected. I tried and tested various simple and ingenious dodges to trap my tormentor, but everything proved in vain.

Exactly three days after intercepting the first message a repeat followed through the same channels. It was a lengthy document and bore the outward visible signs of genuineness, but inwardly it read nothing but nonsense. The object my enemies aimed at had failed. I had provided for that. But whether the police, or the naval or military authorities, were behind the attempt, or whether it was an experiment of Hun origin, I never could unravel.

Several quaint experiences following one another in rapid succession made me wish I could carry through the work I had in hand to a rapid conclusion in order that I could shift to a more congenial atmosphere. I had received warning before starting on this particular business that my lot was not likely to be enviable; and that I would probably have to put my head into the lion's mouth. I had also been warned that the place to which I had been sent to stay and to direct certain operations was known to be infested with German agents, whose jealousy and zeal in watching over certain vitally important secrets amounted to a mania.

My visitation might find a good comparison in likening it to a police officer being sent to sit in the entrance hall of an illicit West End gambling hell. He knew every effort would be strained to tempt him away from the main issue or to shift him. My commanding officer had intimated that if I survived ten days he would consider I had done well. As a matter of fact, I stuck it six weeks. I had arranged what was wanted. I had fixed other matters towards a promising and satisfactory conclusion when I received a picture postcard. The illustration represented a motor-boat going at full speed. Underneath it was written: "Skip-per ahoy!"

In the ordinary way this would seem to convey nothing beyond a casual salutation. But the hyphen! It was evidently intentional. I read it as a hint to get quickly away—to skip, in fact—whilst the motor-boat suggested that a private rapid departure would probably not be to my disadvantage.

The weather was much too tempestuous to venture to sea in such small craft as might have been available. No other possible road of retreat, except by sea, was open, so I had to study ways and means. I informed those who waited on me that I should be leaving three days later for a well-known town lying fifty or sixty miles to the southward. Meanwhile the few remaining details necessary to complete the objective of my visit were arranged, and the local time-sheets of every known route touching at the island were studied. I noted with some satisfaction that early in the morning two boats crossed each other's passage at given hours, arriving at the same quay and departing at the same time.

The next day, before six in the morning, I appeared on the quay and booked a ticket for the southern journey. No one appeared to be watching, and when the boats arrived I made the mistake of boarding the boat which sailed north, although I hardly considered it necessary to inform the purser of the fact when he demanded the wherewithal to cover passage on his ship.

No one in the town knew I had left, but I had sent a secret message to headquarters advising of my intentions.

At the next port of call a letter came aboard addressed to Herr Schmidt, which I claimed. It was a transcribed telephone message. Reading between the lines the writing conveyed only one interpretation. Reduced to simple English, it meant: "Eruption—quit."

I promptly left the boat I was on and changed my route by going inland over a peninsula to a small fishing station, where a portion of luck added to a large portion of whiskey secured a berth on a small cargo-boat running direct to another country.

The false agent who had sold his benefactor but was unable to deliver the brand of goods he had promised, then finding that certain monetary demands were not provided for by telegram, although not in accordance with his agreed arrangements, fell a victim to his besetting sin. He indulged in a prolonged debauch during which he divulged the full depths of his iniquity. His confessions were in due course reported to me, and they brought him the order of the boot.

The deep-laid schemes of the perhaps too-muchly-lauded police, like those of mice and men, ganged agley; action on their warrant to arrest had perforce to be postponed *sine die*; whilst the elusive Herr Schmidt, the pivot round which this little teacup drama gyrated, vanished *pro tem.* from the affairs and haunts of the disciples of *kultur* and *goulashes*.

Chapter 13

Dodging Frontier Guards and Searching for One's Self

Crossing the northern frontiers of Germany during the war was by no means so difficult a task as it apparently was to do the same thing further south. *Landstürmers* were on guard during most of the time. Men about forty years of age who took much more interest in food and drink than they did in fighting. They were on very friendly terms with the Danes, particularly with those who lived near to the frontier; whilst a great many marriages had been consummated from time immemorial between Germans and Danes, and Danes and Germans, all along the northern boundaries.

In spite of the vast amount of commodities and necessities of all sorts that poured into the northern ports of Germany during the whole period of the war, until America came in and in a great measure stopped the absurdity, yet the Germans were short of many things which their souls hankered for, whilst many of them, with a thought to the unknown future, were anxious to hoard up all supplies that could by any means be obtained.

Small fishermen, and those who picked up a precarious livelihood from any odd job or from varied and promiscuous dabblings in trading deals of any nature, were not slow to take advantage of these favourable circumstances. Hence a host of smugglers of small operation sprang into being like mushrooms in a night. Those men mostly owned, in part or in whole, a light boat used for fishing or carrying purposes. The majority of these boats were fitted with paraffin motors which propelled them about six to nine knots an hour. The coast of Germany was not more than twenty-five miles away from any part of the southern islands of Denmark and could be made in three hours, even under adverse conditions.

Soap, tobacco, matches, aquavit, and such like were cheap in Denmark, and very dear, if not at times almost unprocurable, in Germany. Rich harvests were thus to be had almost for the asking. In addition to this, the Germans themselves used a great many small boats from their side of the water. They were assiduous fishers for flounders and other luxuries provided by the Baltic, and they were friendly disposed to all Danish fishermen, more particularly so towards those whose boats were known to carry other cargoes besides fish.

Ports like Kiel, Lübeck, and Rostock were naturally avoided by these men as being too active and too lively; but they did not hesitate to mingle with the German fishing-boats and land as near as they could without raising any undue notice or attraction. The coast almost all the way along is low-lying, with shallow water extending out some distance, and consists of vast shoals of sand and mud. There are, however, numerous landing-places for small boats, and many Danish smugglers made the crossing as often as two or three times a week.

At ports like Swinemunde, Stettin, Lübeck, and Kiel, if a traveller of any nationality attempted to pass through on a passport in the usual manner, he or she was subjected to unbelievable indignities and searches which in most instances amounted to insult and violation of the actual person. No wonder that many Danish workmen, who in some instances had actually been employed upon private, even secret, war material for Germany, and who had obtained permission to visit their homes for a spell, preferred any means of making the home passage across the southern Baltic rather than take the regular ferry-boat routes. Thus it was that quite a few of them came across with the smugglers, whereby they avoided the severe investigations and saved considerable money on their passage.

I was not slow at ascertaining these facts and I made several voyages with the Danish smugglers, which were interesting in themselves, whilst they brought me in contact with some of the very workmen who had been employed upon war-work in Germany which was at that time of the very greatest interest to Englishmen engaged in attempting to anticipate and to thwart the wily Hun. I ascertained by this means valuable corroboration of preliminary particulars concerning the super-submarines, the super-Zeppelins, and the preliminary trials of the super-cannon afterwards used on Paris.

In the early spring of 1915 I had returned from one of these little cruises where business and pleasure had been combined. I had landed safely upon one of the southern islands of Denmark and entered a *kro*, or small licensed inn, to obtain a decent meal with a good long drink of the famous Jacob Jacobsen's Gamle Karlsberg porter, which can be obtained everywhere throughout Denmark and is every bit as good as it is famous, when the very dirty waiter whispered in my ear that there was a heap of good money offered for a very little work.

Perhaps I should apologise to the aforesaid waiter for disparaging his personal appearance. Because it might have been possible that at the time in question my outward appearance equalled or surpassed his own in filth and slovenliness. But be that as it may, I naturally inquired further regarding this hinted El Dorado.

"Well," he said, rubbing his chin and gazing at me with great earnestness, "there are a couple of Germans hunting round this town" (every cluster of houses in Denmark is called a town) "looking for an English spy who has been jumping over the frontier a time or two, and they say that they can get ten thousand *marks* for him, dead or alive, if they can only put their hands on him."

I was on the point of quaffing a most delicious draught of the far-famed porter, but somehow I seemed to lose my thirst. The news was of absorbing interest to me, if not actually startling in its purport.

The waiter was obviously avaricious, and the mention of so much money made his fingers itch and his mouth water at the thought of the glorious times he could secure with such vast wealth.

Whilst I was watching the various changes of his face as these ideas chased one another through his narrow brain, it flashed upon me how easy it would be for anyone to capture me and to take me back across that narrow little strip of sea-water whence I had so recently come. A pinch of some drug in one's food or in one's drink. A slight tap on the head. A little chloroform on a pocket-handkerchief. All simple applications, so easy to administer, and so easy to explain away: that one's friend or brother had merely taken a little more alcohol than was good for him, or had been unexpectedly taken ill and now a little help was necessary to get him aboard his ship or boat, so he could be taken home to the dear old Fatherland, where he could be well and properly attended to!

These lightning-like reflections sent a cold shiver down the very marrow in my spine. I drained my mug of porter at a gulp and hastened the waiter away for more.

Whilst he was so occupied I decided what to do. On his return I told him, with all seriousness, that I had seen a strange-looking dude on the quay less than an hour ago whom I was certain was English, and if he could find and present me to the two Germans and I got the reward I would give him a share of it for telling me all about it. To show him I was in earnest I treated him to a bottle of porter. After consuming our drinks he arranged matters, and we left to hunt up the would-be German scalp-hunters.

About an hour afterwards we found them hanging round a very primitive moving-picture show which seemed to thrive on free films supplied by the Hun propagandists. We all four adjourned to another *kro* for drinks and important conference.

The description they gave me of the man wanted tallied exactly with the man I said I had seen. Now that was quite an extraordinary coincidence, and I impressed it on them. Only my waiter friend had sense enough to cross-examine further into my statement, so I had to order more drinks to stop the possibility of still deeper inquiries. Before I agreed to make a move I wanted to have a bargain in writing giving me half the reward. This the Germans would not agree to. They suggested one-third, and my friend the waiter hinted at a possible fourth share for himself. When I said I would not be satisfied with three thousand *marks* on the risks run they explained that a third share would exceed eight thousand *marks*. "It had been ten thousand," they said, "but quite recently the reward had been increased to twenty-five thousand *marks*," which had made them very active and anxious to try and secure it.

I, however, still argued that if I found the man I should get half the reward, whatever sum it was. They disagreed; meanwhile the waiter got intoxicated. Leaving him where he was, we commenced our search and continued it with vigour and persistence for the remainder of that day and all the next. I assure you, gentle reader, I never had such an interesting hunt before, and I have hunted big game in many lands under extraordinary conditions. That trail, however, was the trail of my life.

About noon next day we ran a suspect to earth in a lonely spot and put him through the mill with a vengeance. But he conclusively proved his identity and we were very lucky to escape trouble over the episode. I think our salvation was that we so frightened the unfortunate captive that he was glad to be able to leave the town as quickly as possible and get away from us back home to his little farm inland.

Towards the afternoon of our second day's man-hunt my Hun colleagues began to hint their suspicions regarding myself and as to my actions. They had been very ungentlemanly towards me from the first on the question of dividing the reward. They were very mean over spending money on drinks and smokes; and, taking one consideration with another, I thought it far wiser to lean on discretion as the better part of valour. So as soon as the shades of night once more darkened the land I regret to have to admit that *I borrowed* a boat belonging to some native, whose forgiveness I trust was granted if he ever found it again, and I left the island, never to set foot in that township again; at least for the duration of the war.

★★★★★★

Entering Germany from the Schleswig frontier was not very difficult unless one attempted to pass through the custom house, with all its surrounding formalities and searches. In the angles of the frontier near Ribe, and on the mainland, of course the whole line was trenched and guarded, and any attempted passing or even approach was both difficult and dangerous. But by skipping round either end, at sea on the east, and between the islands on the west, no insurmountable difficulty presented itself.

I never attempted a landing on the immediate east side, but I did go round on the west, and the trip was not worth the risk or the trouble. There was nothing to learn that one did not already know from scores of others who had been permitted to pass the lines on business or otherwise. There was nothing to gain by going again, and I had no desire to attempt to repeat the experience.

Living on an island which is unnamed except upon the best maps of the southern Baltic I had a friend—a Danish sailorman who was rarely at home, but when he did take a holiday from his sea-going wanderings it was invariably marked for its riotousness on shore or for its devilment afloat.

Dare-Devil Christian was one of the best men I ever met except for his one great weakness. Provided that was guarded against, he was fine company and a great sportsman. Any class of sport satisfied him, from rat-hunting upwards, and if a spice of danger could be added it gave him a greater zest proportionately.

I had the great luck to bump into him twice during one winter season, and for some time we thoroughly enjoyed life together. Just before the New Year of 1915 I had been advised of a possible and probable naval engagement somewhere near the North Sea entrance to the Kiel Canal. It had been hinted to me it would be interesting to know what German war-vessels there might be cruising in the Baltic that would or might be recalled if such an event took place. It was also hinted that the water defences to Kiel harbour, and the Canal entrance on the east, might be ascertained for certain with some advantage to England's Naval Intelligence Department.

I was accordingly on my way down towards the island of Aero when, by great good fortune, I met my friend Christian on the second occasion above referred to. Needless to add, we at once joined company.

In order to occupy our time in a manner congenial to both, and as ice bound the streams inland and made work at sea far from pleasant, I suggested to Christian an expedition having for its object a direct attack upon the short-winged fowl which thronged the outer coastline. These birds are not generally considered good eating, and in England nobody will buy them for such purpose. But in Scandinavia the natives soak them for twelve to twenty-four hours in vinegar and water, and by these and other preparations eventually bring them to table as a most appetising dish.

The waters all around Kiel *fjord* are reputed as good hunting-ground for flounders and for diving ducks. The fjord, however, is situate twenty miles away from Danish territory, and to reach it in those times one would have to rim the gauntlet of numerous patrol craft of various designs and size. Yet a small fishing-boat, resembling in all outward appearance other small boats which are used for coast-fishing along the east of Schleswig Holstein as well as along the Danish coasts, was not so likely to draw particular attention.

When my scheme, embracing an expedition to these waters, was casually brought up with Christian, as though it was a mere matter of utter indifference whether the boat drifted there or anywhere else in Europe, he looked at me with an incredulous expression of pained surprise upon his genial countenance, which seemed to convey the unspoken sentiment:

"Have you forgotten that the Germans are at war? That to go and fish or shoot ducks anywhere near their precious, guarded harbour—about the most sacred spot in their whole empire—could only be equalled in sacrilege to spitting the eternal holy fire out before the Priests in the Temple on Mount Ephesus?"

So I hastened to attempt to assure him by saying: "Well, we need *not shoot* when we get in; nor, for that matter, if and when we see any ships or people about whom we might disturb. Also, my dear friend Christian, don't you appreciate the fact that it would indeed be interesting really to know the truth just at the present time concerning the much-discussed outer Kiel defences?"

"That's all very well, but—"

He stopped short at the "but," whilst he became more serious than I had ever known him to be before. For a long spell he smoked in silence, then looking up with a half-smile, exclaimed: "I don't want to know what I ought not to know, and I don't want you to tell me what I don't suppose you ought to tell me, but I reckon I know what you want to go to Kiel for; *it is not flatfish and it is not ducks.*"

"My dear friend, you are totally wrong. I assure you it was merely idle curiosity coupled with a love of the venturesome which prompted the suggestion. But if you funk it, or do not care about the risk, then we had better steer east."

Christian looked up sharply at the conclusion of this sentence. He did not reply, nor was the subject again referred to for several days.

One eventful morning, however, we found ourselves silently inspecting a small, well-built and compact fishing craft, just such a boat as we would have selected had we determined upon the trip before referred to. The boat was good and so was her gear. Christian, without a word regarding future movements, engaged her, and she was promptly victualled with several days' supplies.

It was announced to the local natives that Christian had determined a cruise around Stryno and the shores of Laaland where ducks and geese were known to abound. In due course a start was made and the boat was headed in that direction. But as soon as darkness set in she was veered completely round by tacit mutual consent, and steered south, then south-south-east.

By daylight next morning we were fishing merrily and apparently quite unconcerned off the land of the Hun, abreast of that particular wealthy tract of rich soil and pasture which the Germans had robbed from Denmark in the 'sixties. As the day wore on the little boat drew nearer in shore and towards the afternoon she sailed boldly up the Kiel *fjord.* It was much safer doing so in broad daylight than at any other time; whilst it is true beyond all shadow of doubt that an impudence which is impudently bold enough generally succeeds where a hesitating cautious policy would be sure to fail.

Christian said little, but he evidently knew the ropes. With the aid of his timely assistance and cool assurance several dangers were passed over, any one of which might have terminated the cruise in disaster. He also appeared to know exactly how to disguise and mark the boat so that she would be, and was, mistaken for a longshore boat in home waters. There was, however, much to try the nerves, not the least strain of all being the overshadowing knowledge that at any moment the boat and her contents might be blown to a thousand fragments by a floating or anchored mine; although by hugging the shore as much as possible this danger was greatly minimised. When a warship seemed to take more than ordinary interest in that frail craft of peace and industry Christian's discretion rather than his valour caused him to steer direct for the nearest hamlet on the shore as though he belonged there.

He would often anchor and down sails, but he wisely refrained from landing, apparently because he had much too much to attend to in connection with his gear. By creeping inshore when other craft were too near, and keeping well away from it at other times, the boat drifted nearer and nearer to the localities desired to be reached and seen. Observations were taken by stealth and with the assistance of good field-glasses, their user first invariably concealing himself under a mass of fishing net, which amused Christian, although he refrained from making any comment upon the peculiar eccentricity or caution of the observer.

At night searchlights played over parts of the water and advantage was taken of any intervening promontory, rock, or anchored craft that could in the smallest degree hide the boat from the searching beams. Having nosed around and observed all that one could have expected to be able to locate in such a venture, advantage was taken of favourable breezes and the return journey accomplished with due care and caution. Fortunately snow-squalls were frequent. Probably the flakes acted as a mighty host of guardian angels to the little amateur privateer; for although she was pushed into the security of shallow waters again and again during the exciting if somewhat risky voyage, she evaded capture, even overhauling; and eventually returned like a migratory bird at the end of a season, to her natal resting-place.

Fortunately a fair supply of birds had been gathered in, both on the outward and homeward journey, whilst the fishing had not been in vain. Thus there was plenty to show to account for our industry. Little did the natives reck the importance of the data and information thus collected, under their very noses, so to speak; or that anything out of the ordinary had taken place; or that risk of instant death had been laughed at and ignored by the two happy-go-lucky sportsmen, who appeared to them as mere overgrown schoolboys taking life as but a ray of sunshine and never seeming to regard it seriously.

Between themselves the trip was not talked about, nor was it ever afterwards referred to beyond one interrogation, and that was when the sweet music of the grating keel upon a Danish beach announced our safe and successful return.

"Now are you satisfied?" asked Christian. The laconic reply given him back was limited to one word—"Quite."

CHAPTER 14

Avoiding Cold Murder

Germans in neutral countries during the war were circumspect. They swarmed everywhere, and never in the history of commercial enterprise since the world began were seen so many commercial travellers as the Fatherland provided, at such "*kolossal*" expense and for such little return.

Nearly every one of those men without exception was in the direct pay of the German Secret Service. It was part of their work to nose into everything, to shadow everyone believed to be foreign to the land they visited, or who showed any sympathy for the enemies of Germany, or antagonism towards their country.

If they desired to or had received a direct order to stop by any means the activities of another, those men rarely came out into the open. They much preferred ways that are dark and tricks that are deep to achieve their desired ends. The depths to which their cunning sank had to be experienced to be believed.

During the years 1914 and 1915, when I was employed in the B.F.S.S. in Northern Europe, several most extraordinary accidents occurred, from which I had miraculous escapes. At the time I put them down to incidents. I think very differently now.

Verily Prussian methods in all things seem to be Jesuitical, in that it is believed the end justifies the means. If one of their employees in their own, Secret Service, no matter what his station of life may be, gets to know too much, his fate may be sealed by a secret sentence of death passed in the Wilhelmstrasse, and the supreme penalty is inflicted in a manner unsuspected by the unfortunate victim.

Dr. Armgaard Karl Graves records in his book, *The Secrets of the German War Office*, how the woman Olga Bruder, whose death in an hotel on the Russian frontier was returned to the Press as suicide, was

156

in reality poisoned; how young Lieutenant Zastrov was challenged to repeated duels until he was killed in one of them; and how others suspecting trouble avoided it by escape. Otto Diesel, we know, disappeared from the Harwich boat when on his way to England to exploit his engines which the Germans had bought. What happened to Frederick Krupp of Essen, no one knows.

Presumably executive workers in the German Secret Service knew as much about these things as Dr. Graves did himself. Perhaps it is part of their training and instruction to attempt to involve representatives of other nations with whom they come in contact and whose energies may be considered prejudicial or annoying to them, in quarrels or in brawls where a blow can be struck which it might be difficult if not impossible to trace. It must be more than a coincidence that Secret Service agents often find themselves in the middle of a small crowd where the pick-pocketing fraternity are undoubtedly represented. Be as careful, polite, and inoffensive as possible, quick-tempered, irascible irreconcilables will at times attempt to pick a quarrel. Boats, motorcars, and other vehicles by which Secret Service agents travel often meet with mysterious and altogether unaccountable accidents, whilst a challenge to a duel, for some trifling cause, is an experience which more than one of them has had to endure and to evade as best he can.

I chuckle now as I remember how I passed through one of these ordeals, not a hundred miles from the Rathhaus of Kiel. The incident took place very shortly before this world-war had actually begun. I have happily only received the very doubtful honour of one challenge since, which I insisted on treating as a practical joke, wisely absenting myself before developments could make the situation serious and untenable.

Both these incidents arose through polite assistance being rendered to a lady in distress.

The former typically exemplifies German methods, whilst its details cannot be considered devoid of interest.

I had for some years been prowling round on erratic wildfowling expeditions in the Baltic and along the western coast of Schleswig Holstein. My operations were at times based from the Esbjerg *fjord*, but I was no respecter of frontiers and there had been trouble whenever I had drifted too far south with the officious and zealous guardians of the German coast. I had previously, when travelling on business and pleasure combined, known trouble at both Berlin and Potsdam;

later on at and near to Hamburg. Apparently I was not popular with a certain section of German officialdom. Perhaps I had become too well known; that might or might not have been. Anyhow, for a long period before the war all German officials showed nervous hysteria in relation to suspected espionage regarding any Britisher who exhibited the smallest interest in the Heligoland district or the western islands, Kiel Canal, and Kiel Harbour. Yet I paid about as much attention to official fussiness as I would have done to a pinch of salt.

One memorable winter I had travelled north as usual, little thinking that any adventure would befall me.

At Osnabruck, where the lower level railway connects up with the higher, passengers have to ascend a steep flight of steps, the only means of communication between the two platforms. A certain young lady of Hungarian extraction, on the occasion in question, regarding whom it had better be stated at the outset that she was exceedingly fair to look upon and still more attractive in her manners, was overloaded with small hand-parcels and wraps. No porter was available, and common politeness dictated that such assistance as one was capable of rendering should be proffered.

The natural sequence of events led to an informal acquaintanceship, and the journey was continued in a jointly-occupied *coupé*. This compartment was also shared by other travellers, including a small, extraordinary-looking eccentric who covered his head with a kind of wire entanglement resembling the skeleton framework of a lampshade, over which he drew a green silk cover in order to shade his eyes from the glare of the lamplight, so that he could sleep without any inconvenience. The whole thing looked so ludicrous that one's risible faculties were tickled. I laughed so much I had to retire to the gangway in order to relieve my feelings without hurting the stranger's feelings by outward rudeness. The aforesaid Hungarian lady found herself in similar straits. Mutual converse naturally ensued.

Ascertaining that Kiel happened to be our common destination, what more natural than we should select the same hotel to stay at? After dinner, in order to kill time as pleasantly as could be, we visited a local place of amusement where a musical farce was being performed and the stalls were filled with military and naval officers. My companion had informed me that her father was the commander of a fortress on the Baltic, that she had two brothers, one a lieutenant in the navy and the other in the army. Whilst waiting between the acts a young officer of overbearing, vulgar, swaggering type, which Zabern brought into world-wide prominence, entered our private box and claimed acquaintanceship. He was more or less intoxicated, and obnoxiously effusive. He would order champagne, and plenty of it, in spite of all protests to the contrary. He also fetched another officer, whom he stated to be a connection by marriage with the lady, but whom she failed to recognise or to remember.

Not appreciating nor being flattered by these attentions, an early attempt was made to cover a polite quittance with plausible excuses, but such an escape was not permitted. In due course, as the wine flowed, the officer's temperament changed from gushing effusiveness to the quarrelsome stage. Instinct foretold unpleasantness, which was not long in the coming. The two officers first quarrelled between themselves, then one of them accused me of an unfriendly act. Whether it was imagination or wilful design on his part I know not, but the accusation was followed by open insult in action as well as words.

Wishing to do everything I could to smooth matters over and avoid as much publicity as possible, I rapidly collected my companion's wraps and got her out of the box. As I was doing this one of the lieutenants threw a glass of champagne in my face accompanied by an epithet against which even Job himself would have protested. It therefore became necessary to administer one of those gentle little all-British reminders, which landed home so unexpectedly and suddenly that the aggressor tripped backwards over the chairs and collapsed on the bosom of his companion, both falling in a mixed heap upon the floor. It was difficult to distinguish which limbs belonged to each respectively, intermingled as they were with the table, the chairs, the bubbling wine and broken glass.

I escorted my lady friend back to the hotel.

Two hours later a couple of very serious middle-aged officers of some rank and distinction visited me. They demanded an audience with the foreigner and sent up their cards. They had come to arrange matters for their friends, and they refused to listen to any explanation or arguments relating to the true facts of the case. All they knew or would admit was that a blow had been struck, their uniform insulted, and the dignity of the two officers of the Imperial Forces had been rolled in the dust. Satisfaction to both must be accorded at the first available opportunity and in accordance with the custom of Imperial Germany. As the principal actor in the affair happened to be a stranger in a strange land, the hospitality of two friends of unimpeachable integrity should be provided to his commands.

Meanwhile full apologies were tendered for the lateness of the hour of calling and for the rather informal procedure; but the visitors seemed over-anxious to fix preliminary arrangements, presumably as a caution against the possibility of any sudden departure.

Which of the usual weapons did I prefer?

Perhaps it is needless to say that my then inclinations leaned towards neither of them, nor to anything of a pugnacious character. I freely said so. They replied that "a choice must be made or a difficulty would arise which could not be easily surmounted. No; it must be in accordance with the recognised code of military honour."

"Very well, then," I quietly replied; "fists or single-sticks are good enough for me."

The look on their faces seemed to imply that insult had been added to injury. Such a proposal was most unacceptable and preposterous. They came back to the original weapons and insisted upon a selection being named, which I settled by telling them to provide both. Their next proposition caused a deadlock to further negotiations. They wanted to fix the meeting in a named wood, some little distance from the suburbs of the town, at the early hour of six on the following morning.

Bowing very politely, I smiled. It was the first smile that had crossed the countenance of anyone of the participants at that memorable interview. "Gentlemen," I commenced, "you may like early hours; they may agree with your constitution and methods of living, but you cannot persuade a civilian gentleman to rise until the world has been properly aired. We English are as regular in our habits as you may be. We go to bed at midnight. We are called at 8 a.m., and we have breakfast—a good substantial repast à la fourchette—at 9 a.m. We must read the morning's news-sheet. After 10 a.m. we are at the disposal of our friends. You may have your own way in any other details or particulars of this unfortunate little misunderstanding you please, but upon this point I remain adamant."

Again I bowed to each of them, and although serious enough to all outward appearances, I was chuckling inwardly, because at last I saw a silver lining to the ominous clouds which had so suddenly and so unexpectedly enveloped me.

The English nation flatters itself and is justly proud of its sporting instincts. But it looks with horror upon duelling as being little short of murder. Our national sense of fair play and justice abhors the thought of any expert being matched against an amateur; more particularly in a contest where the skill of each party is unequal, or one of them can easily overmatch the other.

I personally would never attempt the permanent injury of a fellow-being, unless forced into a fight and the doing of it was the only way of saving life. I knew nothing of swordsmanship, nor had I ever practised with the foils. As a revolver shot I was a very doubtful performer, and they are difficult little things to use at any time. I had no quarrel with the two unmannerly cads who had forced themselves uninvited and unwelcomed upon my privacy. All differences had been settled and wiped off the slate with one small wave of the arm. Why, therefore, should I now seek their lives, or to do them some serious bodily harm? If anyone was aggrieved, surely I was entitled to all sympathy. Why, therefore, should they now seek to destroy me? Little did I know that "*Am Tag*" was hovering so near at hand.

On these points, however, my mind was not only quite clear but it was quite made up. The meeting must be arranged for 11 a.m. on the morrow or it must be postponed to some more convenient and suitable date.

When my visitors shook their heads and demurred I became indignant. I reminded them of the condition in which I had left those whom they represented. I pointed out the obvious fact that the intervening time was not sufficient for them to sleep off the fumes and effects of the excess of alcohol which they were undoubtedly suffering from; whilst as a final and unanswerable argument I hammered home the fact that I had not yet been introduced to the gentlemen who would act as my friends at this very important meeting. If not an insult to them it certainly would be an insult to me, to be invited or even expected to meet in honourable (?) combat, opponents who were not perfectly sober, or who might be severely handicapped in consequence of the continuing effects of their over-night insobriety.

I enlarged on this, speaking in latent sarcasm which, needless to say, was absolutely lost upon my visitors. Perhaps it was best for my personal safety that it was so. Their highly-educated super-*kultur* would prevent them from appreciating such, or understanding it. I said that any combat in which a preponderance of advantage rested on one side or the other could not be tolerated by any honourable gentleman, who never minded accepting odds, providing these odds were against himself. But he would consider it low and mean and altogether unworthy to take advantage of an opponent unless equality and fair play could be ensured. For my part I insisted that those whom they represented should have full opportunities of equal combat; in other words, that they should have time to get sober.

These honeyed sentiments clinched the business. My visitors bowed most politely and replied, "Having heard your explanations, we fully realise, as gentlemen speaking for and acting on behalf of gentlemen" (God save the *mark!*) "that we cannot do otherwise than accept your reasons and act accordingly." Thus they agreed to fix the meeting by mutual consent for eleven the following morning, and with an exchange of courtesies on all sides we parted company.

★★★★★★

According to the local railway time-tables, a slow train was advertised as departing south for Hamburg at the early hour of 4 a.m. or a little after; whilst a fast train, running between Hamburg and the north of Denmark, stopped a few minutes at Neumunster about 7 a.m. Neumunster is the junction station for the Kiel Canal on the main Hamburg, Altona, Rensburg, Schleswig, Flensburg, Wogens, Vamdrup, Kolding line, and connecting up Fredericia and Copenhagen by the boat train *via* Esbjerg.

★★★★★★

At 3.30 a.m., long before the hour of dawn, a silent shadow glided along the deserted streets of Kiel. A meek voice at the palatial railway-station in very guttural German requested a third-class ticket by the slow train to Hamburg. This modest traveller left the train at Neumunster, but no one appeared to notice he had broken his journey, or that he quietly disappeared from view on the station platform until the fast northward-bound train bustled in. In fact, he was so muffled up, and he gripped his handbag so tightly, that he did not appear to be worth ten *pfennig* in return for any railway official's attention; whilst other travellers were far too occupied by their own concerns to trouble about his existence.

★★★★★★

When the world had indeed become properly aired and the morning sun had risen far above the housetops, the landlord of a certain hotel in Kiel might have been seen standing at the entrance of his hostelry. A self-satisfied smile suffused his fat face, and both his hands were dived well down into capacious trouser-pockets, wherein he kept turning over coin after coin, whilst he puzzled his slow-working brains in vain to find a solution to account for the mad eccentricities of all foreigners in general; in particular those lunatics who seemed to prefer night-travelling on any uncomfortable train to snug, warm

162

beds; and who left notes of unintelligible explanation, enclosing double the remuneration necessary for the so-called luxuries supplied by his hotel.

★★★★★★

About the same time a lattice window in an upper storey of the same hotel was thrown open, and a sweet-faced maiden, having an Hungarian type of beauty, leaned out upon the window-sill, permitting the full rays of the morning sun to light up the beauties of her face, form, and figure. She was reading a letter which she had found pushed under her bedroom door whilst she had wandered in dreamland through the fairy glades of fancy during her innocent girlish repose. She frowned as she read it and stamped her foot in disappointment at the postscript, muttering the while to herself:

"No, we shan't meet in Paris next month, because I don't know whether I can get there. I'll come after you now."

★★★★★★

At twelve noon, in a small clearing on the outskirts of a wood a few *kilomètres* from the town of Kiel, three carriages were drawn into the seclusion of the tree-trunks. The horses attached thereto stamped impatiently. Either they were very fresh or they had been waiting too long. Further in amongst the trees was a party of men talking earnestly to one another. They were military officers, and a doctor was with them. They appeared to be expecting somebody to arrive, or something of importance to happen. At last one of them, kicking furiously at a small bush, asked his companion, a man much older than himself, "What was that idiotic proviso you spoke about? 'You cannot persuade a civilian gentleman to rise until the world has been properly aired'? We ought to have spitted him when we had the chance!"

"My dear Fritz," replied his companion, "you never did have the chance; what is still more clear to me now is the fact that you never will. But if he's one of those *Swinehund Engländer*—if so, then—*mein Gott! Am Tag!*" Saying which he viciously spat upon the turf.

CHAPTER 15

Escaping From a Submarine

On one occasion, after I had left the British Foreign Secret Service, I had to undertake a voyage to the outer islands of the Hebrides, situated about one hundred miles into the Atlantic, due west of Scotland, and well away to the north-west of Ireland.

It was known at the time to be a place which was infested with German submarines, which had perpetrated many atrocities whilst operating in that region: senseless, coldblooded murder of innocent fishermen, by blowing up their frail craft to atoms at close range with deck-guns; and the sinking of innumerable ships irrespective of the chances of their crew to make land in the small boats that might be left undamaged by their shell-fire.

It was summer time and no suggestion of a submarine attack troubled anyone concerned on contemplating the voyage.

"I don't like that boat. She looks like a bird of ill-omen," I remarked to my companion as we stood on the high quay at Oban looking downwards at a very small and very dirty steamer which was moored thereto.

She was about one hundred and sixty feet long, with as much available space as possible devoted to cargo and cattle transit. Her decks seemingly had never been scrubbed since the day she was launched. Paint had been relegated to the background if superior tar was available. The saloon cabin, so-called, reeked with a conglomeration of ancient and nauseous smells, whilst the two private berths matchboarded off from it were altogether impossible to anyone holding the smallest ideas on sanitary principles.

"Well, my son, she's the only ship available. She is designated a mail-boat and she carries a thirteen-pounder aft, which is some consolation at least in these days of stress and submarines," replied my friend.

"Maybe, maybe; but for all that I don't like her. My prejudice is instinctive. She's about the most repulsive, uninviting boat I ever boarded, excepting an old coasting tub in Alaska and a pirate junk on the Yellow Sea; but in Europe one does expect a little more in return for even wartime passage money."

"All the grumbling in the world, my son, won't alter or improve the accommodation of this hulk, so come along and make the best of it."

I was silent. I selected one of the largest of my blackest cigars and lighting it with deliberation, proceeded aboard, and turning my back upon the private cabin which had been retained for my special occupation, I proceeded to make myself as comfortable as circumstances admitted in a space which was reserved for luggage at the far end of the saloon above the settee.

It had the advantage of being situate immediately below the only skylight, which, as soon as the ship had started, I prised open and thereby obtained some few whiffs of fresh air during the long night.

The following day brought about an improvement to the comfort of the travellers. The sun shone brilliantly, the sea was as smooth as a lake, and one could bask on the poop with some degree of comfort, although such things as deck-chairs or cushions were conspicuous by their absence.

I, however, had a thick ulster, which, spread over part of the tarpaulin covering the mails, made an efficient couch, and after a coarse yet satisfactory meal I sunned myself to my heart's content and whiled away the time smoking and reading a book, which I was compelled from time to time to characterise as rotten reading, much to the amusement of my companion de voyage.

According to regulations, a notice was hung over the main companion that the ship carried two lifeboats with capacity for thirty-three persons, eleven floating apparatus capable of sustaining one hundred and seventy-six persons, and her passenger allowance was stated to be one hundred and ninety-nine in all. How or where they could have slept did not seem to have occurred to the authorities.

A merciful Providence ordained that on this eventful voyage not more than one hundred people all told happened to come aboard at any one time.

A few calls were made along the rock-bound coast. Cargo was unshipped and more cargo taken in. Travellers disembarked, others took their places.

About midday all vestiges of land disappeared below the horizon and a course was steered for the open sea.

Although during the earlier part of the voyage many wrecks were passed and many a gallant ship of noble proportions could be seen piled upon the rocks, the result of German outrages, and the zone was known to be a particularly dangerous one, no one anticipated or thought of danger; least of all from the much-dreaded submarine.

Had not this obsolete and wretched apology for a mail-boat ploughed a weary course along this familiar route for many, many months during the war, whilst her engines wheezed and coughed and leaked in every pore, and her rusty plates collected weed and barnacles week by week, without molestation? Was she worth a torpedo? She was hardly worth a shell! Why should she be noticed now, even by the most amateur belligerent, or by the freshest novice at the game? Yet to the Hun who dreams of the glories of an Iron Cross, or other coveted decoration, a ship sunk is a ship to his credit, however insignificant that craft may be.

Suddenly and all-unexpectedly a low, resounding boom echoed across the waters, followed almost immediately by a whizz and a bang which made the ship's company jump and quake in their shoes.

What was it?

Where did it come from?

Eyes were strained and the horizon searched in vain, whilst some of the women-folk sent up a premature wail of fear of the unknown.

Doubts were soon dispelled. From the sea about fifty yards away from the starboard quarter of the ship a column of water rose into the air, towering far higher than her masts. It was followed within a few seconds by a second boom, whizz, bang, and another column of similar dimensions rose equi-distant from her port quarter.

"My God! It's a submarine," exclaimed my friend.

"Well, let her sub," I lazily replied, and I continued to read my much-abused book. I should explain to the reader that I had for quite a long time previously experienced attacks from bombs and shells, and I was not unduly disturbed by what I believed to be a mere casual temporary attention.

"You can't lie there, man. Get up!" And suiting his action to his words, he kicked me into activity, although according to him I was very slow to rise.

"The book cannot be as bad as you say it is, if you can continue reading it like this," he added.

"I know all about that," I replied, "but one must finish a paragraph."

As I rose from my recumbent position the ship's gunner rushed up on to the poop, and climbing on the mails, searched the sea for the whereabouts of the enemy.

"There she is!" he excitedly exclaimed, as he pointed to the horizon on the port quarter. "She's about two miles away. Look out!" and he ducked as another whizz-bang sounded all too close overhead.

We followed the direction he had indicated and observed, well below the horizon, a long, low-lying craft, upon the deck of which men were distinctly visible working the gun.

Shot followed shot in rapid succession and all around us great columns of water sprang into the air, the descending spray from which in some instances splashed our decks.

Our own gun, however, was soon in action and it plugged away merrily, seemingly giving as good as we received.

The fourth or fifth shell from the submarine landed just short of our vessel's stern. The explosion jerked it upwards and knocked both our gunners off their feet. This was followed by a shrapnel shell which exploded a little higher than our masts in the air above and hissed into the sea all around. The glass in the saloon skylight was splintered to atoms, the din of the constant explosions seemed like hell let loose and the fear of God was located in almost everyone aboard.

It was too much for the rough element—about sixty or more Hebrideans, some of whom spoke little English. They made an ugly rush for the boats, shouting that the ship was doomed and every man must save himself.

Fortunately there happened to be three military officers aboard who had recently returned from the trenches in France. They tried to control the crowd, and acted with a quiet heroism worthy of much praise.

All their efforts, however, were in vain. Men pushed women aside or knocked them over, and fought like beasts of prey for places in the boats.

By the efforts of the mate, who threatened the maddest of the crowd and fought strenuously for some discipline, an extra small boat was launched first, but about half a dozen frantic passengers jumped into her and without waiting for her complement pushed off from the ship. The two other boats left in the davits were filled with a fighting, snarling, swearing mass of individuals, some of whom hacked away with knives and a hatchet at the falls, whilst the great strain in weight put upon the davits bent them down like twisted wire. As the strands of the falls parted, the boats fell into the sea, shipping much water, whilst some of those left aboard jumped into them. Some fell out of the boats, whilst others jumped into the sea and were pulled into them as they left the vessel's side all too dangerously crowded.

It was a revolting sight; a memory that, however hard one may try to forget, must yet forever live; an act unworthy of all form of manliness, which can only remain a lasting shame to those whose selfish cowardice impelled their madness.

With my friend, I stood near the funnel looking on. What could we do? Had we, or had the officers had a revolver, the rush might have been checked, or possibly a life or so might have been sacrificed to try to save others.

The man handling the axe probably might have suffered first. I did attempt one small effort. I approached the fighting mass and tapped a man, who was struggling ineffectually to get through, on the shoulder. When he turned round I asked him why he was forgetting the women and children. The man swore at me, adding, "Women be damned! the boats are the only thing for us." Then I asked him if he had a match. "What for?" he demanded.

"To light a cigarette with, of course."

"To hell with you and your cigarettes!" he yelled, and springing on the backs of those in front of him he crawled over their heads and jumped for the boat below as it was falling from the davits. I was gratified to see him miss the boat and plunge headlong into the sea.

When all three boats were well away from the ship, those left behind, who could think at all, expressed their thankfulness that the rough element had departed. It gave the much-needed opportunity to talk quietly to many who were demented with fear, and to attempt to soothe others whose quiet weeping and wailing was heartbreaking to listen to.

Meanwhile the small thirteen-pounder aft and the submarine exchanged shots with ceaseless regularity. But the attacking craft appeared to have two guns in action. Her shells came faster and the high explosive was from time to time varied with shrapnel.

Shrapnel is much more unpleasant at sea than on land. One sees it hiss down on the surface of the water like spray from a water-cart. Whilst I was forward taking stock of the hatchway battens for possible floating purposes, I had two fragments pass all too close to either cheek—so close that I actually felt them. I put my hand up to my left cheek expecting to find it laid open, but the skin had not even been broken. A fortunate and most lucky escape. It was the nearest approach to an individual casualty throughout the scrap. When the panic crews in the boats appeared to be about a mile away a high explosive shell from the submarine actually scraped along the whole of the port side of our ship, bursting just in front of her forefoot. I was forward again at the time getting some lifebelts from the fore-hatch. The explosion knocked me off my feet.

Everyone aboard felt the shock. The side of the ship seemed to be stove in, and the captain commanded a member of his crew to see what water the vessel was making.

"You damn well go yourself, mister," was the reply he got; which showed the state of nerves aboard. Being almost next to the man in question I volunteered to go, which seemed to somewhat shame the mutinous seaman, as he went below at once. Then the captain did an extraordinary thing. He stopped his ship, hoisted a flag (the W) half-mast high, blew three long blasts on the siren, and came down from the bridge on deck.

I met him as he descended the companion and asked him what he was playing at?

"I mean to save what lives I can," he said. "The ship is holed and it is useless to carry on."

"That's the way to sacrifice the lot," I told him. "You don't suppose those pirates will spare either ship or us."

Whilst we were slanging each other, a wild-eyed woman whose hair was all down her back clutched the captain and demanded him to surrender at once. "Save us, save us!" she wailed. Her embrace had to be forcibly removed.

None of us aboard who took interest in life were agreeable to a stoppage of the ship or to a surrender in any form. We bluntly said so. But the captain claimed he was master aboard his own ship and should do as he thought fit. Having thus delivered himself he proceeded aft and cut away the lashing of three small rafts, each about ten feet by four, which appeared to be the only hope of safety left for the forty or more people aboard.

The engineers had stuck to their posts—all credit to their bravery!—but the ship, having lost way, was drifting broadside on to the submarine, which would soon have made her an easier mark to hit. Whereupon one of the three military officers, a second lieutenant of infantry, as arranged quickly between ourselves, mounted the bridge and rang up the engine-room for full speed ahead.

He managed to heave her round and got her going again; and very, very slowly she was made to steal further and further away. As soon as the captain realised his vessel was moving he went back to the bridge, reassumed command, and remained there.

For emergencies there is no school of learning to equal that of wide-world travel. In a search for more floating accommodation my friend and myself went forward and released the heavy coverings of the fore-hold, which provided ten or a dozen good planks quite equal to surf boards, such as we had seen used by Kanakas of the Sandwich Islands, and where we had participated with them in the joys of surf-riding on the Pacific breakers rolling in over the coral reefs. It was undoubtedly a wise forethought.

Although the fighting lasted, from first shot to last, forty-two minutes, it but seemed a few seconds to those whose minds were occupied with the safety of the ship and the lives of all aboard her. We had quite a lot to do and we were kept busy. Lifebelts had to be handed out and correctly put on, cigarettes obtained from below and supplied to all who cared for that form of nerve tonic, a great proportion of the terrified women pacified, and the rafts arranged on deck with a captain to each and fresh-water supplies provided.

As soon as necessary matters had been completed I got hold of my friend, who was taking matters quite philosophically, and we ascended the poop together to help take observation of our shell fire. Then we noticed that our gun-layer was serving the gun alone, so I slipped down to him to help get out more shells and to hand them up to his platform.

After a few rounds someone shouted, "Smoke boxes." At the moment I was struggling to the gun with a live shell, but I received a push from the all-too-energetic originator of the idea which sent me sprawling over a coil of rope and a pile of empty shell-cases.

Picking myself up as quickly as I could, I returned to the main deck in time to see the first of these useful and ingenious devices brought into practical utility. It was an oblong box, about three feet long and one foot deep, which was lighted at the end by a fuse, then thrown overboard to windward. Others followed in quick succession.

The smoke formed a light brown haze which with the help of a broadside-on breeze drifted across our wake and in a very short time obliterated our hull from the view of the deserting boats as well as those on board the submarine; which latter did not seem too desirous of following on, nor of decreasing the distance separating us.

From statements made by those in the boats (one of which was not recovered until some five days afterwards), the flag hoisted to half-mast, the three blasts on the whistle, and the obliterated hull gave every appearance of the foundering of the ship. If they formed this impression, *a fortiori*, the Germans, who were more than a mile behind them, must have been still more convinced that their shell-fire had done its dastardly work. This would also be strengthened by the sight of the three boats crowded with refugees rowing frantically away in the foreground; they must have appeared like rats (as they indeed were), deserting what they believed to be a doomed vessel.

Be it as it may be, after this the submarine ceased fire and submerged. Our gun-layer also ceased fire because he could see nothing further to shoot at.

Those on board, although relieved of the horrible din of bursting shells and continuous gun-fire, were not happy. They were haunted by a deeply-rooted idea that the submarine had only submerged with the intention of concealing her course so that she could head off the ship and attack her again from another quarter. Some were quite unable to conceal their anxieties. However, after the cessation of active hostilities a more hopeful and cheerful tone prevailed throughout. Some of the engineers came on deck for a breath of fresh air, whilst those below redoubled their efforts to pack on every ounce of steam the overstrained boilers would stand. With much wheezing and groaning, jerks and spasms, the machinery ground away and the battered old tub really did appear to make an effort to get along. What her speed actually was is not likely to be known, but if the log had been used and had recorded anything over eight knots an hour her passengers would have doubted its accuracy.

After sunset the elements favoured those of us on board who had certainly endeavoured to help ourselves. A rain-squall dropped from above, mists rolled up from the surface of the ocean which had hitherto been so calm and tranquil, and soon it became rough and unpleasant. Womenfolk who had been sick beyond belief through fear and shell-shock now became genuinely sea-sick. Perhaps it was a counter-irritant ordained for the best.

As soon as firing ceased and the enemy had disappeared from view, I sneaked away alone to a coal-bunker, where I carefully buried deep under the black nuggets a small packet of precious documents which would undoubtedly have proved of absorbing interest to the Hun. I thought this would probably be the last place anyone would be likely to look for anything of the kind, even if a boarding had become actual.

On returning to my friend, I much amused that gentleman by reason of a rather argumentative dispute I was drawn into with a Reverend raft captain regarding the salvage of certain fishing gear which I suggested would be the best help to kill the monotony whilst drifting and waiting to be picked up; assuming naturally that we were shortly to be sunk by the submarine.

But by degrees twilight gave place to gloaming. Sturdily the engines throbbed and the vessel pushed steadily ahead; whilst every eye that could, searched the sea around for any sign of periscopes.

What a relief it was to all when the faint outline of land gradually showed up far ahead! Greater still some hours afterwards when a bay was entered and the vessel reached safe anchorage. This, however, was far from the destination we had had in view, and however beautiful the scenery might be said to be, my companion and myself had no desire to linger there for an indefinite period.

How we fared eventually; how the soul of one of our small coterie collected on a rock-bound island, a general recently returned from Gallipoli, passed over the Great Beyond in a storm; how ships that passed and repassed were attacked by submarines and sunk or escaped; how wreckage, empty lifeboats galore and dead bodies daily piled up in the alcoves and on the rare sand-patches of the shore; how a wireless, with plant and adjacent buildings, was blown sky-high; how we were all burnt out of house and home, and other passing episodes of that short but adventurous trip, do not concern the subject-heading of this narrative. They remain another story.

Suffice it, therefore, to say that after a meal of sorts ashore a bargain was struck with some rough but honest island fisherfolk, whose knowledge of English was limited, although they knew well the value of a "John Bradbury;" and an hour after entering that peaceful haven of refuge a small fishing-craft stealthily crept out to sea, steering northwards over the scene of our recent fight, where she was soon lost in the silences and the shadows of the night.

CHAPTER 16

The Casement Affair

In February, 1915, a veritable bombshell was burst in the diplomatic circles of Northern Europe.

A letter had appeared in the German newspapers containing very grave allegations against a British minister, extracts from which had apparently been sent round broadcast to the Press of neutral countries.

On Wednesday, February 17th, the *Aftenposten* of Christiania published the document in its entirety. Other papers may have copied it, but the demand for copies immediately became so great it was difficult to secure them. Those which were purchased were read aloud in public places and discussed and commented upon until excitement reached fever-heat.

The general public in Scandinavian countries knew little or nothing concerning the writer of the letter—Sir Roger Casement.

The *Norske Argus* described him as "a man who had held positions; a British consul in various places in the Colonies; consul-general in Rio de Janeiro; the exposer of the Putumayo affair."

In Norway British consulships are most eagerly sought after, and considered enviable positions carrying high honour.

The *Norske Argus* stated that:

Sir Roger Casement belonged to the faction in Ireland which had opposed the war and recruiting; that he had been to Berlin to intercede with the Germans for better treatment towards Ireland if it came to an invasion of the British Islands; and that he felt satisfied with the answer he had obtained from the highest quarters, that 'in such case Ireland should obtain her full freedom'; and because of this visit the English were very bitter

173

against him and in many places he was stamped as a traitor.

Now Norway is a country infused with a very strong Socialistic element. It holds deep sympathies with the Irish, and believes them to be much abused and a much ill-used race. It knows nothing of the wildly absurd, headstrong obstinacy of certain Irishmen who make it their business to stir up dissent and to oppose their best interests; or that they apparently do this out of sheer "cussedness." Rightly or wrongly, Norway believes that Ireland is a poor, downtrodden country which during the past hundred years has received nothing but harsh and un-sympathetic treatment at the hands of the English. Hence Norwegians, not being fully advised of facts, looked upon this bogus hero, who had voluntarily taken upon himself such great risks as his action and journey involved, in the light of a modern Garibaldi, rather than as a traitor to his country, which he had and since has fully proved himself.[1]

In his letter Sir Roger Casement stated that he landed from America on October 29th, 1914, and that within a few hours of his arrival his abduction or murder was planned by the British Minister person-ally. Some Norwegians looked upon this allegation almost as a breach of good faith with them and their country. They somewhat doubted that the representative of King George of England, the brother of their beloved and popular Queen Maud, could stoop so low as to be a party to such acts as were alleged against him in this letter. But they wanted and waited for a denial direct.

There was no evidence whatever before them that this man (Sir Roger Casement) had done anything contrary to the interests of Eng-land, or that he could well have done anything between the outbreak of war and the dates quoted. If he was a traitor or a criminal their own ministers and police should have been informed thereof and the man arrested and extradited for a fair trial. The alleged revelations thus came as a shock to the country, and consternation filled the faces of many thinking persons.

Translation of Sir Roger Casement's Letter to Sir Edward Grey, as Published in the *Aftenposten* on the 17th day of February 1915[2]

1. Roger Casement was hanged as a traitor at Pentonville prison on August 3rd, 1916, after having been landed from a German submarine on the west coast of Ireland.
2. This letter was circulated in the Berlin Press on February 13th, and most of its material parts appeared in the London *Times* on February 15th, 1915, having been officially circulated through German wireless stations and received by the Marconi Company.

Sir Edward Grey,

I understand that my pension has been the subject of an interpellation in the House of Lords.[3] I have already renounced my claim to the same upon going to Germany to ascertain the German Government's intentions towards Ireland. In the course of the discussion, according to what I hear, Lord Crewe said that 'Sir Roger Casement's behaviour deserves a severe punishment.'

This gives me an opportunity of clearing up once and for all the question under discussion, especially as I now am in possession of incontestable proof of the kind of punishment secretly meted out to me. I acknowledge that from the first day three months ago when I first set foot on Norwegian soil, I was aware of your intentions, but it has taken me some time to get your diplomatic agent to give me written evidence of the assault that His Majesty's Government planned against me.

Allow me first to show my own method of proceeding before comparing it with yours. Between the British Government and myself there has never, as far as I am aware, been any talk of a pension, reward, or order. I have served the British Government truly and loyally as long as I possibly could. I resigned as soon

---

3. The interpellation above referred to is probably the following: On January 8th, during a debate in the House of Lords on the national responsibility with regard to voluntary recruiting or compulsory service, Earl Curzon said: "I should like to mention the case of Sir Roger Casement, which is one in which I take a personal interest, for in the old days at the Foreign Office I was his official superior. This gentleman went to Germany after the outbreak of war, where he has been accused of disgraceful and disloyal acts. His friends wrote to the papers that not too much attention should be paid to those acts, as they were doubtful about his mental condition. Since then his proceedings seem to me to have been characterised by perfect possession of his faculties. The last thing of which we have read is that he has prepared a pamphlet which has been printed by the German Government and circulated by the German Foreign Office pleading for an alliance between Germany and Ireland. I do not desire to comment upon it; it is unworthy of comment, but I wish to ask if this official who has received a title is to continue in the enjoyment of his pension." The Marquis of Crewe, on behalf of the government replied: "I have no particular information in regard to Sir Roger Casement. Even if he is still entitled to a pension it is evident, from what we have heard of his whereabouts, that he is not in a position to draw it, nor is he likely to become so; but I agree that such action as he is reported to have taken ought to be followed, as far as possible, with the infliction of the severest penalties. With that I couple the melancholy reflection that a man who has done such good services in the past, assuming that he is still in possession of all his faculties, should have fallen so low as he appears to have done."

as I found it no longer possible. As it also became impossible for me to enjoy the pension legally due to me I have also renounced it voluntarily, as I had previously given up the position which entitled me to it and as I now give up all orders and distinctions that have at different times been awarded me by His Majesty's Government.

I came last October from America to Europe to see that my Fatherland Ireland should suffer as little as possible from the results of this luckless war, however it may end.

My point of view I have sufficiently clearly published in an open letter from New York dated September 17th,[4] and which I sent to Ireland for distribution amongst my countrymen. I have the honour to enclose a printed copy of this letter. It gives exactly my views which I still hold to and the duties which an Irishman owes his Fatherland during this crisis.

Shortly after having written this letter, I left for Europe.

The possibility of my being able to assist Ireland to escape some of the horrors of war was in my opinion worth the loss of outward honour and my pension, as well as the committing the act of high treason in the technical meaning of the word. I had naturally reckoned on taking all personal risk and any punishment which the law could possibly threaten my actions with. I had, however, not considered that I should be sought after with means in excess of the law in spite of my action being without the moral limits.

In other words, I reckoned with English Justice and legal punishment and the sacrifice of name, position, and income, and willingly agreed to pay this price, but had not reckoned with the present government. I was ready to face a legal tribunal but I was not prepared against being shadowed, kidnapped by force, my servant being bribed, and that I, in short, might be struck down; I was, in fact, not prepared for the precautions your representative took upon hearing that I was stopping in this country.

The criminal attack which M. de C. Findlay, the British ambassador, planned on the 30th in the British Embassy, together with a Norwegian subject named Adler Christensen, included all this and more. The plan included not only an illegal attack

---

4. No copy or trace of this letter can be found.—*Author.*

upon my person for the execution of which the British Ambassador promised my servant £5,000 sterling, but also included an infringement of international law and common justice, and the Norwegian was guaranteed by the English Ambassador in Norway that he should go free of punishment.

I landed from America on October 29th. A few hours after my landing a Secret Agent of the British Ambassador approached the man I had taken into my service and whom I fully trusted, and conducted him in a private motorcar to the English Embassy, where the first attempt was made to induce him to commit an act of treachery against me.

Your agent at the embassy pretended not to know me and said he only wanted to identify me and get to know my plans.

As this attempt did not succeed, Adler Christensen the next day, October 30th, was accosted by a new agent and requested to go to the embassy, where he would hear of something to his advantage. The next meeting was conducted by the ambassador himself. Mr. Findlay went straight to the point. His assumed or real ignorance of my identity, as shown the day before, he now abandoned. Findlay acknowledged that he knew me but declared that he did not know where I was going, what I was going to do, and what my intentions were. It was enough for him that I was an Irish Nationalist. He confessed that the British Government had no proof that I had done, or intended to do, anything wrong which could give him right, either moral or legal, to interfere with my freedom.

All the same, he was determined to do so. He therefore boldly and without further consideration used illegal means and gave my servant to understand that if I 'disappeared' it would be a very good thing for whoever managed it. He specially emphasised that nothing should happen to the perpetrator, as my presence in Christiania was known to the British Government, and that that government would protect and be responsible for those who effected my 'disappearance.' He suggested clearly the means that could be used, intimating to Adler Christensen that the man who 'knocked him on the head' would not need to do any more work for the rest of his life, saying, 'I presume that you would have no objection to taking it easy for the rest of your days?' My faithful servant hid the indignation he felt at this proposal and continued the conversation so as to become more fully acquainted with details of the assault being planned on my person. He remarked not only that I had been good to him, but that 'I absolutely relied on him.'

Upon this absolute confidence Mr. Findlay built his whole plot against my freedom, Norway's common justice, and the well-being of this young man, whom he tried to bribe with a large amount to commit a cowardly crime upon his well-doer. If I could be seized or disappear, no one would know it, and no question could be raised, as no one outside the British Government knew of my presence in Norway, and there was no authority from whom I could get help as the one authority would protect the accused and care for his future. Thus, according to my information, spoke Mr. Findlay, the British Minister, to the young man who was tempted into the embassy for this purpose. That this young man was faithful to me and to the law of his land is a triumph of Norwegian straightforwardness over the vile manner in which the richest and mightiest government in the world tried to tempt him to treachery against both.

After thus having sketched out his plan, Mr. Findlay asked Christensen to 'think it over' and 'come again at three o'clock if you agree.'

He gave him twenty-five *kroner*, just to pay the automobile with, and let him go. As I naturally was interested to hear how they proposed to get rid of me, I gave the man whom they had tried to bribe orders to return to the embassy at three o'clock and pretend to agree with the wishes of your envoyé extraordinaire. I advised him to 'sell me dearly' and demand a respectable sum for such a dirty job. Christensen, who had been a seaman and naturally seen many strange people, assured me that he felt quite at home with His Majesty's representative. He returned to the Legation at three o'clock and remained alone with Mr. Findlay until nearly five o'clock. An exact account of the conversation will duly be sent to you and others. My servant pretended to agree to the British Minister's plans and only demanded a moderate sum for his treachery. Mr. Findlay promised on his word of honour (this strange phrase was used to guarantee the transaction) that Christensen should have £5,000 on his handing me over to the British authorities.

If by this abduction any harm should happen to me, or any personal injury be inflicted upon me, no question would be raised and full impunity would be guaranteed to the abductor.

My servant emphasised that I should travel in the afternoon to Copenhagen, and he had already reserved my place in the train, unless he had some immediate opportunity to carry out the commission.

Mr. Findlay admitted that it would be necessary to defer the attempt until there appeared a favourable opportunity to lure me to the coast, to one or other place by the Skagerak or North Sea where there would be an English warship which waited to catch me.

He confided further in my servant the commission to steal my correspondence with my supposed colleagues in America and Ireland, particularly in Ireland, so that they could be made a party to the 'sympathetic punishment' which was intended for me.

He explained a system for secret correspondence with him which Christensen should use and write through a confidential address in Christiania, to which he should communicate the results of his endeavours to steal my papers and report my plans.

This address in Christiania was written down in block letter capitals by Mr. Findlay on a half-sheet of the ambassador's letter-paper. This precaution, said he, would prevent the handwriting from being identified.

This document, besides 100 *kroner* in Norwegian notes which Mr. Findlay had given him as earnest money, with more to follow later, was immediately brought to me, together with a full account of what has already been told.

As I was obviously in a dangerous position I changed my plans, and instead of travelling to Copenhagen I resolved to change the method of travelling and the route.

Thus it was that I, with secret knowledge concerning the full extent of the crime which was planned by your representative in Norway, left Christiania on October 30th.

The remainder of the history is soon told.

You are doubtless apprised of all that happens, as you are both by telegraph and by letter in constant communication with your representative.

You also know the Imperial German Government's declaration which was published on November 20th last year in answer to my question.

The British Government had, both through Press correspondents as well as through special agents, allowed to be spread over the whole of Ireland the lie that the Germans began the most abominable crimes in Belgium, and they had also pointed out that a similar fate awaited the Irish people if Germany came victorious out of this war.

Your government's intention was to excite the Irish to apprehend a predatory attack by a people who never had done them any harm and by false reports make them believe that this was their plight. It was my intention not only to obtain a binding benevolent assurance from the German Government, but also to free my countrymen from the false position which this lying exciting campaign would develop; finally, as far as it stood in my power, I would prevent them from entering into an immoral conflict against a people who had never done Ireland an injustice.

This declaration from the German Government, which, as far as I know, was delivered in full sincerity, forms a justification for my 'treason.' I leave it to you, sir, to find justification for the British Government's and the minister's criminal plan, which was fully prepared before I had even set foot on German soil and, furthermore, in a land where I had perfect right to remain, this plan, which was attempted to be carried out by the miserable means of bribery and corruption.

You will not find justification in the many conversations which Mr. Findlay in November and in December last year had after his own wish with my faithful servant. The correspondence between them couched in the ambassador's arranged cipher speaks for itself. These conversations have brought one thing to the light of day which I later on will make public.

It is certainly correct to say concerning all this, which passed between your representative and mine, with these opportunities, that you during the constant negotiations had half the thread in your own hand.

Your object was, as Mr. Findlay openly has confessed before the man whom he believed he had bought, to get me out of the way in the most disgraceful manner. My object is to expose your plans to the whole world, and by the help of the agent whom you yourself have selected for your plans and whom you have attempted to bribe in order to get him to perpetrate an exceptionally vile crime.

Once, when my man pretended that he was not satisfied with the sum which was bid him for the treachery, your agent ventured to raise the amount to £10,000. I have a precise inventory of the negotiations put forward and the promises which were given in your name.

Your ambassador has twice given A. Christensen large money rewards—once 500 *kroner* in Norwegian money, another time a like sum partly in Norwegian money and partly in English gold. On one of these occasions, in order to be precise, December 7th, Mr. Findlay handed to Adler Christensen the key to a back door in the English Ministry so that he could come and go unobserved. This key I intend to return personally to the owner, together with the various money rewards which he has forced upon my servant.

The tales which Mr. Findlay told in these conversations would not deceive a schoolboy. All mentioned proofs of my plans and intentions which Adler Christensen produced, the mentioned letters, the fingered land and sea maps, etc., I must put together for my own defence to expose your criminal plan and thus come into possession of the indisputable proof which I now have.

First.—On January 3rd Mr. Findlay exposed himself thus, that he, in the English Government's name, gave my betrayer a safe undertaking from himself in which he promised him reward and impunity from any punishment if he committed the arranged crime. This piece of writing is in my hands. I have the honour to enclose a photograph of it.

Then, the English ambassador in Norway obviously is in a position to give secret guarantees and safe impunity from punishment for crime, so I reserve myself for a time when I am not exposed to his persecutions to place before the Norwegian authorities the original letters and the whole of the proofs which are in my possession and as glaring illuminations of the British Government's methods.

I now permit myself, through you, Sir, to surrender to this government my Order of St. Michael, the King George the Fifth's Coronation Medal, and all the other distinctions which the British Government has given me.

I am, your obedient and humble servant,

Roger Casement.

Englishmen in Norway, or indeed throughout the whole of Scandinavia, who could have given the true history of Sir Roger Casement at that time might have been counted on the fingers of one hand. (see note following).

✶✶✶✶✶✶

Note:—The following extract from the *Daily Telegraph* lifts the veil as to the English position to October 7th, 1914. Sir F. E. Smith, K.C. (Attorney-General) was appearing for the Crown at the trial of Sir Roger Casement in opening the case for the prosecution, on June 26th, 1916, before the Lord Chief Justice of England and other judges, the charge being one of High Treason without the Realm contrary to the Treason Act, 1851, and the account goes on:

> After stating that prisoner was born in County Dublin in 1864, the Attorney-General proceeded to recite the various offices he had filled as Consul at Rio de Janeiro, Lorenzo Marques, West Africa, the Gaboon, Congo Free State, Santos and Para. During the South African War he was employed on special service at Cape Town, and when hostilities ended he did not refuse the Queen's South African Medal, although that was a war of which many Irishmen profoundly disapproved. They might perhaps therefore assume that at the age of thirty-six the crimes and delinquencies of this Empire had not engaged prisoner's attention or affected his intelligence.

> On June 20th, 1911 he was made a knight, and the same year he received the Coronation Medal. In August, 1913, he retired on a pension. That pension had been honourably earned, and it would have been neither necessary nor proper to refer to it were it not for the sinister and wicked activities of prisoner which ensued. Government pensions were paid quarterly, and on each occasion must be formally claimed by a statutory declaration setting forth the services for which the pension was awarded and the amount claimed. Prisoner made five such declarations, the first on October 2nd, 1913, and the last on October 7th, 1914.

> When notification was sent to prisoner by Sir Edward Grey of the intention to bestow a knighthood upon him,

this enemy of England, this friend of Germany, this extreme and irreconcilable patriot, replied in the following terms:

'Dear Sir Edward Grey.—I find it very hard to choose words in which to make acknowledgment of the honour done me by the king. I am much moved by this proof of confidence and appreciation of my service in Putumayo conveyed to me by your letter, wherein you tell me the king has been graciously pleased, upon your recommendation, to confer upon me the honour of knighthood. I am indeed grateful to you for this signal assurance of your personal esteem and support. I am very deeply sensible of the honour done me by His Majesty, and would beg that my humble duty might be presented to His Majesty, when you might do me the honour to convey to him my deep appreciation of the honour he has been graciously pleased to confer upon me.'

What happened to affect and corrupt prisoner's mind he did not know.

Sir F. E. Smith then went on to describe Sir Roger Casement's visits to the internment camps in Germany, etc., which was after October, 1914.

Norwegians naturally argued that one side of a story was good until the other was told. Meanwhile the newspapers did a remarkably fine business, as most editions were greedily bought up day after day and week after week, in the expectation of finding the reply of His Britannic Majesty's Minister to the scathing indictment propounded against him.

According to the *Berliner Tageblatt*, and other German newspapers, this letter was sent to Sir Edward Grey on February 1st, but no answer had been received up to February 15th, when some of the most material allegations were being quoted in the Press. Nor did any answer ever appear, to the writer's knowledge, from Sir Edward Grey, Mr. Mansfeldt de Cardonnel Findlay, or any other person; even after the letter had been republished in full by the *Aftenposten* in Christiania, and commented upon by other papers, and discussed from one end of Scandinavia to the other by men and women in every station of life.

That omission was publicly and privately stated to be a colossal mistake which would cost England, and the countries fighting by her side, very dearly indeed.

One would have thought that Mr. M. de C. Findlay would instantly have sent a short explanation in reply to every newspaper in Norway which reproduced any part of this fatal letter. He, however, remained in the seclusion of his castle on the hill of *Drammensvei* and observed a prolonged and unbroken silence.

The honest, open-minded, and clean-thinking Norwegian people were disgusted beyond words. They looked to him for an explanation as of right. They waited long, but they did not see, neither did they hear, a word of denial. Sorrowfully but very naturally they actually began to believe these extraordinary accusations to be true in substance and in fact.

Now, references are made in this letter to "secret agents of the British ambassador approaching the man whom Sir Roger Casement refers to as his servant." Therefore the writer takes this, his first opportunity, of most clearly and emphatically denying that any member of the British Secret Service was in any way employed or engaged in this affair. Such Secret Service agents as were then working in Scandinavia were known to him (the writer), also their locations; not one of them was within hundreds of miles of Christiania at the time of the alleged transaction. It should also be obvious that if any person exhibited such an amateurish display of incompetence and bungling as the accusations allege, that person would be more than useless for any Secret Service work, however simple it might be.

It seems quite impossible to believe that any man could have acted as Mr. M. de C. Findlay is said to have done.

What use was block letter-writing to conceal identity if it was ciphered on ambassadorial note-paper?

Why use English gold when Norwegian money was available?

Why permit such a man to come near the Embassy at all?

Why see such a man personally?

Why give a key to a gate, or a door, which could be left open?

Why give a scrap of writing or paper of any sort?

Why offer such ridiculous sums of money to a stranger, who, if he were such a man as suggested, would have accepted a fraction of the amount for such work?

If an investigation of the alleged proofs could show there was any semblance of truth in this story, then, indeed, "it certainly would not have *deceived a schoolboy*," as the letter quotes.

Assuming, for the sake of argument, that an alien to a neutral country (whosoever that person might be or in whatsoever walk of life he might happen to be placed) had made himself a danger to the realm; that it might have been considered an advantage to the Allies if he were kidnapped and taken to a place of safe keeping so that he could be looked after until peace was declared. What more simple and inexpensive than to bring about a consummation of such wishes? Our friend Nixie Pixie, or Jim, or another of that ilk, any one of those individuals could have acted secretly and absolutely independently.

What could have been easier or more inexpensive than a quickly-cultivated acquaintanceship by a Secret Service agent with a person so named? A little dinner or light refreshment at a *café*, or a hall; drugged food or drink, followed by the natural announcement that one's companion was temporarily indisposed or suffering from a slight excess of alcohol; assistance to a cab or other vehicle, nominally to convey him home but actually a quick journey to the docks and quay side, with rapid transport to a friendly ship! Thus such a job could have been accomplished for a few pounds without fuss, inconvenience, or publicity.

It would probably not be wide of the mark to venture the statement that many a man has been, perhaps even now is being, temporarily detained in the seclusion of some lonely lodging upon far less pretexts than the alleged revelations of Sir Roger Casement, until this tangled European skein be fully and completely unravelled. The annals of that grim fortress of Peter and Paul, the dungeon walls of which are washed by the turbid waters of the Neva (wherein the author has had personal experience of his own), could perhaps add histories of some interest, but if they are to be told they must form the pages of another chapter.

CHAPTER 17

Pertaining to Mystery Ships

The year 1915 saw much havoc at sea from the ravages of German submarines. I was located in the midst of it. I saw many a noble craft torpedoed direct or sunk by gunfire or mines. Such is a sight which leaves impressions and gives much to reflect upon.

The Germans, I knew, adopted subterfuges to lure their victims to destruction. The British apparently scorned to descend to such levels. Bitterly I remembered the words of the captured officer: "You British will always be fools and we Germans shall never be gentlemen." It was maddening to know that all our acts of chivalry and knightly conduct throughout the war only provoked the mirth and contempt of our adversaries.

Something should be done to meet blow with blow, subterfuge with subterfuge, and violence with equal retaliatory force.

The outcome of my reflections on this subject are hereinafter divulged.

To
The Admiralty,
Whitehall,
London.

June 15th, 1915.

Sir,

I would, with all deference, submit to your consideration a suggestion which has occurred to me as possibly worthy of trial. It is as follows:

"In the Port of —— I observed trawling vessels fitted with guns conspicuously mounted upon a platform raised just abaft the funnel and over the engine-room, obviously for patrol purposes.

I assume that a German submarine could not but at once observe the gun and at a considerable distance, as it is raised well above deck-levels. She would naturally resort to the torpedo without coming to the surface and without warning. But if the submarine could be deceived that these trawlers were fishing vessels, or mine-sweepers, she would hardly waste an expensive torpedo when she could sink such insignificant craft by gunfire or bombs, and she might come to the surface to warn the crew to take to the boats, or to hail the vessel, thus giving a chance for our men to get a bit of their own back.

"In my humble opinion the guns which are now mounted (twelve-pounders, I believe) on these trawlers could be concealed with the greatest of ease in more ways than one; and as the vessels are in all other respects unaltered in their ordinary appearance, I see no reason why the experiment should not be tried. Also remembering that submarines as a rule attack at dawn or gloaming.

If I may be so presumptuous as to go further and outline one of the means of concealment foreshadowed, I would construct in light framework covered with painted canvas the sides of a small row-boat or lifeboat in two silhouettes, which I would place on each side of the gun, whereby it would be completely covered up. The stanchions erected round the gun platform I would unship, or if their continuance is essential I would mount imitation davits of painted steam-bent wood, which could easily ship or be jointed with hinge and hook fastenings, so that they could be unshipped at a moment's notice. To these davits I would add light blocks and tackles, so that in a few seconds the whole dummy show could be swept on one side and the gun brought into play.

I have carefully examined the platform and gun on one of these vessels and firmly believe that the idea is practical and feasible and would act effectively and to advantage.

When I was cruising in the Baltic opposite Kiel and Femern (December-February) I was successful with somewhat similar devices of a simple nature, fitted to small boats, and calculated to deceive as to distances and in other ways, which originated the present ideas as soon as I saw our trawlers.

If you consider the idea worthy of a moment's further consideration, I would, if you so desired, at once set to work and have a working model made.

I remain, your obedient servant,

Nicholas Everitt,
('Jim' of the B.F.S.S.)

★★★★★★

Intermediary correspondence and actions would not perhaps interest the reader. Suffice it to say that my ideas found favour in the eyes of the powers-that-be, and I was given *carte blanche* to carry my designs into effect.

It may now be divulged that many weeks prior to the writing of the letter mentioned above I had confided an outline of my invention to a certain naval officer, a friend of mine in charge of a patrol-boat. We had between us manufactured a rough model from such materials as could be collected, which had been fitted to a vessel, and it had been effectively and successfully used in action at sea, although not officially known or recognised.

Now that I had free access to, and full authority to make use of, several Admiralty yards for material and assistance, it was an easy matter to improve on former ideas and to produce a complete efficient and creditable result.

★★★★★★

To
The Admiralty,
Whitehall,
London.

July 14th, 1915.

Extracts from My Report

The completion of the model was pushed along as quickly as circumstances would permit, and the first week in July, 1915, was fitted to a completed gun platform on the steam trawler —— then lying in —— Harbour.

The silhouette boat and chocks which support it on the gun-deck are made all in one piece, the deception being brought about simply by shading in the painting.

The boat is held in position by the dummy blocks and falls above, and to the gun-deck below by short iron clips at the foot of the chocks, which slip into small iron sockets screwed on the gun-deck and so slightly raised that they are not noticeable. The two silhouette boats are kept firm by two iron connecting rods.

To clear the gun-deck.—Two men are required to handle the gun, which gives one man at each end of the boats.

To clear the gun-deck for action each man would simultaneously push up the iron connecting-rod between the silhouettes and at the same time instantly kick clear the clip at the foot of the chock from its socket. A slight push to the swinging boats releases the hinged davits, which fall backwards, pulling each dummy boat clear over the top of the lifeline stanchions, whilst they automatically drop into the bend of the davits, which holds them there until wanted for further deception purposes.

The boats can be pulled back and fixed into their original positions in about a minute, or even less time if necessary.

Both sides of the dummy silhouette boats are covered with canvas and painted white with gunwhale streak brown, so both sides match each other. The gun should be laid pointing towards the stem of the vessel and the gun itself, mounting and pedestal, painted white.

Then in whatever position (whether the ends are covered with canvas or not) the dummy boats are viewed, within ten yards or further away the deception is complete.

A very close observer, viewing the apparatus end-on, might assume that a couple of collapsible lifeboats were being carried aboard over the engine-room.

★★★★★★

Immediately after the official inspection (July 10th), which was said to be quite satisfactory, the vessel so fitted was ordered to sea, and in due course I received a registered letter marked "Personal and Private." The envelope covered an inner envelope also marked "Private." The inner envelope contained a short note conveying the thanks of the Lords of the Admiralty to me, the inventor.

To what further uses, or with what results the design was utilised, remained as closely guarded a secret as the inner letter of thanks.

★★★★★★

Meanwhile I was more than anxious for active service which would give me a chance of getting at short grips with the dastardly submarines which I had hunted in the frozen north so long but never fairly and squarely behind a gun.

Further reflections caused the following letter to be written:

(TAKEN AT 25 FEET) SHOWS THE DUMMY BOAT IN POSITION READY TO GO TO SEA.

(TAKEN AT 25 FEET) SHOWS THE DUMMY DAVITS DOWN, THE BOAT GONE AND THE GUN DECK CLEARED FOR ACTION *WITHIN THREE SECONDS* FROM THE WORD OF COMMAND HAVING BEEN GIVEN.

To
The Admiralty,
Whitehall,
London.

August 17th, 1915.

Sir,

Since I wrote you with completed report on my gun-screen-dummy boat, submarines have continued to favour these waters in particular. Three large steamers have quite recently been torpedoed. They have sunk in this neighbourhood alone over fifty sailing trawlers, *every one* bombed or sunk by gunfire, and *from the surface*, but not a mine-sweeper nor a patrol-boat seems to have been attacked!

There are plenty of sailing trawlers lying idle in ports.

I therefore humbly venture to suggest to the Admiralty that if half a dozen of these were mounted with guns, covered by the dummy-boat-screen and manned by a small, smart crew, dressed in *ordinary fishermen's* clothes (not the naval uniforms with gold braid and *white-topped* ornamental caps, so much in vogue at present), those submarine pests would be caught napping without much difficulty; whilst the fishermen, who are mostly ruined, would at least feel that we had got a little of our own back with every pirate so sunk.

It would also be easy to place a motor and propeller in the vessel so employed which would help manoeuvring in no small measure; whilst as to manning them, there is plenty of material of the very best to select from for such a job—men who have been patrolling in gunboats and trawlers for a year without a smell of powder which their nostrils hunger for. I personally know plenty who would willingly abandon good positions and hail such an opportunity with eagerness; whilst, if the chance was given, I myself would willingly and gladly volunteer my services with them in the first boat sent out, or under them in "If this seeming presumption on my part should be acted upon you may rely upon my wholehearted service for any assistance that I may be able to give in the fitting-out, etc., or otherwise, and it will be my pleasure to execute your smallest commands.

I remain, your obedient servant,

Nicholas Everitt,
('Jim' of the B.F.S.S.)

★★★★★★

This letter only produced further "secret" thanks. The suggestion for active service was not responded to!

Cold comfort to one burning with such unquenchable desires. Poor gratitude for services rendered. Depressing recognition for future effort.

But what could a mere civilian expect! It was the same in both Services at that period of the war. Civilians were as nothing; merely to be used as conveniences—if they had to be used at all. Or as stepping-stones for service men to trample upon towards their own immediate advantage, utterly regardless of position, ability and status, and whether they had voluntarily or compulsorily sacrificed position, property, or dearer belongings.

Had any such ideas as these originated with a junior in the service he would have had to have taken them at once to his superior officer. That dignified individual would in all probability have personally commended him in private, then put forward the ideas to those above him with much weight, but at the same time conveniently neglecting to couple the name of the real originator.

The secret annals of the service could many such a tale unfold.

Should a junior officer have dared to presume to have sent in his original ideas direct to Whitehall, woe betide the day for his immediate future and his chances for early promotion.

The above opinions are no flights of imagination; they are founded solely on many bitter complaints which have come direct to the ears of the writer from junior officers in both arms of the service, whose inventive ideas have either been summarily squashed by superior officers, or who have been compelled in their own future interests to stand aside, silent and disgusted, whilst they have observed others far above them taking what credit was to be bestowed for ideas or suggestions which were never their own, and often followed by decoration without any patent special service.

★★★★★★

Shortly before this book went to press the author happened to meet a naval gunner who had served for a prolonged period aboard mystery ships. He was most enthusiastic on the subject of camouflage, and he related how he had served in 1915 in a ship which had one gun only, placed amidships, which was concealed by a dummy silhouette boat.

According to his account the stunt was great. He narrated in detail the completeness of the deception, the instantaneous manner in which the gun was brought into action, and the success which had attended the introduction of the idea. He affirmed that no less than ten submarines had been sunk during the first few weeks this invention had been first introduced. But, as he explained, one day a vessel so fitted was attacked by two submarines at the same time, one being on each quarter, and the secret became exposed. After that, he added, the Germans became much more suspicious how they approached and attacked fishing vessels, and successes fell off considerably.

It had been an Admiralty regulation that when a submarine was sunk and its loss proved, the successful crew was awarded £1,000 for each submarine recorded, which was divided proportionately according to rank. Submarines claimed to have been sunk run to over two hundred. Many and various were the methods by which they were sent to the bottom of the sea; but so far as a number of inventors or the originators of ingenuity were or are concerned, it would appear that virtue alone remains their sole reward.

★★★★★★

Since this book was accepted for press my attention has been called, in the February number, 1920, of *Pearson's Magazine*, to an article by Admiral Sims of the U.S.A. Navy, entitled "How the Mystery Ships Fought," in which he says:

> Every submarine that was sent to the bottom, it was estimated, amounted in 1917 to a saving of about 40,000 tons per year of merchant shipping; that was the amount of shipping, in other words, which the average U-boat would sink, if left unhindered to pursue its course.
>
> This type of vessel (Q-boats) was a regular ship of His Majesty's Navy, yet there was little about it that suggested warfare. *Just who invented this grimy enemy of the submarine is, like many other devices developed by the war, unknown.* It was, however, the natural outcome of a close study of German naval methods. The man who first had the idea well understood the peculiar mentality of the U-boat commanders.

Extracting further paragraphs from Admiral Sims' article:

> There is hardly anything in warfare which is more vulnerable than a submarine on the surface within a few hundred yards of a four-inch gun. A single well-aimed shot will frequently send it to the bottom. Indeed, a U-boat caught in such a predica-

ment has only one chance of escape; that is represented by the number of seconds which it takes to get under water.

"Clearly the obvious thing for the Allies to do was to send merchant ships armed with hidden guns along the great highways of commerce. The crews of these ships should be naval officers and men disguised as merchants, masters, and sailors.

At p. 104 of the magazine Admiral Sims refers directly to my invention as described and illustrated:

Platforms were erected on which guns were emplaced; a covering of tarpaulin completely hid them; yet a lever pulled by the gun crews would cause the sides of the hatchway covers to fall instantaneously. *Other guns were placed under lifeboats, which, by a similar mechanism, would fall apart* or rise in the air exposing the gun.

From the greater part of 1917 from twenty to thirty of these ships (Q-boats) sailed back and forth in the Atlantic.

The February number of the *Wide World Magazine*, p. 361, also contained a most interesting article by Captain Frank H. Shaw entitled, A "Q," and a "U," in which he describes how he personally helped to sink a submarine with the aid of a camouflage apparatus on the lines of my invention as illustrated:

Meanwhile the fitters were making most of their opportunities aboard the *Penshurst* (the Q-boat in question). A useful twelve-pounder gun—one of the best bits of ordnance ever devised for short range work—was mounted on the fore-deck. A steel ship's lifeboat was cut in two through the keel, and so faked that on pulling a bolt, the two halves would fall clear away. This dummy boat was then put in place over the twelve-pounder and effectively concealed its presence.

So far as the outward evidence was concerned, the *Penshurst* was simply carrying a spare lifeboat on deck—a not unnecessary precaution, considering the activity of the enemy submarines.

Captain Shaw describes in stirring narrative and vivid detail how a submarine held up his ship, how part of their crew abandoned the ship, and how the Hun boat was lured well within easy gun-fire range, and how my ideas worked in practice:

The foredeck boat opened beautifully like a lily and the gun came up, with its crew gathered round it. The twelve-pounder was not a second behind its smaller relative. Her gunlayer, too, was a useful man. He planted a yellow-rigged shell immediately at the base of Fritz's conning-tower. It exploded there with deafening report and great gouts of water flew upwards with dark patches amongst the foam.

★★★★★★

By my friends I was disparaged for foolishness in not putting forward a claim for compensation in connection with these ideas, followed by an accepted invention of recognised utility. In the U.S.A. in the spring of 1919 I heard this invention considerably lauded; in New York, Boston, and Washington. It was also described and illustrated in certain American periodicals.

If the figures given by Admiral Sims are true estimates, and, say, only twenty-five submarines were sunk by the direct assistance of this simple contrivance, then it follows that about 1,000,000 tons of shipping were saved each year it was in active use.

Eventually I communicated with Admiral W. R. Hall, C.B., through whom I had submitted my suggestions in the first instance. From him I received a charming letter in which he regretted the matter had passed beyond his department. Therefore on January 26th, 1920, I wrote to the Secretary of the Admiralty referring by number to previous letters conveying the *secret* thanks of the Lords of the Admiralty to me in 1915 and asking him whether (now that the war was over) I was entitled to any recognition for this invention, and if so, how and to whom I should apply.

I wrote again on April 29th, asking for a reply to my previous letter, but being only a civilian, I suppose he did not consider either myself or the subject matter I enquired about worthy even of simple acknowledgment.

CHAPTER 18

The Sinking of the "Lusitania" by German Treachery

So long as the memory of mortal man endures, this dastardly act of German treachery will never be forgotten.

On May 7th, 1915, the SS. *Lusitania*, a passenger ship of 32,000 tons of the Cunard Line, was sunk by torpedoes, fired at short range from a German submarine off Kinsale. She carried on board 1,265 passengers and a crew of about 694 hands. From this number 1,198 were drowned, including 113 Americans and a large number of women and children.

It is no exaggeration to say that the event staggered the humanity of the world, yet the *Kölnische Volkeszeitung* on May 10th, 1915, stated: "With joyful pride we contemplate this latest deed of our navy," etc. The commander of the submarine which struck the fatal blow was decorated, and a special medal was struck in the Fatherland commemorating the event, and dated May 5th—*two days before she was actually attacked and sunk.*

A copy of it is now before the writer.

It was struck with the object of keeping alive in German hearts the recollection of the German Navy in deliberately destroying an unarmed passenger-ship together with 1,198 non-combatants, men, women, and children.

On the obverse, under the legend "No Contraband" (*Keine Banvare*), there is a representation of the *Lusitania* sinking. The designer has put in guns and aeroplanes, which (as certified by United States Government officials after inspection) the *Lusitania* did *not* carry, but he has conveniently omitted to put in the women and children, which the whole world knows she did carry.

On the reverse, under the legend "Business above all" (*Geschäft über alles*), the figure of death sits at the booking-office of the Cunard Line, and gives out tickets to passengers who refuse to attend to the warning against submarines given by a German.

This picture seeks apparently to propound the theory that if a murderer warns his victim of his intention, the guilt of the crime will rest with the victim, not with the murderer.

How the foul deed was plotted and accomplished is told in concise and simple language by Mr. John Price Jones in his book entitled, *The German Spy in America*, which has an able introduction by Mr. Rogers B. Wood, ex-United States Assistant Attorney at New York; also a foreword by Mr. Theodore Roosevelt.

Summarising detail and extracting bare facts from Mr. Price Jones' work, it is shown that Germany had made her preparations long before war was declared. She had erected a wireless station at Sayville with thirty-five kilowatt transmitters and had obtained special privileges which the U.S. Government never dreamed would be so vilely abused.

Soon after the declaration of war, Germany sent over machinery for tripling the efficiency of the plant, *via* Holland, and the transmitters were increased to a hundred kilowatts. The whole plant was in the hands of experts drawn from the German Navy.

On April 22nd, 1915, the German Ambassador at Washington, by direction of Baron von Bernstorff, inserted notices by way of advertisement warning travellers not to go in ships flying the British flag or that of her Allies, whilst many of the ill-fated passengers received personally private warnings; for example, Mr. A. G. Vanderbilt had one signed "*Morte.*"

It is also stated than one of the German spies who had helped to conceive this diabolical scheme actually dined, the same evening the vessel sailed, at the home of one of his American victims.

The sinking of the vessel was also published in the Berlin newspapers before she had actually been attacked.

On reaching the edge of the war-zone, Captain Turner, who was in charge of the *Lusitania*, sent out a wireless message for instructions in accordance with his special orders.

By some means unknown the German Government had stolen a copy of the secret code used by the British Admiralty.

A copy of this had been supplied to Sayville, which used it (*inter alia*) to warn Captain Turner against submarines off the Irish coast—

which evidence was revealed at the inquest.

Sayville was very much on the alert, looking out for and expecting Captain Turner's request for orders.

As soon as it was picked up the return answer was flashed to "proceed to a point *ten miles* south of Old Head of Kinsale and run into St. George's Channel, making Liverpool bar at midnight."

The British Admiralty also received Captain Turner's call and sent directions "to proceed to a point *seventy to eighty miles* south of Old Head of Kinsale and there meet convoy."

But the British were slow and the Germans rapid. Captain Turner received the false message instead of the genuine one, and over a thousand unfortunate beings were sent to their doom.

At the inquest the two messages were produced and the treachery became apparent. Further investigations pointed direct to Sayville, Long Island, New York, to which place the plot was traced.

The German witnesses who swore the *Lusitania* had guns aboard her were indicted in America and imprisoned for perjury.

To use the wireless for any such cause as above described was contrary to and in violation of neutrality laws; also of the United States of America's statutes governing wireless stations.

In many chapters full of vivid detail Mr. Price Jones gives extraordinary particulars of conspiracies and plots against persons and property.

In scathing terms he condemns Captain Franz von Papen, von Igel and Koenig, Captain Karl Boy-Ed, Captain Franz von Rintelen, Dr. Heinrich F. Albert and Ambassador Dumba as spies, conspirators, or traitors; men without conscience, whom no action, however despicable, would stop.

CHAPTER 19

Ministerial, Diplomatic, and Consular Failings

The Press, it will be remembered, was during the first few years of the war periodically almost unanimous in its outcry against the government, particularly the Foreign Office. Having regard to the facts quoted, well might it be so. But the Foreign Office is somewhat in the hands of its ambassadors and ministers abroad, who unfortunately sometimes appear to put their personal dignity before patriotism, and threaten to resign unless some ridiculous, possibly childish, whim is not forthwith complied with. It seems hard to believe such things can be in war-time; yet it was so. If our ambassadors and ministers were selected by merit, and not by influence, a vast improvement would at once become apparent, and such things as were complained of would not be likely to occur or be repeated.

One Press writer pointed out that "Great Britain lacked a watchful policeman in Scandinavia." Perhaps he will be surprised to learn that about the most active non-sleeping watchmen that could be found were there soon after war started. But these watch-dogs smelt out much too much, and most of them were caught and muzzled, or driven away, or chained up at the instigation of the embassies. The heaviest chains, however, get broken, whilst the truth will ever out.

Naturally one embassy would keep in constant touch with another, and with regard to this question of supplying the enemy all three Scandinavian Embassies knew, or should have known to a nicety, precisely what was doing in each country.

We in the Secret Service had been impressively warned before leaving England to avoid our ambassadors abroad as we would disciples of the devil. In so far as we possibly could we religiously remembered and acted upon this warning. But the cruel irony of it was, our own ministers would not leave us alone. They seemed to hunt us down, and as soon as one of us was located, no matter who, or where, or how, a protest was, we were told, immediately sent to the Foreign Office, followed by hints or threats of resignation unless the Secret Service agent in question was instantly put out of action or recalled to England.

I was informed that several of my predecessors had been very unlucky in Denmark. One had been located and pushed out of the country within a few hours of arrival. Another I heard was imprisoned for many months. I was further very plainly told by an English official of high degree that if the British Minister at —— became aware of my presence and that I was in Secret Service employ, if I did not then leave the country within a few hours of the request which would with certainty be made, I would be handed over to the police to be dealt with under their newly-made espionage legislation.

Considering that the German legations in Scandinavia increased their secretaries from the two or three employed before the war to twenty or thirty each after its outbreak; considering that it was a well-known fact, although difficult to prove, that every German Embassy was the local headquarters of their marvellously clever organisation of Secret Service[1] against which our Legations possessed rarely more than one overworked secretary, whilst the British Embassies were a menace rather than a help to our Secret Service, it did seem to us, working on our own in England's cause, a cruel shame that these men, who posed not only as Englishmen but also as directly representing our own well-beloved king, should hound us about in a manner which made difficult our attempts to acquire the knowledge so important for the use of our country in its agony and dire peril. Dog-in-the-manger-like, they persisted in putting obstacles in the way of our doing work which they could not do themselves and probably would not have done if they could.

If unearthing the deplorable details of the leakage of supplies to Germany evoked disgust and burning anger in the breast of Mr. Basil Clarke, the Special Commissioner of the *Daily Mail*, surely I, and those patriotically working in conjunction with me, always at the risk of our

---

1. As evidence in support of this, see the papers seized from von Papen at Falmouth, December, 1915; the papers seized at Salonika, January, 1916; the reports from Washington, U.S.A., 1915-6; and the numerous paragraphs in the Press to date since November, 1914.

liberty and often at the risk of our lives, might be permitted to feel at least a grievance against the Foreign Office for its weakness in listening to the protests of men like these, his Britannic Majesty's Ministers abroad; real or imaginary aristocrats appointed to exalted positions of great dignity and possibly pushed into office by the influence of friends at Court, or perhaps because, as the possessors of considerable wealth, they could be expected to entertain lavishly although their remuneration might not be excessive. Had they remembered the patriotism and devotion to their king and country which the immortal Horatio Nelson showed at Copenhagen a hundred years previously, they too could just as easily have applied the sighting glass to a blind eye, and have ignored all knowledge of the existence of any Secret Service work or agents; unless, of course, some unforeseen accident or circumstance had forced an official notice upon them.

The Foreign Office would have lost none of its efficiency or its dignity, had it hinted as much when these protests arrived; whilst England would today have saved innumerable lives and vast wealth had some of the British ministers in the north of Europe resigned or been removed, and level-headed, commonsensed, patriotic business men placed in their stead as soon after war was declared with Germany as could possibly have been arranged.

That the Germans themselves never believed England would be so weak as to give her open doors for imports is expressed by General Bernhardi in his *Germany and the Next War*. He writes: "It is unbelievable that England would not prevent Germany receiving supplies through neutral countries." The following extract is from it:

> It would be necessary to take further steps to secure the importation from abroad of supplies necessary to us, since our own communications will be completely cut off by the English. The simplest and cheapest way would be if we obtained foreign goods through Holland, or perhaps neutral Belgium, and could export some part of our products through the great Dutch and Flemish harbours. . . . Our own overseas commerce would remain suspended, but such measures would prevent an absolute stagnation of trade. It is, however, very unlikely that England would tolerate such communications through neutral territory, since in that way the effect of her war on our trade would be much reduced. . . . That England would pay much attention to the neutrality of weaker neighbours when such a stake was at

issue is hardly credible.

To understand what was actually permitted to happen the reader is referred to the succeeding chapter. What possible excuse is there which any man, that is a man, would listen to, that could be urged in extenuation of this deplorable state of affairs and of its having been permitted to exist and to continue so long without drastic alteration?

Our Foreign Office, hence presumably the government, were fully informed and knew throughout exactly what was going on. Every Secret Service agent sent in almost weekly reports from October, 1914, onwards, emphasising the feverish activity of German agents, who were everywhere buying up supplies of war material and food at ridiculously high prices and transferring them to Germany with indecent haste.

Cotton[2] and copper were particularly mentioned. Imploring appeals were sent home by our Secret Service agents for these to be placed on the contraband list; but no Minister explained to the nation why, if it were feasible to make them contraband a year after the war commenced, it was not the right thing to have done so the day after war was declared.

German buyers openly purchased practically the whole product of the Norwegian cod fisheries *at retail prices*; also the greater part of the herring harvests. Germany absorbed every horse worth the taking, and never before in the history of the country had so much export trade been done, nor so much money been made by her inhabitants.

The same may be said of Sweden, with the addition that her trading with Germany was even larger.

The British ministers in Scandinavia seemed to carry no weight with those with whom they were brought in contact. Their prestige had been terribly shaken by reason of the decision to ignore entirely the Casement affair. An ambassador of a then powerful neutral country referred to one of them as "what you English call a damned fool." It was only the extraordinary ability and excellent qualities of some of the subordinates at the Chancelleries which saved the situation.

All this had its effect in these critical times. I, who was merely a

2. Cotton was not made absolute contraband until 381 days after the war had broken out, August 20th, 1915. Sir Edward Grey, speaking in the House of Commons on January 7th, 1915, said: "His Majesty's Government have never put cotton on the list of contraband; they have throughout the war kept it on the free list; and on every occasion when questioned on the point they have stated their intention of adhering to this practice."

civilian Britisher and not permanently attached to either the army or the navy, and hence was not afraid to refer to a spade as a spade, was called upon continually by others in the Service to emphasise the true state of affairs with the Foreign Office.

Those with whom I associated in the Secret Service agreed that if the ministers in Scandinavia could be removed and good business men instated at these capitals it would make a vast amount of difference to Germany and considerably hasten along the advent of peace. But by reason of circumstances which cannot well be revealed in these pages, my hands were tied until such time as I could get to London in person.

In March, 1915, I attended Whitehall, where I in no unmeasured terms stated hard convincing facts and explained the exact position in the north of Europe. I strongly emphasised the vital importance of stopping the unending stream of supplies to Germany and of making a change at the heads of the Legations mentioned. Direct access to Sir Edward Grey was denied me, but an official of some prominence assured me the essential facts should be conveyed to proper quarters without delay, although the same complaints had previously been made *ad nauseam*.

But facts have proved that no notice whatever of these repeated warnings was taken, and matters went from bad to worse.

On June 21st, 1915, I had returned again to England, and I wrote direct to Sir Edward Grey, at the Foreign Office, a letter, material extracts from which are as follows:

Sir,

Being now able to speak without disobedience to orders, I am reporting a serious matter direct to you from whom my recommendation for government service originates.

★★★★★★

It is exceedingly distasteful having to speak in the semblance of disparagement concerning anyone in His Majesty's service, and I am only anxious to do what I believe to be right and helpful to my country, whilst I am more than anxious to avoid any possibility of seemingly doing the right thing in the wrong way. But it is inconceivable that any Englishman should push forward his false pride, or be permitted to place his personal egoism, before his country's need; more particularly so at the present crisis, when every atom of effort is appealed for.

—— now being *a centre and a key to so many channels through which vast quantities of goods* (as well as information) *daily leak to Germany*, the head of our Legation has become a position of vital importance. Much of the present leakage is indirectly due to the present minister, in whom England is indeed unfortunate.

I therefore feel that, knowing how much depends upon even little things, it is my bounden duty to place the plain truth clearly before you. I have often before reported on this, so far as I possibly could, but those whom I could report to were all so fearful of the influences or opinions of the all-too-powerful gentleman in question, that none of them dare utter a syllable concerning his status or his foolish actions—although in secret they sorrowfully admit the serious effects.

1. Since the commencement of the war —— has committed a series of indiscretions and mistakes, entailing a natural aftermath of unfortunate and far-reaching consequences.

2. Since February, 1915, he has stood discredited by the entire—— nation, and in other parts of Scandinavia.

3. He is bitterly opposed to the Secret Service and paralyses its activities, although he states that his objections lie against the department and not individuals.

★★★★★★

In conclusion, please understand that I am in no way related to that hopeless individual, 'the man with a grievance,' but, being merely a civilian and having nothing whatever to expect, nor to seek for, beyond my country's ultimate good, I can and dare speak out; whilst the fact that in the course of my duty I went to Kiel Harbour (despite the German compliment of a price on my head), should be sufficient justification of my patriotism and give some weight to my present communication.

I have the honour to remain,

Your obedient servant,

Nicholas Everitt,

('Jim' of the B.F.S.S.)

★★★★★★

It seems hard to believe, but this letter was passed unheeded, not even acknowledged.

A week later, on June 28th, I wrote again, pointing out the importance to the State of my previous communication and emphasising

205

further the danger of letting matters slide.

Both these letters were received at Whitehall or they would have been returned through the Dead Letter Office. What possible reason could there be behind the scenes that ordered and upheld such a creed as *Ruat cœlum supprimatur veritas*? Or can it be ascribed to the much-talked-of mysterious Hidden Hand?

My letters pointed only too plainly to the obvious fact that I had information to communicate vital to the welfare of the State, which was much too serious to commit to paper; serious information which subservients in office dared not jeopardise their paid positions by repeating or forwarding; information which affected the prestige of our own king; information which might involve other countries in the war, on one side or the other; information which it was the plain duty of the Foreign Secretary to lose no time in making himself acquainted with. Yet not a finger was lifted in any attempt to investigate or follow up the grave matters which I could have unfolded, relating to the hollowness of the Sham Blockade with its vast leakages, which the government had taken such pains to conceal, and to other matters equally vital which I foreshadowed in my letter, and which might have made enormous differences to the tide of battle and to the welfare of nations.

No wonder the Press of all England made outcry against the Foreign Office, as and when some of the facts relating to its dilatoriness, its extreme leniency to all things German, and its muddle and inefficiency in attending *in time* to detail gradually began to become known.

Abroad I had heard the F.O. soundly cursed in many a consulate and elsewhere. I had, however, hitherto looked upon Sir Edward Grey as a strong man in a very weak government, a man who deserved the gratitude of all Englishmen and of the whole Empire for great acts of diplomacy; the man who had saved England from war more than once; and the man who had done most to strive for peace when the Germans insisted upon bloodshed. I would have wagered my soul that Sir Edward Grey was the last man in England, when his country was at war, who would have neglected his duty, or who would have passed over without action or comment such a communication as I had sent him.

I waited a time before I inquired. Then I heard that Sir Edward Grey was away ill, recuperating his health salmon-fishing in N.B. But there were others. Upon them perhaps the blame should fall.

The Foreign Office knew of, and had been fully advised, that the so-called Blockade of Germany by our fleet was a hollow sham and a delusion from its announced initiative. It was also fully aware that the leakages to Germany, instead of diminishing, increased so enormously as to create a scandal which it could hardly hope to hide from the British public. Why, then, were these ministers abroad allowed to remain in office, where they had been a laughing-stock and were apparently worse than useless? It can only be presumed that they also had been ordered to "wait and see."

Perhaps our ministers, particularly at the Foreign Office, believed that they could collect, through the medium of our Consulate abroad, practically all the information that it was necessary for our government to know. In peace times this might have been probable. These self-deluded mortals seemed to have forgotten entirely that we were at war. Furthermore, it must be admitted to our shame that our English Consular Service in some places abroad is the poorest paid and the least looked-after branch of government service of almost any nation.

Sir George Pragnell, speaking only a few days before his lamentably sudden and untimely end, at the great meeting called by the Lord Mayor of London at the Guildhall on January 31st, 1916, a meeting of the representatives of Trade and Commerce from all parts of the British Empire, said:

> Our business men maintained that our Consular Service should consist of the best educated and the most practical business men we could turn out. Not only should these men be paid high salaries, but I would recommend that they should be paid a commission or bonus on the increase of British Trade in the places they had to look after.

If this sound, practical wisdom had only been propounded and acted upon years ago the benefits that England would have derived therefrom would have been incalculable. But look at the facts regarding the countries where efficient and effective Consular Service was most wanted during the war. In Scandinavia there were gentlemen selected to represent us as British *Vice-Consuls* who received a *fixed salary of £5 per annum*, in return for which they had to *provide office, clerks, telephone,* and other incidentals. Although the fees paid to them by virtue of their office and the duties they performed may have amounted to several hundred pounds *per annum*, they were compelled to hand over the whole of the fruits of their labours to the English Government, which thus made a very handsome profit out of its favours so bestowed. Our Foreign Office apparently considered that the honour of the title "British Vice-Consul" was quite a sufficient recompense for the benefits it demanded in return, the laborious duties which it required should be constantly attended to, and the £20 to £50 or more per annum which their representatives were certain to find themselves out of pocket at the end of each year. Soon after the war commenced one or two members of the service were removed from the largest centres and other men introduced, presumably on a special rate of pay; but in almost all the vice-consulates the disgracefully mean and unsatisfactory system above mentioned seemed to have been continued without any attempt at reformation.

Is it to be wondered at that so many vice-consuls who are not Englishmen did not feel that strong bond of sympathy either with our ministers abroad or with our ministers at home, which those who have no knowledge of the conditions of their appointment or of their service might be led to expect existed between them?

Further light is shown upon this rotten spot in our governmental diplomacy management abroad by an article entitled "Scrap our Alien Consuls," written by T. B. Donovan and published in a London paper, February 20th, 1916, short extracts from which read as follows:

Look up in Whitaker's *Almanack* for 1914 our consuls in the German Empire before the war—and cease to wonder that we were not better informed. Out of a total of forty old British consuls more than thirty bear German names! Other nations were not so blind. . . . Glance through the following astounding list. In Sweden, twenty-four out of thirty-one British consuls and vice-consuls are non-Englishmen; in Norway, twenty-six out of thirty; in Denmark, nineteen out of twenty-six; in Holland and its colonies, fourteen out of twenty-four; in Switzerland nine out of fourteen—and several of the few Englishmen are stationed at holiday resorts where there is no trade at all. And we are astonished that our blockade 'leaks at every seam'! This type of British consul must be replaced by keen Britishers who have the interests of their country at heart and who are at the same time acquainted with the needs of the districts to which they are appointed. If we could only break with red tape, we could find numerous men, not far beyond the prime of life, but who have retired from an active part in business, who would gladly accept such appointments and place their knowledge at the disposal of their fellows. . . .

The state of things in our Consular Service is such as no business man would tolerate for a moment.

Turning attention to our diplomacy on the shores of the Mediterranean and the Near East, those in the Secret Service knew that during the early days of the war at least our Foreign Office had nothing much to congratulate itself upon with regard to its representatives in Italy.

For the first eight months of war an overwhelming volume of supplies and commodities, so sought after and necessary to the Central Powers, was permitted to be poured into and through that country from all sources. Even the traders of the small northern neutral states became jealous of the fortunes that were being made there. Daily almost they might be heard saying: "Why should I not earn money by sending goods to Germany when ten times the amount that my country supplies is being sent through Italy?"

The tense anxiety, the long weary months of waiting for Italy to join the Entente, are not likely to be forgotten. When at last she was compelled to come in, it was not British cleverness in diplomacy that caused her so to do, but the irresistible will of her own peoples, the men in the streets and in the fields; the popular poems of Signor D'Annunzio, which rushed the Italian Government along, against its will, and as an overwhelming avalanche. The popular *quasi*-saint-like shade of Garibaldi precipitated matters to a crisis.

It is interesting as an object lesson in the ironies of fate to compare the fevered enthusiasm of the Sonnino of 1881 for the cultured Germans and Austrians, and his exuberant hatred of France, with the cold logic of the disabused Sonnino of 1915, who suddenly acquired widespread popularity by undoing the work he had so laboriously helped to achieve a quarter of a century before. European history, ever since Germany began to obtain success in moulding it, has been full of these piquant Penelopean Activities, some of which are fast losing their humorous points in grim tragedy.

Thus wrote Dr. E. J. Dillon in his book of revelations, *From the Triple to the Quadruple Alliance, or Why Italy Went to War.* From cover to cover it is full of solid, startling facts concerning the treachery and double-dealing of the Central Powers. It shows how Italy was flattered, cajoled and lured on to the very edge of the precipice of ruin, disaster and disgrace; how she had been gradually hedged in, cut off from friendly relationships with other countries, and swathed and pinioned by the tentacles of economic plots and scheming which rendered her tributary to and a slave of the latter-day Conquistadores; how for over thirty years she was compelled to play an ignominious and contemptible part as the cat's-paw of Germany; how Prince Bulow, the most distinguished statesman in Germany, also the most resourceful diplomatist, who by his marriage with Princess Camporeale, and the limitless funds at his disposal, wielded extraordinary influence with Italian senators and officials as well as at the Vatican, dominated Italian people from the highest to the lowest; how, in fact, the *Kaiser's* was the hand that for years guided Italy's destiny.

The book is a veritable mine of information of amazing interest at the present time, given in minutest detail, authenticated by facts, date, proof, and argument. But it is extraordinary that in this volume of nearly 100,000 words, written by a man who perhaps, for deep intimate knowledge of foreign politics and the histories of secret court intrigue, has no equal living, not a word of commendation is devoted to the efforts made by our own British diplomacy or to the parts played by His Britannic Majesty's ministers and ambassadors. There is, however, a remote allusion on his last page but one, as follows: "The scope for a complete and permanent betterment of relations is great enough to attract and satisfy the highest diplomatic ambition." This seems to be the one and only reference.

As quoted in other pages of this book, the reader will perhaps gather that Dr. Dillon, who has been brought much in contact with the Diplomatic Service and who has exceptional opportunities of seeing behind the scenes, believes in the old maxims revised; for example: *De vivis nil nisi bonum.*

A brief *resumé* of the material parts of this book which affect the subject matter of the present one shows that on the outbreak of the European war Italy's resolve to remain neutral provoked a campaign of vituperation and calumny in the Turkish Press, whilst Italians in Turkey were arrested without cause, molested by blackmailing police, hampered in their business and even robbed of their property. But Prince von Bulow worked hard to suppress all this and to diffuse an atmosphere of brotherhood around Italians and Turks in Europe.

In Libya, however, Turkish machinations were not discontinued, although they were carried on with greater secrecy. The Turks still despatched officers, revolutionary proclamations, and Ottoman decorations to the insurgents, and the Germans sent rifles in double-bottomed beer-barrels *via* Venice. Through an accident in transit on the railway one of these barrels was broken and the subterfuge and treachery became revealed. The rifles were new, and most of them bore the mark "St. Etienne," being meant not only to arm the revolt against Italy but also to create the belief that France was treacherously aiding and abetting the Tripolitan insurgents. And to crown all, during the efforts of fraternisation, in German fashion, Enver Bey's brother clandestinely joined the Senoussi, bringing 200,000 Turkish pounds and the Caliph's order "to purge the land of those Italian traitors."

The never-to-be-forgotten "Scrap of Paper," the violation of neutral Belgium, the shooting and burning of civilians there, the slaying of the wounded, the torturing of the weak and helpless, at first chilled the warm blood of humane sentiment, then sent it boiling to the impressionable brain of the Latin race. Every new horror, every fresh crime in the scientific barbarians' destructive progress intensified the wrath and charged the emotional susceptibility of the Italian nation with explosive elements. The shrieks of the countless victims of demoniac fury awakened an echo in the hearts of plain men and women, who instinctively felt that what was happening today to the Belgians and the French might befall themselves tomorrow. The heinous treason against the human race which materialised in the destruction of the *Lusitania* completed the gradual awakening of the Italian nation to a sense of those impalpable and imponderable elements of the European problem which find expression in no Green Book or Ambassadorial dispatch. It kindled a blaze of wrath and pity and heroic enthusiasm which consumed the cobwebs of official tradition and made short work of diplomatic fiction.

Rome at the moment was absorbed by rumours and discussions about Germany's supreme efforts to coax Italy into an attitude of quiescence. But these machinations were suddenly forgotten in the fiery wrath and withering contempt which the foul misdeeds and culmination of crimes of the scientific assassins evoked, and in pity for the victims and their relatives.

The effect upon public sentiment and opinion in Italy, where emotions are tensely strong, and sympathy with suffering is more flexible and diffusive than it is even among the other Latin races, was instantaneous. One statesman who is, or recently was, a partisan of neutrality, remarked to Dr. Dillon that "German *kultur*, as revealed during the present war, is dissociated from every sense of duty, obligation, chivalry, honour, and is become a potent poison, which the remainder of humanity must endeavour by all efficacious methods to banish from the International system. This," he went on, "is no longer war; it is organised slaughter, perpetrated by a race suffering from dog-madness. I tremble at the thought that our own civilised and chivalrous people may at any moment be confronted with this lava flood of savagery and destructiveness. Now, if ever, the opportune moment has come for all civilised nations to join in protest, stiffened with a unanimous threat, against the continuance of such crimes against the human race. Europe ought surely to have the line drawn at the poisoning of wells, the persecution of prisoners, and the massacre of women and children."

The real cause of the transformation of Italian opinion was no mere mechanical action; it was the inner promptings of the nation's soul.

The tide of patriotic passion was imperceptibly rising, and the cry of completion of Italian unity was voiced in unison which culminated on the day of the festivities arranged in commemoration of the immortal Garibaldi. Signor D'Annunzio, the Poet Laureate of Italian Unity, was the popular hero who set the torch to the mine of the peoples which, when it exploded, instantly erupted parliamentary power, ministers' dictation, and the influences of the throne itself. It shattered the foul system of political intrigue built up by the false Giolitti and developed the overwhelming sentiment of an articulate nation burst into bellicose action against the scientific barbarians; by which spontaneous ebullition Italy took her place among the civilised and civilising nations of Europe.

Most people who have followed events closely are convinced that Turkey could, with judicious diplomacy, have been kept neutral throughout the war. It was whispered in Secret Service circles that a very few millions of money, lent or judiciously expended, would easily have acquired her active support on the side of the Entente.

One need not probe further back in history than to the autumn of 1914 to ascertain the blundering fiasco that was made in that sphere of our alleged activities.

Sir Edwin Pears, who has spent a lifetime in the Turkish capital and who can hardly be designated a censorious critic, because for many years he was the correspondent of a Liberal newspaper in London, published, in October, 1915, a book entitled *Forty Years in Constanti-*

nople. In that book he describes how the Turks drifted into hostility with the *Entente* because the British Embassy was completely out of touch with them. Sir Louis Mallet, H.B.M. Ambassador, appointed in June, 1913, had never had any experience of the country; he did not know a word of Turkish, whilst he had under him three secretaries also ignorant of the language and of the people. Sir Edwin Pears thus describes them:

> Mr. Beaumont, the counsellor, especially during the days in August before his chief returned from a visit to England, was busy almost night and day on the shipping cases. . . . He also knew nothing of Turkish, and had never had experience in Turkey. Mr. Ovey, the First Secretary, also had never been in Turkey, and knew nothing of Turkish. Unfortunately, also, he was taken somewhat seriously ill. The next secretary was Lord Gerald Wellesley, a young man who will probably be a brilliant and distinguished diplomatist twenty years hence, but who, like his colleagues, had no experience in Turkey. The situation of our embassy under the circumstances was lamentable. . . . It was made worse than it might have been from the mischievous general rule of our Foreign Office which erects an almost impassable barrier between the Consular and Diplomatic Services. . . . There were three men in the Consular Service whose help would have been invaluable.

It thus seems to be implied that this help, which would have meant so much in the saving of valuable lives and the wasted millions in gold, was absolutely barred by the false dignity or inefficiency of someone at the Foreign Office. England's only chance of attaining any success with the wily Turks apparently rested upon one man. According to Sir Edwin Pears:

> Nine months before the outbreak of war we had at the British Embassy a *dragoman* (interpreter), Mr. Fitzmaurice, whose general intelligence, knowledge of Turkey, of its ministers and people, and especially of the Turkish language, was, to say the least, equal to that of the best *dragoman* whom Germany ever possessed. His health had run down and he had been given a holiday, but when, I think in the month of February, 1914, Sir Louis Mallet (the British Ambassador) returned to Constantinople, Mr. Fitzmaurice did not return with him, and was never in Constantinople until after the outbreak of war with

England.

It is said that he did not return because the Turkish Ambassador in London made a request to that effect......I think it probable that if such a request was made it was because Mr. Fitzmaurice did not conceal his dislike of the policy which the Young Turks were pursuing.

As his ability and loyalty to his chief are beyond question, and as he possesses a quite exceptional knowledge of the Turkish Empire, and has proved himself a most useful public servant . . it was nothing less than a national misfortune that he did not return with Sir Louis Mallet.

Baron von Wangenheim, the German Ambassador, possessed a superbly equipped staff. It is known that he distributed money, favours, and distinctions broadcast with a free and bountiful hand. He played upon the weaknesses and characteristics of the Orientals with such diplomatic skill and cunning that he entirely won over the Young Turkish party to his way of thinking. And the Young Turkish party ruled and dictated to the whole country.

The blame and responsibility for this extraordinary state of affairs has been put by our indignant Press upon our Foreign Office at home, which sent out, organised, and controlled such a representation. The terrible defeat we suffered at the Dardanelles has also been referred to as the natural aftermath to such a sowing; for proof of culpability as to this see further on.

Our position in Turkey, says Sir Edwin Pears:

. . . . was made worse than it might have been from the mischievous general rule of our Foreign Office, which erects an almost impassable barrier between the Consular and Diplomatic Services, a barrier which I have long desired to see broken down. When, some months afterwards, I returned to England, I received a copy of the *Appendix to the Fifth Report of the Royal Commission on the Civil Service*, published on July 16th, 1914, in which (on p. 321) there is a letter written by me two years earlier in which I made two recommendations. The first was adopted, the second unfortunately was not. I claimed that the Consular and Diplomatic Services should be so co-ordinated that a good man in the Consular Service in Turkey might be promoted into the Diplomatic Service, and I instanced the case of Sir William White, one of the ablest ambassadors we ever had in Constantinople, who had risen from being a consular clerk to the embassy. The facts under my notice from July to the end of October, 1914, afforded strong proof of the common sense of my recommendation.

The inexperience of the ambassador and his staff heavily handicapped British diplomacy in Turkey: yet there were three men who had been or were in the Consular Service whose help would have been invaluable. They had each proved themselves able *dragomans* and each had many years' experience in Turkey. The only explanation that I can give of why their services were not at once made available in the absence of Fitzmaurice was the absurd restriction to which I have alluded.

The Press has also stated that the unsatisfactory precedent exhibited by the embassy at Constantinople typified the British Legations at the Balkan capitals. We know how badly we were disappointed, deceived, and let down in the whole of that theatre of war. The best *resumé* may be found in an admirable series of articles, published, February 3rd to 8th, 1916, in the London *Daily Telegraph*, by that most brilliant and experienced of Continental correspondents, Dr. E.J. Dillon. They reveal the pitiful failings, weaknesses and miscalculations of our Balkan Diplomatists in such glaring vividness that the reader wonders at the marvels performed by our gallant troops and navy in the face of the difficulties and obstructions they had to contend with.

Dr. Dillon wrote:

High praise is due to the intentions of Entente diplomatists, which were truly admirable. They did their best according to their lights during the campaign as they had done their best before it was undertaken. That the best was disastrous was not the result of a lack of goodwill. What they were deficient in was insight and foresight. Their habit is not to study the mental and psychical caste of the peoples with whom they have to deal, but to watch and act upon the shifts of the circumstances. Amateurism is the curse of the British nation. Their vision of the political situation in the Balkans was roseate and blurred, and their moral maxims were better fitted for use in the Society of Friends than in intercourse with a hard-headed people whose morality begins where self-interest ends.

By these methods, which, unhappily, are still in vogue, the diplomacy of Great Britain, France, and Russia lost the key to

Constantinople, and contributed unwittingly to deliver over the Serbian people to the tender mercies of the Bulgar and the Teuton. Turkey is still fighting us in Europe and Asia. Roumania is neutral, and mistrustful, and the war is prolonged indefinitely. The facts on which our statesmen relied turned out to be fancies; their expectations proved to be illusions; and their solemn negotiations a humiliating farce devised by the Coburger, who moved the representatives of the Allied Powers hither and thither like figures on a chess-board.

Mr. Crawford Price, the Balkan war correspondent, writing in the *Sunday Pictorial* of February 27th, 1916, alleges that the Greeks wanted to join the Allies in active aggression on several occasions, but the Hellens were effectively snubbed by our Diplomats. Although the General Staff and the King were both willing at one time to intercede, they opposed unconditional participation in the Dardanelle enterprise, because they believed our ill-considered plans would end in disaster. Mr. Price says that our Diplomatists refused to consider their matured ideas based upon a lifelong study of local conditions and the adoption of which would probably have given us possession of Constantinople in a month. Again, after we had failed, the Greek Government submitted a plan on April 14th, 1915, for co-operation, but we would have nothing to do with it. Finally, when in May following King Constantine offered to join forces with us upon no other condition than that we should guarantee the integrity of his country (surely the least he could ask!), he received a belated intimation to the effect that we could not do so, as we did not wish to discourage Bulgaria.

After this, it will be remembered, England offered to bribe Bulgaria with the Cavalla district belonging to Greece.

No wonder Greece refused to be bribed with Cyprus when Bulgaria had declined to be moved by the blind and incomprehensible enthusiasm which seems to have dominated English diplomacy in the Near East. Or was a certain Continental wag, well known in Diplomatic circles, nearer the mark when he facetiously lisped, "Your English Government is said to be slow and sure, which is quite true, in that it is slow to act and sure to be too late"?

It is a matter for consideration that the British minister at Sofia was changed during the war, whilst almost his whole staff were only short-timers in Bulgaria, where such a gigantic failure was proved by the subsequent actions of that misguided and unfortunate country.

What small advantages were once obtained in this sphere of action seem all to have been lost through our everlasting and repeated procrastinations and unpardonable delay. Had the permission of Venezelos to land troops at Salonica been immediately acted upon and the proffered co-operation of the Hellens accepted with the cordiality it deserved, and half a million men been marched to the centre of Serbia, that country would never have been conquered by the enemy, whilst Bulgaria and Roumania would have come in upon the side of the Entente, and Turkey would have been beaten at the outset; thereby saving hundreds of thousands of valuable lives, and hundreds of millions of pounds sterling.

What a difference this would have made to the length of the war! Our diplomacy failed.

Our then government showed an utter lack of possessing the art of foreseeing. The fruits of its policy, "Wait and see," materialised into muddle, humiliation, slaughter, and defeat.

Just criticism fell from Lord Milner, who, speaking at Canterbury on October 31st, 1915, said:

If the worst of our laches and failures, like the delay in the provision of shells and the brazen-faced attempts to conceal it, or the way we piled blunder upon blunder in the Dardanelles, or the phenomenal failure of our policy in the Balkans—if the nation was induced to regard these as just ordinary incidents of war, then we could never expect and should not deserve to see our affairs better managed in the future. Truth all round and clearness of vision were necessary to enable us to win through.

A few days later Mr. Rudyard Kipling in the *Daily Telegraph* wrote:

No man likes losing his job, and when at long last the inner history of this war comes to be written we may find that the people we mistook for principals and prime agents were only average incompetents moving all hell to avoid dismissal.

History repeats itself, and George Borrow was not very wide of the mark when he wrote in 1854:

Why does your (English) Government always send fools to represent it at Vienna?[3]

---

3. *Romany Rye.*

The work of all foreign ministers should consist in providing for contingencies long foreseen and patiently awaited. Surely we must have some good and able men who do or can serve us abroad? Or does the fault lie with the Foreign Office at home?

The *English Review* of February, 1916, contained a serious article entitled "The Failure of Sir Edward Grey," the logic of which causes one to reflect. Its author, Mr. Seton-Watson, argues as follows:

> From the moment that the mismanagement of the Dardanelles Expedition became apparent to the Bulgarians (and it must be remembered that the whole Balkan Peninsula was ringing with the details at a time when the British public was still allowed to know nothing) only one thing could have prevented them from joining the Central Powers, and that was the prompt display of military force, as a practical proof that we should not allow our ally to be crushed. . . . Prince George of Greece was sent to Paris by his brother, the King, with a virtual offer of intervention in return for the Entente Powers guaranteeing the integrity of Greek territory. The French were inclined to consider the offer, but it was rejected by London on the ground that no attention could be paid to 'unauthorised amateur diplomacy.'
>
> This astonishing phrase was allowed to reach the King of Greece, and having been applied to his own brother on a mission which was anything but unauthorised, naturally gave the greatest possible offence.
>
> As a matter of fact, the Treaty was much more comprehensive than is generally supposed. Under its provisions the *casus fœderis* arises not merely in the event of a Bulgarian attack on Serbia, but also of an attack from any other quarter also; and therefore Greece, in not coming to Serbia's aid against Austria-Hungary in 1914, had already broken her pledge. Hence Sir Edward Grey, who must have been well aware of this fact, was surely running a very grave risk when he relied upon Greek constancy in a situation which his own diplomatic failures had rendered infinitely less favourable.
>
> On September 23rd Bulgaria mobilised against Serbia; yet on September 27th Sir Edward Grey practically vetoed Serbia's proposal to take advantage of her own military preparedness and to attack Bulgaria before she could be ready. Next day (September 28th) in the House of Commons he uttered his

famous pledge that, in the event of Bulgarian aggression, 'We are prepared to give to our friends in the Balkans all the support in our power, in the manner that would be most welcome to them, in concert with our Allies without reserve and without qualification.'

At the moment everyone in England, and above all in Serbia, took this to mean that we were going to send Serbia the military help for which she was clamouring; but on November 3rd Sir Edward Grey explained to an astonished world that he merely meant to convey that after Bulgaria had joined Germany 'there would be no more talk of concessions from Greece or Serbia.' The *naïveté* which could prompt such an explanation is only equalled by the confusion of mind which could read this interpretation into a phrase so explicit and unequivocal. Greece's failure in her Treaty obligations towards Serbia alone saved Britain from the charge of failure to fulfil her pledge to Greece. Nothing can exonerate Greece's desertion of her ally, but in view of our tergiversation and irresolution, some allowance must be made for King Constantine's attitude towards the Entente.

Sir Edward Grey, throwing to the winds all his public pledges to Serbia, definitely urged upon the French *generalissimo* complete withdrawal from Salonica and the abandonment of the Serbs to their fate. General Joffre replied with the historic phrase: 'You are deserting us on the field of battle and we shall have to tell the world.' General Joffre carried his point, and in the biting phrase of Sir Edward Carson, 'the government decided that what was too late three weeks before was in time three weeks after.' But those three weeks, which might have transformed the fortune of the campaign, had been irretrievably lost through Sir Edward Grey's lack of a Balkan policy. Even then our hesitation continued.

In Paris the question is being asked on all sides why Sir Edward Grey, after such repeated *fiascoes*, did not follow his late colleague, M. Delcasse, into retirement, and what everyone is saying in Paris, from the Quai d'Orsay to the Academie Française, surely need no longer be concealed from London. The German Chancellor was unwise enough to hint this in his speech, when he ascribed Germany's Balkan success in large measure to our mistakes. The fall of Sir Edward Grey, as the result of a demand for a more energetic conduct of the war and for still closer co-operation with our Allies, and the substitution of a man of energy and first-rate ability, would be far the most serious and disconcerting blow which the Germans had yet received.

The halting, hesitating, vacillating "wait-and-see" policy which seems to be revealed in such startling vividness by Mr. Seton-Watson causes a deep thinker to ponder further. Is it not possible that Sir Edward Grey, like the late Lord Kitchener, may not have been his own master? That he in turn may have been held down and dictated to by the one man whose own valuation of his personal services so greatly exceeded the worth put upon them by the nation at large?

It is easy to state in the House of Commons, "I accept entire responsibility," as Mr. Asquith did when the Gallipoli disaster was questioned, but he surely ought then to have been the questioner! *His statement*, which the members of the House were bound down by national loyalty not to attack as they would have liked to have done, *prove* that the prime minister had been *meddling with military matters* which should have been left absolutely and entirely to military experts. Hence it was that the nation learnt that the halting, hesitating, vacillating "wait-and-see" policy had paralysed not only the whole Gallipoli campaign, but particularly the Suvla Bay expedition, which if properly exploited would undoubtedly have given our arms one of the greatest victories of the war.[4]

---

4. It has been said by those who were there that the English troops were kept back and permitted to play about on the beach bathing and building camp, etc., for three days after the first landing, thus giving the Turks more than sufficient time to bring up opposing forces and successfully dig themselves in where required, whereas it was but nine miles across the peninsula, which could presumably have been straddled in a few hours with little, if any, opposition at the time of landing. Was this the suppressed episode "within a few hours of the greatest victory of the war," which the Right Hon. Winston Churchill referred to in his memorable speech, and which has been the subject of so much surmise and comment?

CHAPTER 20

The Sham Blockade

During the first year of the war Secret Service agents busied themselves much concerning the vast stream of goods, necessities and munitions in the raw state which poured into Germany direct and through neutral countries like the waters of a rising flood over weirs on the Thames. Night and day these ever-restless beings flitted as shadows along the secretly or openly favoured trade routes. Persistently and energetically they followed up clues and signs of the trails of enemy traders, from ports of entry to original sources. Week by week, almost day by day, they flashed home news of then present and future consignments of such importance and value to the enemy that he paid exorbitant prices and ridiculous commissions to help rush them over his frontiers.

Seemingly all was in vain. These efforts were but wasted. The work was apparently unappreciated and unresponsively received. England, to all intents and purposes, was slumbering too soundly to be awakened. Meanwhile, during every hour of the twenty-four, unending processions of trade ships of every shape, make and rig sneaked along the coasts of neutral waters, as near to land as safety permitted, on their way to the receiving ports of Germany.

Observers, stationed in lighthouses or on promontories, who watched this abnormal freighting activity, could not but help noticing that, whenever smoke showed itself upon the horizon seawards, consternation at once became manifest on the decks of these cargo carriers. They would squeeze dangerously inshore, lay to, or drop anchors, bank up their fires and damp down every curl of smoke which it was possible to suppress; in short, they adopted every conceivable ruse to conceal their presence and identity.

If this trade was honest and legitimate, why should these tactics be followed, and these precautions taken? *Res ipsa loquitur.*

As the year 1915 progressed and the inertia of the British Government became more and more realised abroad, the captains of freighters grew bolder and bolder, and the confidence of the thousands upon thousands of get-rich-quick-anyhow dealers ashore increased and multiplied accordingly. No one, except the Germans themselves, knew or could get to know the actual extent of this enormous volume of their import trade. The chattels came from so many different countries and were consigned through so many channels that accurate records were rendered impossible; whilst the greater part was shipped in direct.

The English Press, which had been so self-denying and loyal to the government in spite of the shameful manner in which it had been gagged and bound down, until the Censor's blue-pencilling amounted almost to an entire suppression of news, began to grumble and to hint very broadly that the bombastic utterances of our ministers regarding the effectiveness of our blockade and the starvation of the Central Powers were exaggerations and not facts. Men who had always put their country before any other consideration began to proclaim that the so-called blockade was a delusion; whilst they quoted figures of imports to neutral countries which were embarrassing to the government. Something therefore had to be done.

The notorious Danish Agreement[1] was accordingly framed in secret (in secret only from the British public), and a very highly-coloured and altogether misleading interpretation of its limitations and effectiveness was hinted at in Parliament. In spite of terrific pressure upon ministers by members of both Houses, not a clause of this extraordinary document was permitted to be published, although its context was freely circulated or commented upon in the Press of neutral countries and the whole Agreement was printed *in extenso* on December 12th, 1915, in the *Borsen*, at Copenhagen. What a sham and a farce this whole arrangement turned out to be will be seen later.

It has ever been the proud boast of Englishmen that Britannia rules the waves. Until this war the British Navy had been supreme mistress of the seas, and no loyal person within the empire whereon the sun never sets has grudged a penny of the very heavy taxation which has been necessary to keep up the efficiency of our fleet. From the commencement of the war, however, our fleet was tied up body and soul, shackled in the intricacies of red tape entanglements woven round its

---

1. Completed on November 19th, 1915.

keels, guns, and propellers by lawyer politicians who never could leave the management of naval affairs to the navy, any more than they could leave the management of military affairs to the army. In theory these pedantic illusionists may be superb, whilst some of them even stated (1915-16) that if they were removed from office during the continuance of the war it would be a calamity. But in practice the British public has seen proved too vividly—and at what a cost!—only an incessant stream of terrible disasters and mishaps; "milestones" in their policy of makeshift, dawdle and defeat.

The first chapter in this book shows that our party system government was probably directly responsible for the war itself, or at least for our being precipitated unprepared into it. Without a shadow of a doubt it is solely accountable for the wild and riotously extravagant waste, for our colossal supererogation, and for our excessive losses.

What would have happened to the Mother Country and to her extensive Colonial Possessions had not Lord Northcliffe, through the powerful newspapers he controls, stepped in from time to time and torn off the scales which had been plastered and bandaged upon the eyes of an all-too-confiding British public, and just in the nick of time to save disaster upon disaster too awful to contemplate?

It is not necessary to enumerate the many and vital matters which Lord Northcliffe helped an indignant and a deluded public to consider and discuss, whereby the government was roused from its torpor and pushed into reluctant activity, but the greatest of all canards which it had attempted to foist upon Europe does very much concern the subject-matter of this volume, hence it must be separately dealt with. It is this so-called blockade, which amongst Teuton traders in Northern neutral countries was looked upon as the best of all "war jokes"!

It seems to be universally believed that had the British fleet been given a free hand and its direction left to the discretion of a good, business-like, fighting Sea Lord, the war would have been over within eighteen months from the first declaration. As it has happened, the freedom of action of our fleet has been so hampered that our enemies have actually been permitted to draw certain food supplies not only from our own Colonies, but from the United Kingdom itself. How can it be argued that this suicidal policy has not helped to drag out the war and add to its terrible and unnecessary wastage of life and wealth, with the aftermath of woe and misery consequent thereon?

For our ministers to affirm that Germany has been starved by our blockade is as untrue as it is ridiculous. The bunkum which has filled the thousands upon thousands of Press columns in different countries on this subject has been mere chimerical effort, in great part subsidised from indirect pro-German sources of more or less remote origin in accordance with the value of the publication used.

Now for a dissection of the facts concerning the main subject.

Passing over innumerable paragraphs in the Press which hinted at much more than they disclosed, attention should be given to an article which appeared in the January (1916) number of the *National Review* (pp. 771-780), in which a naval correspondent gives record of a startling amount of supplies of cotton, copper, oils, foodstuffs and other commodities that were permitted to pass into Germany by permission of our benevolent government.

The *Edinburgh Review* of the same month also contains an article worthy of perusal upon the same subject. Many other periodicals directly and indirectly touched upon it, but for proof positive and authentic evidence the reader is referred to the files of the *Daily Mail*. That paper, in its persistent and praiseworthy patriotism, by pushing forward everything it honestly believed to be for the Empire's good, or which it hoped might help shorten the war, determined to get to the bottom of the matter. In order to ascertain how far this alleged supplying of Germany was permitted it arranged for one of its Special Commissioners to visit Scandinavia for the express purpose of collecting evidence on the spot and for publication in its columns. The author has taken the liberty of extracting freely therefrom. On January 12th, 1916, the special series of articles commenced as follows:

> In setting out the facts I will try hard to keep from my presentation of them any distortion due to the disgust and burning anger that they evoked in me, as they must do in every patriot of this Empire.
>
> Lest even for a moment a wrong and cruel suspicion rest upon little Denmark—namely, that she is unfriendly towards the Allies and has been 'two-faced' in the many tokens of friendliness and respect she has shown us, I say with conviction that there is not a truer or deeper love for England and the English than exists today in Denmark. These Danes, forefathers of so many of our race, warm still to Britain and the British. Their hearts glow to our successes, yearn to our reverses. Deep down they are for us through and through. The best Danes revolt at the work Denmark is now forced to do. A big and greedy German

fist hangs over her—threatening, bullying, driving. 'So far as in you lies,' says the bully behind that fist, 'you must be useful to us—as useful at least as you are to our enemy'—(aside, 'even more useful if we can make you so')—'and should you fail by one iota to yield us such surplus food commodities as you produce and such food commodities as you can get'—(aside, 'by hook or by crook')—'from abroad, then the consequences for you will be serious. We shall seize Denmark.'

Here follow several columns of statistics relating to the importation of foodstuffs to Denmark, showing increases in some instances of upwards of 1,000 *per cent.* upon her normal supplies.

Denmark's total population is under 3,000,000, and to argue that she would, or even could, use these commodities herself is mere foolishness. Extracting further:

The vast bulk of Denmark's pork goes to Germany—either directly, by train or ship, or *via* Sweden, where obliging workmen, dignified *pro tem.* with the title 'merchant consignee' (but whose whole stock-in-trade consists perhaps of a hammer, some nails and a batch of labels), change the labels on the goods and perhaps turn upside down the marked ends of the packing-cases, and then re-consign the goods to Germany.

And they may even leave Sweden in the very railway trucks and cases in which they have arrived and travel to Germany back through Denmark in sealed trucks over which the Danish Customs have no control. Or there may be no need to trouble to send them to Sweden. They may leave Copenhagen docks direct for Lübeck, Warnemunde, Stettin, or Hamburg, in direct steamers, of which some 500 sailed during the year. Or they may go by train. Huge trains leave every day. The trains and ferries and boats connecting Denmark and Germany are so full that there is competition for room. How often may one see the Danish shippers, in advertising their sailings for German ports, add the significant words, 'Cargo space already full' days before the actual date of sailing!

Now more Swedish traffic than ever crosses the water from Malmö or Helsingborg and makes its way to Germany across Denmark by rail. I have stood about the railways at many points in the two countries and watched truck after truck go by—all to cross the German frontier below Kolding, in Jutland. The great wagons were closed and a little seal gleamed red on their black doors. I have stood, too, on the quays at these ports and watched the dock cranes lifting and lowering sack after sack, box after box, and barrel after barrel, from the quays to German-bound steamers, to German words of command, and on the main or mizzen-mast of the steamer would be as often as not the gloomy little German flag, black and white and red, still blacker and gloomier with the smoke drifting from the funnel before it.

On the quays at Copenhagen I watched the steamers *Hugo Stinnes*, of Hamburg, *Esberg*, *Snare*, *Haeland*, *Hever*, and others, of Sweden, loading wine from Spain and Portugal; oil, lard, coffee and petroleum from America; meat from Denmark, and many other goods, *all for German ports*. I travelled to Malmö, in Sweden, with a cargo of oils and fats and iron and boxes with no marks on them, and at Malmö saw these things put ready on the quay to await the next German steamer. At the same port I saw pork in boxes, meatstuffs in boxes and barrels labelled 'Armour and Co.,' oils and fats bearing the names Swift or Morris or Harrison or Salzberger, and some of them adding the information that the contents were 'guaranteed to contain 30 *per cent.* of pure neat's-foot oil'; also petroleum of 'Best Standard White' and other brands; pork 'fat backs,' and many other things besides, *all labelled 'Lübeck'* and going into lighters for transport thither.

Fussing tugs, with a litter of 400-ton lighters behind, may be seen travelling these waters all hours of the day bound for Germany, and no one can say what mysterious cargoes slip from country to country at night. The glut of traffic at these link-points is tremendous. *At some ports there is such a glut of stuff that Danish traders complain that they cannot get their own Danish produce over to Germany 'because of the amount of foreign stuff' there is to be ferried over.* A pretty position, indeed!

And it is we in Great Britain who are allowing all this 'foreign stuff' to reach these countries. It is British licences and permits and recommendations which make possible this pouring of the world's goods into Germany. Little wonder the Danish merchants and other onlookers less friendly to us look with wonder upon us. 'My word, but you are truly a Christian people,' they say. 'You love your enemies all right—well enough to feed them. And if you, England, will allow the stuff over, it is not for us, little Denmark, to stand in Germany's way.'

"But how is all this possible, you may ask, this feeding of Germany through neutral Scandinavian countries? Are there not strict undertakings and promises and guarantees given to England against these goods, supplied from outside, ever reaching our enemy, Germany?

Our navy does its part. Ships are hauled into —— and searched. Guarantees are exacted and forthcoming. And the whole performance, admirably and bravely done, is so much waste of effort. *For the guarantees are not worth the ink they are written with;* they are not worth a single tinker's expletive. To show this will be a little intricate, perhaps, but it is worth trouble to follow.

Goods leave Great Britain and America, Spain and other countries for Danish ports. The shipper, now wary of the British Fleet, which has done wonderful police duty on the high seas, generally exacts a declaration that the goods are not for export to an enemy country. The declaration is signed right willingly, for the consignor can quite easily believe, or pretend to believe, that his goods are merely for Denmark. A British warship overhauls the boat, and perhaps takes her into —— (a certain British port) for examination.

The declaration with each consignment is in order. But, not satisfied (the Navy all through have been suspicious, and rightly), the officer communicates with London. 'The s.s. *so-and-so* has big consignments of foodstuffs for Copenhagen under the names So-and-So. Can we release them?' London communicates with our Legation at Copenhagen, in whose hands they are in this matter. 'Can we let through consignments to So-and-So in your capital?' And our Copenhagen Legation replies with a list of the Danish people whose consignments must be let through and a list of those (if any) whose goods must be stopped or forwarded only on declaration that the goods must not leave Copenhagen Harbour or Copenhagen City.

It all looks admirable—most businesslike; quite systematic and thorough. *It is so much nonsense. For in point of fact the ideas of our Legation at Copenhagen on the good faith of some Danish traders and the bad faith of others are childish beyond words. Their rulings are the laughing-stock of Denmark.* And the joke would be all the more appreciable were it not that there is so much anger caused by the arbitrariness of the Legation's trade rulings and the baiting of some honest men, while less honest go free and trade with impunity. Struck by the frequency with which one or two names appeared in the Copenhagen importers' lists, I made some calculations, then some personal inquiries. I found that 'X' alone had imported during the year 4,000,000 lbs. pork, 3,000,000 lbs. lard, 2,500,000 lbs. oleo, 1,000,000 lbs. other pork and meat. 'Y,' another man, imported in September, October and November alone, 1,045,000 lbs. of cocoa.

Neither of these men was engaged in these trades before the war. They were men of quite humble business attainments. *Yet both enjoyed the full confidence of our trusting British Legation at Copenhagen*, who would have taken solemn affidavits, no doubt, that neither of these men traded with Germany. I would have done the same myself. But these men traded with others who did trade with Germany, either directly or through third and fourth and maybe fifth parties.

What is the result? You have in Copenhagen that amazing modern war phenomenon the trader of the *n*th degree. Plain Trader imports his goods and basks and grows fat under the ægis of the British Legation in Copenhagen. Trader 2 buys from Plain Trader under a 'guarantee' not to sell to Germany, and if he does not dare to break that guarantee himself he sells to Trader 3 or Trader 4 or Trader 5, one of whom will undoubtedly do it. And the less money that Trader 5 has the better, because then, even if he is caught, which is not likely, for nobody worries, no one can squeeze him for the amount of the guarantee because he has not got it.

The result is that every Tom, Dick and Harry of Copenhagen is a trader—from the *bona fide* merchant downwards. Your hotel porter may be trading with a Hungarian for flour or rice or fat; the "Boots" can get you a ton or two of meal. Imagine the amazement of the Danish housewife when her maid came in one day and, with hands clasped in enthusiasm, said, 'Oh, madam, I've got three wagon-loads of marmalade to sell'! And that happened in Copenhagen not long ago.

The newspapers are daily blackened with great display advertisements offering goods for sale. I have before me as I write a whole sheaf of such advertisements, offering anything, from American lard to potash and oil and cocoa and coffee. And not one of

228

these advertisements has a name or an address to it; nothing but a telephone number. One or two of these I tracked down, only to find as vendors simple, kindly souls, such as old shopwomen, caretakers, porters, shop-girls, and the rest waiting for an offer for their goods. *Per contra*, as the book-keepers say, there are advertisements from those wanting goods, and these are often more outspoken. Some of these nameless advertisements treat of great quantities. 'Ten thousand kilos fat, with permit to export; 20,000 kilos salted half-pigs; 50,000 kilos salt meat'; and much more says one advertisement alone. And the good soul answering to your inquiry may prove a simple little typewriting girl—one of Copenhagen's new traders to the *n*th degree.

The machinery that has been established by Great Britain in Denmark for preventing imported foodstuffs from reaching our enemy might be very admirable—if only it worked.

There has been little or no enforcement of the trading laws imposed upon Danish traders by Great Britain. We have supplied them with goods and have allowed them to help themselves to goods from all the ends of the earth upon set conditions— namely, that those goods should not go to Germany, our enemy. They go to Germany, nevertheless, and *they go because we have no one in Denmark who sees to it that they shall not go.* Great Britain, in short, lacks a watchful policeman in Denmark. Great Britain also lacks a live sergeant at home to see to it that her Denmark policeman does not sleep on his beat. *The British Foreign Office* is the sergeant I mean; *the British Legation at Copenhagen*, or its commercial department, is the policeman. *Theirs is the duty. And both have failed us.*

Take the written declarations made by traders that goods supplied to them by or through us shall not go to Germany. Without control and enforcement they are perfectly useless. I myself found traders who told me point-blank that they would consider such agreements as this not morally binding upon them. 'Your navy seizes our ships,' said one, 'and your Foreign Office releases them only on condition that the goods they contain shall be subject to your own conditions. I sign those conditions, but they are exacted from me by force, and I don't consider them as worth a snap of the fingers. If you put a pistol to my head and said, "Sign that cheque," I'd sign it, but I'd telephone to the bank the minute you'd gone and stop payment. And I'll do the same thing with your British import agreements.' These agreements are perhaps 'backed' by a money penalty.

The banks undertake this guarantee part of the business. For a modest 3 *per cent.* or so they will put up your money guarantee against your goods ever reaching Germany and contravening the agreement clause. And when the goods go on to Sweden the Swedish banks relieve the Danish banks of their obligations. And when the goods go on from Sweden to Germany, who relieves the Swedish banks? I have it on the word of a man I believe to be thoroughly honest and well informed that the North German Bank of Hamburg alone has taken over from Swedish banks of late in one transaction as much as £78,000 worth of guarantees—that the goods will not reach Germany! *Was ever there such a comedy? A German bank guaranteeing that much-needed goods will not reach Germany!*

The Germans are not 'let down' by their diplomacy in Copenhagen. A constant weight is poised carefully and with a silken brutality over little Denmark's head and von Ranzau smiles and assures Denmark he is really preserving her from his powerful master. And he gets his way, of course. The little matter of a permit for export? Well, perhaps it can be managed for you, Baron—*especially as the British watchman is asleep just now!*

So the great game goes on. If Denmark has goods that cannot obtain a permit for direct export to Germany they can go *via* Sweden. *Vice versa*, if Sweden has goods about which our active British Legation there is too curious, send them to Denmark and re-export them. That is simple. And I have seen for myself at Denmark's port of Copenhagen Swedish goods (casks of American oil) which had been refused permits for shipment direct from Sweden to Germany, being loaded into the steamer *Heinrich Hugo Stinnes*, of Hamburg, for shipment to Hamburg. Also, on the quay at Malmö (Sweden) I have seen goods for which Denmark had refused a direct export permit being loaded into nameless lighters for shipment to German Lübeck.

Thus agreements, promises, guarantees, and prohibitions—*the whole commercial code that Great Britain has devised for regulating imports into Denmark and for checking their re-export to Germany*(and, incidentally, for displaying to us at home) *are so much meaningless pantomime.* They have become so simply because the honester traders of Denmark, and the dishonest parasites of all nations who work under them and through them, have found that there is no supervision, no punishment, no judge to answer. *Our watchmen, both in London and in Copenhagen, have slept.*

On January 13th, 1916, Lord Sydenham in the House of Lords raised the question of "Feeding the Germans," and in his speech stated that in cocoa alone our exports for August-July, 1913-14, were 6,138 tons as against 32,083 tons for 1914-15. For the sixteen months preceding the war our exports were 8,883 tons, as against 33,357 tons during the first sixteen months of the war.

Lord Lansdowne, following, admitted that *"there was an enormous balance unaccounted for which it was reasonable to suppose found its way to enemy countries."*

The following are the exports of cocoa to the countries named in the years 1913, 1914, and up to December 30th, 1915:

COCOA EXPORTS

In lbs. To (to Dec. 30)	1913	1914	1914
Holland	2,205,282	12,203,463	9,298,805
Denmark	50,782	1,853,948	10,615,873
Scandinavia	343,573	3,079,904	14,606,309

A leading article in the *Daily Mail* of January 14th, 1916, stated:

The strength of the greatest navy in the world is being paralysed by administrative feebleness and diplomatic weakness. Had our sea power been used, as the sailors would have used it, from the opening of the war, it is possible that Germany would before now have collapsed. The mightiest weapon in our arsenal has been blunted because our politicians imagined they could wage what Napoleon called 'rosewater war,' and were more eager to please everybody than to hurt the enemy, and because our diplomatists are remiss.

On December 29th the *Neue Freie Presse*,[2] a leading Austrian

2. The following illuminating advertisement also appeared in the *Neue Freie Presse* of January 16: "For Sale. 40 tons prime beef, fresh packed in ice from Holland. Condensed milk from —— Amsterdam, Raspberry jam, China tea, 25 chests, Soap, 20 to 40 *per cent.* fatty matter, 8 wagons. Sausages from —— Holland. Cement, linseed oil, a wagon of each every week from —— Denmark. Apply, etc." Not far away from the above advertisement in the same paper is another. "Soup extract, 2½d. a cube. Soup vegetables, Julienne, 1s. 8d. per lb., China tea (Souchong), 5s. per lb., just come from a Danish export house."

newspaper, published for the benefit of the people of Vienna an advertisement offering provisions from Holland. A list of the articles which could be supplied at moderate prices followed. It included cocoa, chocolate, potatoes, flour, sausages, sides of bacon, butter, coffee, tea, sardines, oranges, lemons and figs.

And yet Mr. Runciman tells us that the Germans are on the verge of starvation!

The cure for this state of affairs is to infuse greater energy and insight into our diplomacy and to free the Navy from its paper fetters. Much of the mischief is due to the want of capable advisers at the British Legations in the neutral capitals and of energy and vigilance on the part of the Foreign Office at home. The Germans have been quick to realise the importance of stationing active agents at the vital posts.

The present system of setting diplomatists who have lived all their life in a world of formality to deal with the sharpest business men in Europe in a matter where huge profits are at stake is an immense blunder which may have the most serious consequences.

Our very gentleness with Denmark is being quoted in that country to prove that we are not likely to win the war. This is undoubted and dangerous fact.

On January 14th, 1916, the Special Commissioner in a further article, headed, "The Sham Blockade: British tyres on German Cars," explained in detail the tricks used by unscrupulous foreigners and others to acquire stocks of rubber motor-tyres for German use. He complained, with reason, that the broken promises, broken guarantees, and reckless manner in which permits to trade were granted seemed to be almost entirely the fault of the British Foreign Office representatives at the British Legation. He concludes with the following paragraph:

Is this soft-heartedness towards commercial shortcomings and laxity characteristic of our British control in Copenhagen? On the evidence that I have I honestly believe it to be so. But is this attitude solely the individual attitude of Britain's representatives in Copenhagen or is it merely a reflex of the Foreign Office attitude at home?

I think the true answer is that the Copenhagen Legation attitude is a reflex of our Foreign Office attitude. But *if London is mild, Copenhagen is puny*; if London is a lamb, Copenhagen is a sucking dove.

On January 13th, 1916, the following paragraph appeared in the *Globe*:

We cannot disregard the startling and amazing figures collected in Denmark by the Special Commissioner sent out by the *Daily Mail*. Of course, all these commodities are consigned to Danish purchasers, under guarantees that they are not intended for the enemy. What purposes these guarantees serve except to hold harmless the vessels in which the articles are conveyed we are at a loss to understand.

No sane person will believe that the Danish people have suddenly developed such a passion for pork that they must increase their consumption by 1,300 *per cent.*, or that every man, woman and child in Denmark requires the daily bath in cocoa with which the 23,000 tons they now import would appear to be intended to provide them. *The only possible inference from these figures is that we are being deluded, and are feeding Germany* in our own despite.

The *Pall Mall Gazette* of January 18th, 1916, said:

Revelations like these can only be described as heart-breaking to the men and women who have given their sons and brothers and husbands to the end that Germany may be brought to her knees. Now they find that some malign spell has paralysed the Navy's arm so that, instead of Germany's foreign supplies being cut off, they are in some vital respects more abundant than ever.

The *Quarterly Review*, January, 1916, contains a powerful article on "The Danish Agreement." It suggests how *some blight has been at work in our Foreign Office for years steadily undermining our mastery of the sea.* One paragraph bears particularly on the present point:

No informed man doubts that the winter of 1916-17 must weaken to a marked degree, through lack of food, Germany's armed resistance, always assuming that she is not supplied through neutral countries. The existence of England depends on her victory over Germany. Her victory over Germany depends on the cutting off of neutral supplies. Therefore the existence of England depends on the cutting off of neutral supplies. But *when, in August, 1914, the Cabinet and, above all, the Foreign Office, were confronted by this great possibility of stratagem every psychological force was set in motion against its adoption.*

A telegram from Washington, U.S.A., on January 17th, 1916, to the *Morning Post,* set out the exports permitted to be poured into neutral countries in spite of all the efforts and protests of our navy by our all-too-benevolent Foreign Office, and in face of Mr. Asquith's pledges to the House of Commons in March and in November, 1915, when he emphasised to loud cheering that *he would stick at nothing to prevent commodities of any kind reaching or leaving Germany. That there was no form of economic pressure to which he did not consider we were entitled to win the war.*

EXPORTS TO NEUTRAL COUNTRIES

	To	1913. Bushels.	1915. Bushels.
WHEAT	Holland, Norway, Sweden, Denmark	19,000,000	50,000,000
MAIZE	Denmark	4,750,000	10,950,000
	Holland	6,900,000	11,600,000
	Other neutrals	2,100,000	6,400,000
		13,750,000	28,950,000
		Barrels.	Barrels.
WHEAT FLOUR	Holland	708,000	1,500,000
	Other neutrals	709,000	3,800,000
		1,417,000	5,100,000
		lbs.	lbs.
BACON	Holland	3,900,000	9,000,000
	Other neutrals	27,000,000	82,500,000
		30,900,000	91,500,000
		1914	1915
BOOTS	Neutrals	462,000 pairs	4,800,000 pairs
COTTON	Neutrals	53,000 bales	1,100,000 bales
MOTOR- CARS & PARTS	Neutrals	£260,000	£4,000,000

The New York *Journal of Commerce*, quoting statistics of the U.S.A. export trade for the first ten months of 1915 under a headline, "Increase to Neutral Europe Equals German Loss," shows that "whilst shipments to Germany fell away £31,400,000 for the period named, the gain to the neutral nations on the north of Germany was £32,000,000."

What could give more confirmatory proof? On January 24th, 1916, the *Morning Post* received a further cablegram from Washington, U.S.A., containing the elucidating facts that in the ten months from January 1st to October 31st, 1913, Germany imported from the U.S.A. 9,898,289 lbs. of cotton-seed oil, the Netherlands 31,867,327 lbs., and Norway 6,174,033 lbs.

In the corresponding ten months of 1915 the figures were: Germany, nil; the Netherlands, 93,153,175 lbs.; and Norway 24,110,269 lbs.

Other statistics follow, such as cotton-seed, meal and cake, etc., proving beyond all shadow of doubt that neutral countries were importing far more goods and foodstuffs, etc, than their usual average imports plus the total previous imports of Germany in addition.

A careful analysis of the leading American exports showed, almost without an exception, the striking fact that the prices of peace exports were very much lower in 1915 than in 1913; whilst the prices of war exports all showed large and heavy advances.

Deducing from these figures, leader-writers came to the obvious conclusion that *Germany was enjoying unrestricted imports for which Great Britain directly or indirectly paid.*

Returns from other parts of the world merely corroborated, adding proof upon proof. By way of example the Brazilian official trade returns during the first nine months of 1913, compared with 1915, show the following exports to the countries named:

	1913	1915
	£	£
Sweden	389,475	2,844,787
Norway	63,562	594,900
Denmark	105,637	715,387

In addition to the export figures given and those quoted from the U.S.A. should be added the enormous quantities of corn, etc, re-exported from Liverpool and other British ports under special license issued by our government.

It is therefore reasonably arguable that *our government has used our fleet to convoy our merchantmen in freighting foodstuffs, at our expense, to feed the Germans.* By this incomprehensible tolerance home prices of food in the United Kingdom were directly raised to a high figure and neutral countries were directly helped to pile up fortunes by *bleeding and pinching our own peoples in order to feed their enemies.*

On January 21st, 1916, in the House of Commons Major Rowland Hunt asked the Foreign Secretary "whether the Foreign Office had been aware of the state of things demonstrated by the American trade statistics and if so could he say how much longer our navy was to be crippled by the Foreign Office, the war prolonged, and many more thousands of our men sacrificed?"

Sir E. Grey: "I understand that the subject is to be discussed next week. I must, however, say that the statements in the question are grossly unfair and entirely misrepresent the facts of the case. I reserve any further statement I have to make until next week."

From December 16th to 30th, 1915, just on 25,000 tons of iron ore were openly *consigned to Germany* through Rotterdam and Holland; as to which see further on.

Here is a sample report of the sales one day at Esbjerg (Denmark) cattle market, December, 1915:

Cattle sold today numbered 1,450 head, of which Street, of Hamburg, bought 141; Dar Neilsen, of Kiel, 330; Franck of Berlin, 440; an Austrian buyer, 327.

This leaves 212 for Danish buyers. No wonder best beef was then half a crown a pound in Denmark!

Incidentally great quantities of the fodder with which these cattle for Germany are fed come from British ports and possessions.

Our government was fully, persistently, and impressively advised by the Secret Service agents of this continual and enormous export of cattle and beef direct to Germany in January and February, 1915. Yet it apparently did not lift a finger to attempt to stop or divert it throughout the year following, or at any time.

Sweden, which normally imports 734,720 lbs. of meat in November and exports 2,961,280 lbs., imported during November, 1915, 8,016,960 lbs.

Holland, which usually imports in November 1,843,520 lbs. of meat and exports 11,874,240 lbs., imported in November, 1915, no less than 17,973,760 lbs.

In the light of these figures it seems idle to say that our blockade was tightened or in any degree effectual.

In the House of Commons on January 19th, 1916, Mr. Booth put the following question to Lord Robert Cecil in reference to these exports.

Mr. Booth: "Is the noble Lord aware that the Germans in New York toasted the health of the Foreign Office at Christmas time?"

No answer was returned.

On January 26th, 1916, Sir Edward Grey delivered his promised reply in the House of Commons. It was brilliant oratory, but it was not argument. It was a defence of the navy, which needed no defence. It was a masterpiece of forensic jurisprudence, but it revealed between the chinks of polished sentences and high-sounding declamation, in startling nakedness, the weaknesses, the unwarrantable hesitating caution, or the downright cowardice of the Cabinet. With such grace and skill did the speaker unfold his case that a reader, unaware of the facts concealed behind it, would believe the policy and actions of the government had been hitherto faultless, flawless, and blameless. Reading it at a later date brought to my mind the story of a poacher's wife, who with tears of grateful joy streaming down her countenance, thanked a learned junior counsel for his able and successful defence of her husband, who had been charged with stealing a certain shot-gun.

"My good woman," replied her modest advocate, "it was only a mistake. The judge truly said that your good husband left the court without a stain upon his character. It was only *alleged* that he stole the gun."

"Alleged be bothered," said the woman; "why, we've got the gun at home now!"

If this speech of Sir Edward Grey, as a speech, had a fault at all, it was that the defence he made was too good to ring true. At the time of its utterance it appeared to appease the House. No one wished to hamper the government, which, like the energetic but painfully inefficient pianist at a certain Western mining camp, was protected by proclamation: "Please don't shoot. He's doing his best." But outside the House the underlying effect of the speech upon thinking people was very different. It created satisfaction in Germany and amongst neutral Governments. It caused great jubilation amongst the vast army of mushroom traders and adventurers abroad who were piling up fortunes by illicit trading. But it left Englishmen and our true sympathisers in this tragic war irritable, indignant, and unsatisfied; smouldering in their just wrath at the confessed weak-kneed policy of politicians, who, however good their intentions, proved that they had not yet grasped the difference between a quarrel at law and a quarrel at war.

It left the nation disappointed. The people felt we had been fooling with the war too long; that the time had arrived for some strong and decisive action. That politics and patronage should be shelved and the navy given a free hand. It remembered how the government had hesitated, procrastinated, and vacillated in this so-called blockade, as in other matters. It remembered that Parliament had refused to pass a code of international rules called the Declaration of London because that code, made largely to please Germany, weakened the hands of the Navy. It remembered that *the government had gone behind the back of Parliament and illegally put that very code into operation after war began.* It had not forgotten that this proved such a scandalous weakening of our right and our strength that soon after the Coalition Government came into being that code was said to have been scrapped. Even as to this doubts arose for long afterwards.[3]

It had not forgotten the seventeen long months of public pressure and the trouble there had been to force cotton as contraband; nor the seventeen months of "wait and see" before the navy was permitted to examine mails and extract (*inter alia*) parcels of rubber. It had not forgotten Sir Edward Grey's declaration that "he had no intention of making cotton contraband"; nor Lord Haldane's contention that "it was useless stopping the import of cotton to Germany, because if we did Germany could find a substitute for it."

The nation had been deceived and lulled to sleep before by soft words and gentle assurances. It had been told, "we decline to be bound by judicial niceties." It had been promised "to prevent commodities of any kind from entering or leaving the enemy's country"; "to stick at nothing." It remembered with some misgiving how these promises had been kept.[4]

What, it reasoned, were the disappointments of a few Dutch and Scandinavian adventurers from making fortunes out of a war which to ourselves was a tragedy? The country had unbounded confidence in the navy. It had not unbounded confidence in either the government or the Foreign Office. It hungered with an overwhelming desire

---

3. "Apparently the Declaration of London was valid in the House of Commons, but not valid in the House of Lords."—Lord Beresford, House of Lords, February 23rd, 1916.

4. In referring to the keeping of government pledges, Sir A. Markham (L.) said: "The only thing the Prime Minister has stuck to has been his salary."—House of Commons, March, 1916.

to know why the navy should not be given a free and unhampered hand.

The speaker skilfully evaded too much information on that point, and the nation was compelled to nurse its resentment.

At the outset of his speech, Sir Edward Grey attempted to deal with the mass of statistics and evidence of direct importation of goods into Germany accumulated by the Press. He selected wheat and flour only, whilst he casually referred to a list of figures issued by the Press Bureau from the War Trade Department of the government the day before the debate, which members in the House rightly complained had not been supplied to themselves. This list was stated to have been compiled officially in this country from true copies of the ships' manifests, and it alleged the figures given by the Danish *Borsen* were in many cases wrong and unduly inflated. For instance, the increase in rice imports should have been only 480 *per cent.* as against 580 *per cent.*; lard, 275 *per cent.* instead of 375 *per cent.*; pork only 1,216 *per cent.* instead of 1,300 *per cent.*; and so on.

Now everyone knows that statistics are not infallible and a generous allowance should always be made by a careful calculator. But when all circumstances are taken into consideration it can safely be concluded that the majority of the increases alleged by the various Press writers, as having percolated into Germany, were, if anything, under rather than over the mark.

As to the reliability of the *Borsen*, it is edited by a government statistician, and considered by Danish traders as official.

So far as Norway is concerned, H.B.M. Minister at Christiania had difficulty in obtaining official statistics regarding imports and exports after the Casement affair remained unanswered; certain it is that government assistance was denied to various consuls acting under him; whilst I, when in that country, was informed (by British authorities) I must not collect these figures, although to me and others working with me they were comparatively easy of access.

So far as Foreign Office knowledge is concerned, it is hardly a credit to the ability or even sanity of the British Legations in Scandinavia if they have denied knowledge of these colossal imports of goods into Germany, which were known to almost every inhabitant of seaport towns. If they deliberately shut their eyes to the evidence all around them, they presumably obeyed orders. One could then only wonder as to the reason for such suicidal policy.

As before mentioned, at the commencement of his speech Sir Edward Grey laid stress upon the fact that part of the stated increased import, namely, 2,000,000 barrels of flour were allowed to be exported to Belgium; whilst a little later in his speech he admitted that "She [Germany] had requisitioned the food supplies of the civil population of Poland and Belgium." Almost immediately afterwards Lord Robert Cecil strove hard to back up the Secretary for Foreign Affairs, but he could not give the House any positive assurance that the Belgian Relief distribution was absolutely independent of German control. The disposition of this is therefore obvious.

Sir Edward Grey attempted to whittle down the U.S.A. exports of wheat by stating that nearly half went to Spain, Portugal, Greece, and Malta; but he did not refer to the corn, etc., exported to Northern neutrals from Liverpool and other British ports, nor did he make any allowances for the stream of mysterious ships sailing round far northern seas (many of them choosing the passage north of Iceland), which sighted land on the north-western coast of Norway and carried their course inside neutral waters into the Baltic; which heavily-laden cargo-boats I and others in the Secret Service had watched and reported week by week and month by month with heart-rending persistency. The majority of these ships probably sailed direct to German ports, and no records of their cargoes were likely to be made, or returned from any country concerning them.

Nor did Sir Edward Grey make reference to the grain ships, which although nominally bound for Scandinavian ports, were intercepted by their owners' or consignees' agents in the Baltic, for the purpose of varying orders for their ultimate port of destination; nor to the ships which were held up in the Baltic by German war vessels and taken to German ports under circumstances calling for grave investigation. Nor did he attempt to answer the general American statistics showing that the gain in imports to northern neutral countries exceeded the German loss.

About the middle of his speech Sir Edward Grey said: "If a vessel was held up by the Fleet with suspected cargo on board, the matter was referred to the contraband committee, who decided what *part* of the cargo should go to the Prize Court."

Surely any other nation in the world at war would have arranged from the outset that the capture of a vessel *with contraband* on board *en route for the enemy*, would have meant *confiscation* of the ship and her cargo. Our exceptional and extraordinary leniency was hardly commented upon; it was certainly not satisfactorily explained.

Continuing to quote from the speech: *He would* say to neutrals that we could not give up the right to interfere with enemy trade and must maintain and press that point. *He would* ask those countries in considering our rights to apply the principles which were applied by the American Government in the war between the North and South as affected by modern conditions. *If they agreed* to it, then let them with their Chambers of Commerce and other bodies make it easier for us to distinguish between goods intended for the enemy and goods intended for themselves. *If those* neutral countries said that we were not entitled to prevent trading through, neutral countries with the enemy, *then he* (Sir E. Grey) *must say* to the neutral countries who took that line that it was a departure from neutrality. (Cheers.) But he did not think they would take that line.

What naturally strikes the reader on perusal is this: why not the words, "I had said" and "I have asked" instead of "he would say" and "he would ask" which Sir Edward Grey used in his speech? Why wait eighteen months to arrive at such a decision? Why were not these words used as soon as war was declared? Flagrant breaches arose, as Sir Edward Grey should or must have known, and continued to increase in magnitude from the autumn of 1914. Why he waited until the then date, and why he had not acted before, was not explained. In the next few grandiloquent sentences he admitted the justification and the necessity; whilst the House cheered the words, forgetting past neglected deeds.

Next he admitted that "Germany had, in effect, treated food, when she found it, as absolute contraband since the first outbreak of war."

This admission gave one much to ponder over.

On the point of a stricter blockade Sir Edward Grey suggested that "if a rigorous blockade had been established the whole world would have been against us."

Such a contingency, put into legal parlance, is too ridiculously remote for further consideration. Why did he not explain why our fleet was not allowed to limit particular imports to neutral countries to certain fixed totals per month, or *per annum?* It is unthinkable to suppose that any country would seriously threaten war in face of former well-known precedent and because such limits were imposed by a blockading fleet. More particularly so if any such affected country happened to have been one of the parties to the Treaty of the Hague, which affirmed the integrity of poor innocent, unoffending Belgium; the country which, without justification or excuse, was violated, and ravished, outraged by the barbarian Hun invaders, and which so many other countries watched aghast without attempting to help England to protect or to avenge.

Admittedly it would have been easy for us to close the Baltic and the Mediterranean. Why did we not do so? We could then have regulated to each country not at war its full and fair average annual complement of necessities plus an extra and a generous margin for contingencies. The government of each recipient country would have seen to it that its own respective countrymen reaped full benefits; leaks to the Central Powers would have automatically stopped.

What countries would such a course of action have forced into war against us?

Possibly Sweden, doubtfully Holland, remotely Denmark.

America had boasted she was "too proud to fight." She might have favoured us with a "note," but her love of trade would have been an absolute bar to the possibility of any cessation of supplies and munitions.

No other country would have demurred except Greece, and the vacillating tactics of the Greeks were but the harvest which could have been expected from the seed of "wait-and-see" diplomatic sowing. This is clearly shown by the utterances of King Tino, who said: "I fear the Germans. I do not fear the English." The Greeks have similarly expressed themselves. "We know the Germans would rob, murder, and outrage our land and our people without any hesitation. The English are quite incapable of anything of that kind."

It had been proved that Consulates in Greece had been nests of espionage and arsenals of munitions, and the Islands bases for submarine murderers; and yet their king actually sent us a protest against our movement at Salonika to assist the persecuted Serbians whom he and his country had pledged themselves to uphold and protect; a solemn treaty they had long ago undertaken, but so conveniently forgotten and lamely excused themselves out of as soon as called upon to carry it into active force.

As a general answer to the direct charges of the Press that the Foreign Office had not kept faith with the nation in doing all that could be done to make an effective blockade, as an explanation to sweep on one side the overwhelming mass of evidence relating to the extraordinary number of German agents and dealers who swarmed throughout Scandinavia and Holland, their amazing advertisements, their suddenly accumulated wealth, the balance sheets showing large profits of neutral companies dealing in Germany's requirements, the alleged wholesale dealers of imported goods so suddenly sprung up from the ranks of hotel porters, clerks, typists, adventurers, caretakers, and even charwomen and servant-girls, our own inflated home prices of necessities and commodities—Sir Edward Grey's answer to all this was: The government had lately sent Lord Faringdon to examine the position in Holland and Scandinavia and he reported that on the whole things were very satisfactory and that all was being done that could be done to prevent the enemy obtaining supplies.

Well might the fat stomachs of the *"Goulashes"*[5] extend and shake in merriment when they read these comfortable words!

Sir Edward Grey concluded his speech with this stirring peroration: The whole of our resources were engaged in this war, and our maximum effort was at the disposal of our Allies in carrying on this conflict. With them we should see it through to the end and we should slacken no effort in the common cause. We should exert all our efforts to put the maximum possible pressure upon the enemy, and part of that pressure must be doing the most we could to prevent supplies going to or from the enemy, *using the navy to its full power* . . . and in common with our Allies sparing nothing, whether it were military, naval, or financial effort, which this country could afford, to see the thing through with them to the end.

In the loud cheering with which the House of Commons received the speech no thought was given to the famous words of Napoleon: *"Put no faith in talk which is not borne out by action"*; whilst future events went to show that Napoleon truly forecasted England's present-day weakness when he wrote:

Feebleness in its government is the most frightful calamity that can befall a nation.

Contrast Sir Edward Grey's eloquent words and diplomatic evasiveness upon the treatment of neutrals with the plain, outspoken, thoroughly English opinion of Lord Fisher, who is credited with having said:

There are no such things as neutral powers. Powers are either with us or against us. If they are friendly they will put up with some inconvenience; if they are unfriendly they will squeal. Let them squeal.

---

5. *Goulashe* is the name given to illicit traders with Germany.

Had we acted throughout on this dictum the war would most probably have been over well inside of eighteen months. Men of the calibre of this grand old Sea Lord, whose farsight, foresight, and second sight have endeared him to the nation and made him unique and incomparable, would soon have made short work of the war. Yet they were not wanted by the then present-day party-system government. They were much too blunt and honest and energetically active.

The nation will also remember that when Lord Kitchener of Khartoum returned from the East in the early days of the then present government, it had no use for his invaluable services. He was actually permitted to accept a directorship of one of our poorest railway companies on the south coast for want of a better occupation.[6] But the Press and the public soon brought the government to book, as it seemingly had to do in every matter of real national importance.

The government tried to keep Lord Haldane installed at the War Office, but the Press would have none of it. It also insisted on K. of K. being placed in his proper place and kept there. More's the pity that he was not given a free hand to do as he liked.

The Press also clamoured for Lord Fisher as First Lord of the Admiralty. The nation knows how he was treated. A captain in the navy aptly described the unwanted and slighted admiral expert in *John Bull*, February, 1916, as follows:

> Lord John Fisher is today our second Nelson—a diplomatist among diplomats and a strategist unequalled in our history. What has Lord John Fisher done?
>
> He scrapped 162 obsolete warships which were rotting in harbour at great expense—for which the government tried to reprimand him.
>
> He introduced the water-tube boilers, which, as every engineer and seaman knows, raise a full head of steam in twenty minutes, instead of twenty hours, as formerly.
>
> He introduced the steam turbine, which was adopted by every nation.
>
> He introduced oil fuel into the navy, thus making destroyers capable of steaming further, a great benefit being the almost total absence of smoke. He also applied it to battleships and other large craft.

---

6. Books on the life of Lord Kitchener of Khartoum do not dwell upon this unpardonable fact. Some discreetly omit to mention it.

He introduced the Dreadnought, the bulwark of Britain, and the ship that baffled the German nation and made the Kiel Canal useless for years. The oil-burning, water-tubed destroyer, and the *Queen Elizabeth*—the Secret Service ship and the monitor—all emanated from his brain.

He introduced the battle-cruiser, against the will of a timorous government whose cry was ever, 'Cut down armaments,' 'Cut down the army and navy.' Had Fisher listened, the Germans would today have outraged our wives and crucified our children.

He planned the Falkland Islands battle, and sent the Secret Service ships to chase the German submarines out of the Channel.

He fought hard against the Dardanelles expedition.

He was Sea Lord when we sank the *Blucher*, the German destroyers in the North Sea, the German Fleet at the Falklands.

He is a great man, who seems never to have made a mistake.

Whilst Sir Edward Grey was giving his explanations in the House of Commons, Lord Devonport was busy in another place. He is one of our shrewdest and most experienced business men. As Chairman of the Port of London Authority and former Parliamentary Secretary of the Board of Trade, he would not be likely to go into figures lightly.

He had given notice to ask the government for its official figures of Holland's imports of ore (metal) during 1915.

The Duke of Devonshire replied that the figures provided him were only 650,000 tons. It was admitted that Holland had virtually no smelting plant, nor coal to feed it if it had, and the Government was virtually bound to confess that at least this amount of contraband had mostly gone straight through to Germany.

Lord Devonport clearly stated that in reality one and a half million tons of metal ore had been imported; whilst he produced statistics showing the name of every ship, the date of entry, the place from which the cargo came, the quantity and character of the ore carried, and the agents to whom each was consigned.

To summarise shortly the total shipments for the period named by Lord Devonport, August, 1914, to January 15, 1916, it appears that 298 ships carrying 1,414,311 tons of metal ore entered Rotterdam. The countries from which the ore came included Sweden, Norway, Spain, Algeria, Russia, and Great Britain. The totals shown monthly are as follows:

ORE CARGOES.

1914	No. of Ships	Tons
August	38	174,162
September	11	61,679
October	10	47,900
November	8	37,300
December	14	63,900
		Total 384,941

1915		
January	17	76,200
February	17	79,700
March	13	85,800
April	22	123,800
May	17	68,100
June	21	95,350
July	21	89,150
August	19	82,300
September	19	92,400
October	22	105,270
November	13	59,700
December	12	48,300
		Total 1,006,070

1916		
To January 15	4	23,300
		Grand total 1,414,311

Two hundred and fifty eight ships carried 1,321,456 tons of iron ore; 25 ships carried 41,830 tons of zinc ore, the remainder taking copper ore, pyrites, nickel, manganese, and calamine.

Lord Devonport added:

> What has come of the much-vaunted order in Council declaring that no goods should either enter or leave Germany? What is the ultimate destination of these cargoes? There is no concealment about the matter. Every captain knows exactly. There are no facilities in Holland for converting ore into pig-iron; not a single blast-furnace, and no coal to feed it even if there were.

The cargoes are transhipped into barges and carried up the Rhine to a place in easy communication with Essen, where Krupp's works are situated. Sweden is the main source of the supply. *It is astounding to me that the British Government should sit still while these ores are sent to the enemy* from mines which are virtually the property of the Swedish Government.

Great though *the imports of ore into Rotterdam have been, they are insignificant compared with the importations in German ports* in the Baltic Sea and the North Sea—Lübeck, Stettin, Swinemunde, Emden and others. *From May 1st to December 31st, 1915, the total of those imports were 556 cargoes and 2,089,000 tons of ore.* The question is going to become critical for, *though the country has been tolerant and long-enduring, things have not gone too well.* The sheet-anchor of the situation is the British Fleet.

Fairplay, the shipping paper says:

The figures sufficiently indicate the absurdity of supposing that the Netherlands Overseas Trust or any similar artificial would-be barrier as at present constituted can, in fact, prevent the enemy from receiving vital supplies of raw or manufactured material.

Nineteen days after the delivery of Sir Edward Grey's "blockade" speech in the House of Commons Mr. T. Gibson Bowles, speaking at a great City demonstration in London on February 14th, 1917, under Lord Devonport as chairman and convened for the purpose of protesting against hampering our navy, said: "Since the war began Sir Edward Grey had hampered, shackled, and strangled the fleet in the performance of its duties." Whilst Lord Charles Beresford wrote to the chairman: "If the government had used our sea power as they were legally entitled to do at the commencement of the war, by instituting an effective blockade and making all goods entering Germany absolute contraband, the war would now be over."

Lord Aberconway added:

The matter is far too serious to be trifled with any longer; my personal knowledge intensifies my conviction.

The government having attempted to evade any direct answer to the startling figures and accusations of the *Daily Mail* disclosing the get-rich-quick method of the Scandinavian *Goulashes,* Lord Northcliffe sent a Special Commissioner to Holland, and published the result of his investigations in February, 1916. It showed a repetition of the sordid Scandinavian fiasco, a further proof that the so-called blockade was leaking in every seam.

To enumerate the masses of statistics would be wearisome. It is sufficient for present purposes to quote a few extracts.

Cocoa Beans.—Of the 528 tons imported into Holland in 1916 Germany received the whole.

Cocoa Butter.—England could only obtain half what she had in 1913, whereas Germany obtained five times as much.

Cocoa Powder.—England obtained half 1913 supplies, whereas Germany obtained approximately ten times as much.

Cocoa in Blocks.—In 1913 Germany imported 4 tons from Holland, Belgium none at all; whereas in 1915 no less than 565 tons were exported from Holland into these two countries, all for German use.

Copra.—In 1913 Germany obtained 26,728 tons of copra from Holland, whereas in 1915 the amount rose to the amazing total of 106,613 tons.

It would appear from the figures that England was indirectly supplying Germany *inter alia* with margarine.

In 1913 Great Britain sent to Holland 1,914 tons of the raw material, as against 6,166 tons in 1916. Germany sent no raw material to Holland during either of the years quoted.

In 1913 Holland exported 308 tons of margarine to Belgium and to Germany 401 tons.

In 1915 Holland exported 7,616 tons to Belgium and 21,721 tons to Germany. *Totals of 709 tons suddenly jumped to 29,237.*

Coffee.—Before the war Germany had always exported coffee to Holland in thousands of tons. During 1915 she sent in none at all, but she imported from Holland 129,968 tons; whilst 32,822 tons in addition were sent to Belgium for German use as against a prior yearly average import of about 8,000 tons.

N.B.—England, which during 1911, 1912 and 1918 exported a yearly average of 6,720 tons of coffee to Holland, suddenly increased her exports to this country to 15,672 tons in 1914 and to 28,425 tons in 1915.

In March, 1916, Brazil was seizing German ships because she

could not collect a trifle of about £4,000,000 owing to her for coffee by the Fatherland.

Cotton.—In the three years before the war England exported an average of 7,808 tons of unspun cotton to Holland, but in 1915 she sent no less than 22,856 tons. Germany, which *exported* an average of 33,975 tons before the war, actually *imported* from Holland direct in 1915 no less than 38,750 tons.

The Commercial Treaty of the Rhine, cunningly made by the clever Teutons before war was declared, prevented the Dutch from even examining any cargoes which were thereunder arranged for direct shipment into Germany; whilst from the very first the workings of the much-boasted arrangement made by our Foreign Office with the Netherlands Overseas Trust *piled up evidence, week by week and month by month, that our so-called blockade was an absolute farce.*

In the famous "Kim" case before the Prize Court, the President, Sir Samuel Evans, made the law quite clear. Figures were placed before the court to show that the average monthly quantities of lard exported from the United States to all Scandinavia in October and November, 1913, was 427,428 lbs. Within three months of the outbreak of war one company was shipping to Copenhagen alone *considerably over twenty times that quantity in three weeks.*

When it might have been thought that the public had forgotten this complete and overwhelming evidence, Lord Emmott, speaking on behalf of the government, told the House of Lords that "an abnormal supply to a country is not sufficient reason to stop a cargo." Here was a government spokesman absolutely contradicting the Prize Court Judge—another unwarrantable interference with the rights of Democracy.

On February 22nd and 23rd, 1916, the House of Lords debated an important motion ably advocated by Lord Sydenham.

That in conformity with the principle of international law and the legitimate rights of neutrals, more effective use could be made of the Allied Fleets in preventing supplies, directly conducing to the prolongation of the war, from reaching the enemy.

Lord Lansdowne, Lord Emmott and the Marquis of Crewe spoke in defence of the government, but they brought forward no direct proof to upset the alarming statistics which had been quoted against them.

Some figures, however, were given to show that during the last past month a greater activity had been caused, in consequence of which there had been some diminution of imports to Germany; whilst it was further promised that as an attempt to concentrate the general supervision of the War Trades Committee the work should be placed in the hands of one minister, Lord Robert Cecil, who would be given Cabinet rank.

That Lord Robert Cecil is a man of great ability no one doubts. The stock he springs from is pedigree so far as politics are concerned, but he is a lawyer. For many years past this country has suffered greatly from a glut of lawyer politicians, particularly in the unwieldy Cabinet of twenty-three members. The nation remembered only too well how this noble lord had fought so strenuously and so persistently against cotton being made contraband. His appointment therefore to this post of vital importance, which could influence, affect and control the duration of the war to such a great extent, was strongly objected to by the public at large. Neither the act nor the man carried an iota of confidence.

To have seriously attacked the government and put it out of office would have raised a general outcry. It was considered disloyal even to criticise. "Wait and see" was the only policy Englishmen were permitted to contemplate. Meanwhile this farce, this weakness or this cowardly inaction, whichever epithet is most appropriate to it, was permitted to drift its course. Gleefully the Germans continued to annex the rich cod and herring harvests of Norway, nor did they cavil at the super-price. Gleefully the Norwegian fishermen continued to rake in the deluge of gold, the like of which had never been known within the memory of man.

Gleefully the *Goulashes* of Scandinavia continued to increase and multiply, whilst they prospered and waxed exceedingly rich, in spite of a few widely-proclaimed spectacular fines and confiscations. The advertisements in the papers of neutral countries offering to supply necessities direct into Germany also continued and spread, like the proverbial grain of mustard-seed, until the very mails were glutted with contraband.

One of these multitudinous advertisements is given as an example. It is from the *Fatherland*, March 29th, 1916, the subsidised German-American weekly published in New York:

FOOD TO GERMANY.
Delivered through my Firm at Stuttgart.

Can condensed milk	30 cents
Fruit marmalades, per pound	35 cents
Fifty cigars	$2.00
One pound of rice	40 cents
One pound of bacon	75 cents
One pound of lard	70 cents
One pound of cheese	5 cents
100 cigarettes	$1.70

Also dried fruits, beans, peas, etc. Invigorating wines for sick and wounded.

Information and price lists on request.

E. R. Trieler, Dept. F. 35-37, West 23rd St., New York.

No wonder Lord Grimthorpe, after quoting an influential Frenchman's opinion that "England had muscles of iron but brains of wool," argued that, instead of bringing more lawyers into the management, the country would be much more satisfied if the Ministry of Blockade was put into the hands of a fighting man like Lord Beresford or Lord Fisher.

Those in the Secret Service knew that since the outbreak of war Germans had employed only soldiers and sailors to manage it; and that all their lawyers and civilian politicians had been relegated to a back seat until further notice; furthermore, that only proved ability counted. Patronage, length of service, hereditary and social altitude carried no weight whatsoever at Berlin; whilst the capacity for organisation and thoroughness which Germany exhibited had astonished the world.

Yea, verily, it is a true saying that "*Britishers are the greatest muddlers on earth.*" It seems to be their grim bulldog pertinacity only which pulls them through, and their individuality which gives them the stamina to stay.

As the winter turned to spring and the spring to summer other terrible disasters arose which diverted the attention of the nation from the bogus blockade. Mr. Asquith's "one bright spot," the Mesopotamia expedition, turned to gall and wormwood; the terrible Gallipoli fiasco shocked the nation; the pampered Irish rebels appeared in their true colours; the careless sacrifice of a man whom many believed to be one of the noblest and greatest of army chiefs (K. of K.) this world had ever seen, paralysed and numbed every English-speaking land; whilst

251

German spies were still permitted to press their deadly fingerprints upon our national throat owing to our unbelievable weakness in neglecting to intern all aliens of belligerent nationality.

Meanwhile the Press continued to growl and to publish statistics from time to time to prove that the so-called blockade was still as great a farce as ever; furthermore, it was absolutely and utterly ineffective to stop supplies going to Germany. whilst ministers and members of the government still had the audacity to refer to its alleged effectiveness and to call attention to the unenviable plight of starving Germany.

All true Englishmen should gratefully thank God that we had at least one man amongst the few real men who had the courage of his convictions, namely, Mr. W. M. Hughes, the Australian Premier. He, during his all too short sojourn in the Motherland, rendered noble, great and patriotic service. He called with an unmistakable voice at the British Imperial Council of Commerce in London, on June 8th, 1916, for a real blockade. He said: "Do you realise the tremendous pile of treasure we are pouring out in this contest? Do you think that any nation, no matter how wealthy, can stand indefinitely such a strain on its wealth? It cannot. We are living like spendthrifts, upon our capital. There must come a day when we can no longer live upon it. I want to emphasise the point that we cannot continue this struggle indefinitely. The blockade is one great weapon at our disposal—one of the most effective weapons for shortening the duration of the war—by increasing the pressure upon the enemy. *If the blockade had been effective earlier it would have curtailed the war.*

We now have the power, as Mr. Balfour said, to make that blockade still more effective, and whatever stands in the way of making that blockade effective against the enemy and against neutrals must be swept aside. *We have to choose between offending neutrals and inviting defeat.* We have to choose between pouring out our treasure and losing the lives of thousands of our best and bravest. Let us hedge around this nation (Germany) a ring of triple steel through which nothing shall pass. I have been told there are still things going out of Britain to Germany. I am told the reason given is that we are getting German money in exchange. That argument does not appeal to me. I would not tolerate the practice for another hour. I would treat those who engage in it as I would treat any other traitor to his country. Therefore insist upon the blockade being such a blockade as will compel our enemies to recognise the power of Britain and the Allies."

Lord Hugh Cecil, the Blockade Minister, does not appear to have been amongst those present at this memorable gathering. More's the pity of it! Had he been perhaps he might have had his eyes opened at last to the folly and inefficiency of his previous policy and foolishly expressed fallacies.

To the probable relief and secret joy of the Cabinet, and to the irreparable loss of the nation, Mr. W. M. Hughes was in the early summer of 1916 compelled to return to his duties in Australia. After his regretted departure the so-called blockade continued to leak, as is proved by the following facts and figures which found their way into the Press in spite of all the hushing-up processes of the weaklings in power. Can it be wondered at that many thousands of astounded Englishmen were actually beginning to believe that some of our prominent Ministers did not want to win the war because they were either indirectly interested financially in Teutonic enterprise, or they were pro-German from other mysteriously concealed causes? What other possible reasons seemed arguable in view of their extraordinary actions, their leaving undone those things which they ought to have done, and their doing those things which they ought not to have done?

How German production steadily revived from the shock of the first year of the war is shown by the following table of pig-iron output in tons published in the *Berliner Tageblatt*:

	1914	1915	1916
January	1,566,505	874,133	1,077,046
February	1,445,511	803,623	1,033,683
March	1,602,714	938,438	1,114,194
April	1,534,429	938,679	1,073,706
May	1,607,211	985,968	
June	1,531,826	993,496	
July	1,561,944	1,047,503	
August	587,661	1,050,610	
September	580,087	1,033,078	
October	734,841	1,076,343	
November	788,956	1,019,122	
December	853,881	1,029,144	

Asking the Prize Court on June 5th, 1916, to condemn the Swedish vessel *Hakan*, of Gothenburg, with her cargo of 3,238 barrels of salted herrings, the Attorney-General, Sir F. E. Smith, alleged that the fish were intended for Germany. Writing from Lübeck to Gottfried Friedrichs, fishmongers, of Altona, said the attorney-general, a member of the firm of Witte & Co., their forwarding agents, said: "We have prohibited the export of herrings from Norway, but our firm has obtained a licence to export 50,000 tons. We hope to sell 75,000 tons this winter, so there is plenty of work."

Sir Samuel Evans: How many herrings in 50,000 tons?

The Attorney-General: My assistants and confederates inform me that there are about 450,000,000 herrings. It is a conservative estimate.

These are official figures published by the Netherlands Statistical Department on May 20th, 1916; such great assistance rendered to Germany is more serious owing to the fact that Germany's gain has been our loss.

FOODSTUFFS SENT FROM HOLLAND, IN TONS.
(Covering the months January to April.)

	1914	1916
Eggs—		
To Germany	3,101	11,825
To Britain	2,733	557
Fish—		
To Germany	21,337	29,378
To Belgium	—	—
Meat—		
To Germany	4,156	30,621
To Britain	25,460	555
Potato Flour and its products—		
To Germany	13,991	43,862
To Britain	8,831	5,620
Coffee—		
To Germany	17,429	39,694
Cocoa Powder—		
To Germany	598	3,302
To Britain	2,155	1,437
Butter—		
To Germany	4,010	10,237
To Britain	1,387	33
Cheese—		
To Germany	4,120	25,437
To Britain	5,624	407

One has only to cast the eye down these figures to see what Holland means as a *depôt* for Germany's food.

During the first four months of 1916 Holland had imported by consent of Great Britain 432,702 tons of cereals. No less than 283,792 tons were re-exported from Holland and consequently did not go into home consumption there; 272,630 tons of this went over into Belgium. It is important, also, to note that of the cereals imported 102,722 tons of maize were included in the total. Most of this maize was used for fattening pigs, which were eventually slaughtered and sent to Germany.

This abundance of pig food allowed by us to be consumed by the Dutch pigs in fact enabled the Dutch to fatten the immense supply which they sent over to Germany. The meat figures given above must be read in the light of this fact.

The more we sent into Holland for her home supply, the more she could release of her home-grown products to the enemy. As between Holland, Germany and ourselves, we lost tremendously. Germany and Holland were of immense assistance to each other, at our expense.

A weekly circular of the London Rice Brokers' Association shows the following striking contrasts in exports from London:

EXPORTS OF RICE FROM LONDON.

	January 1st to May 27th, 1915. Cwt	Same period, 1916. Cwt
To Holland	247,869	905,078 (say 45,000 tons)
To France	22,607	430

Thus the export to Holland had greatly increased and the supply to France had dwindled almost out of existence. During the single week ended May 27th, 1916, 224,252 cwt. (say 11,212 tons) were shipped to Holland from London.

On June 2nd, 1916, the London Press wailed over the enormous supplies of grain entering Germany through Roumania, which she was enabled to purchase by exchanging goods made from the raw material permitted so kindly by England to leak through the blockade.

In April one consignment of 1,500,000 eggs passed from Holland to Germany in two days only. Indeed, so vast was the drain of Germany upon Holland that the Dutch people complained in June that they were being stinted of their proper food supply. Norway continued to supply nickel, fish, copper, fish oils, and many other things, although

England at last awoke in the spring of 1916 to the advisability of purchasing part of the Norwegian fish harvests. In this deal, however, her lawyer Government had not the sense to consult the best export fish merchants, who are essentially business men. She went to work in the usual amateurish way, which spelt reckless waste and extravagance; paying £5 to £7 per package for what could have been previously arranged for at about 10s. or less.

The English Government throughout the war had the Norwegian fish trade absolutely in its own hands. Yet one of its own consuls supplied Germany wholesale in 1914; it supplied coal and salt to assist the Germans to garner in practically the entire harvest of 1915; and it was not until the middle of 1916 that some English sluggard in power woke up and paid through the nose for what could have been purchased practically on our own terms.

Sweden continued to supply almost everything and anything that Germany required, openly when possible, smuggled in by all manner of tricks and dodges should any difficulty of transport be likely to arise.

At the end of June, 1916, a Liverpool merchant contributed some remarkable facts and figures to the *Liverpool Courier*, proving that England was helping Germany to obtain what she required at the expense of the home consumer in England. The net result of his arguments was that our shipping and home ports were congested for several months by Dutch imports through private arrangements between Holland and England, whereby Holland was supplying Germany to a colossal extent and frustrating the supreme purposes of the so-called blockade. In conclusion, he plaintively besought the nation to adopt the strangle-knot of Mr. Hughes by so tightening the blockade that Holland would no longer be able to provide the Germans with food for her peoples and materials for the manufacture of guns and explosives to slaughter our sons.

The tables of figures quoted showed in glaring contrast the usual enormous increases of imports upon pre-war returns which the British reader had grown quite accustomed to see. To give but one example: the shipments of margarine from Holland to Germany during 1915 showed thirteen times greater, etc.

On July 20th, 1916, during the hearing of a case in the London Prize Court relating to the S.S. *Maracus*, the solicitor-general (Sir George Cave) read an affidavit by Mr. John Hargreaves, provision merchant, Liverpool, stating that in 1915 the price of lard in Germany was

100s. per cwt., as against 50s. in Liverpool. At that price there was an inducement to American shippers to risk shipment to Germany, and to German buyers to open credits in New York. Should the American shipper succeed in getting two shipments through, he might well make a large profit which would amply compensate him for the loss of one shipment, apart from his chance of recovering compensation from the British Government.

An affidavit by Mr. R. M. Greenwood, assistant treasury solicitor, showed the imports of foodstuffs into Copenhagen during the first six months of 1915 as compared with the similar period of 1913. The figures were:

	1913	1915.
Pork	948,400 lbs.	15,062,060 lbs.
Lard	3,999,700 lbs.	23,458,720 lbs.
Oleo	2,509,900 lbs.	8,775,750 lbs.

The evidence in the case proved that the ship was bound for Germany and her captain had been promised a bonus of £200 if the goods reached their destination.

On June 28th, 1916, Lord Robert Cecil in reply to a question in the House of Commons, said:

"As the result of the Paris Conference His Majesty would be advised to issue an Order in Council withdrawing the successive Orders which had been issued adopting with modifications the Declaration of London, and a general statement should also be issued explaining the reason for this step."

Amidst the loud cheering which followed a voice was heard to exclaim, "After twenty-three months!"

How Potsdam must have hugged itself with delight in 1909, 1910, and 1911 at the absurdly childish simplicity exhibited by the English Liberal Government in nullifying all its geographical advantages by accepting such a one-sided code of sea-law which gave Germany the right to stop food *en route* to British ports, while forbidding Great Britain to stop food *en route* to Germany, and whilst in force rendered any effective blockade of Germany impossible.

But what powerful mysterious motives prompted its re-adoption after it had been rejected by the House of Lords? Again on August 20th, 1914, why did the Cabinet illegally put it into force with modifications—though Article 65 thereof states that the code is indivisible?

What was held in the unseen hand and to whom was it extended?

On August 2nd, 1916, M. Clemenceau published an article in *L'Homme Enchaîné*, headed, "A Fresh Assassination," in which, after commenting upon the brutal murders of Nurse Cavell and the innocent Captain Fryatt, he wrote:

> It is time that Great Britain made the weight of her will felt, especially as regards the strict application of the blockade, which, has too often been relaxed out of a desire not to arouse an unpleasant quarrel with Washington. It is time to end these half-measures. We must make up our minds as to what to do, and do it.

On July 6th, 1916, Lord Robert Cecil admitted in the House of Commons, in reply, what was tantamount to a confession that the British Fleet employed in the blockade was still muzzled, being bound down by red-tape precedents and strict London directions.

On July 9th he was further compelled to confess that 10,708 tons of lard had been permitted to enter Belgium, as well as about 2,000 tons of tallow and other fats. Nominally this was fathered by the Neutral Relief Committee, but in reality it was just so much more assistance granted to the enemy.

FAT (FOR EXPLOSIVES) IN TONS

In the early part of 1914 Germany exported lard to Holland, but this ceased on the eve of war. Great Britain, on the other hand, for some extraordinary and unintelligible reason, permitted her exports to Holland to increase. These are the figures:

	From Germany	From Great Britain.
1914	861	660
1915	Nil	6,591
1916	Nil	12,273

BARLEY FOR MALT

In 1916 Great Britain exported to Holland about fifteen times more barley than normal pre-war exports, so diminishing our home supplies that the British working-man was deprived of his national beverage through shortage and prohibitive prices. Whisky also was similarly affected.

TOBACCO

The Christian spirit of *"love your neighbours and your enemies better than yourselves"* had apparently no limits with the British Government. Their loyal and hard-suffering subjects were deprived of a full supply of the soothing weed on the excuse of economising freight room, but no effort seems to have been made to curtail *Dutch supplies*, which were *thirty-five times greater than the pre-war exports.*

In 1914 Hamburg and Bremen exported 4,544 tons of tobacco to Holland, but in 1915 and 1916 neither of these towns exported any at all.

The amounts exported by Holland from January to June in tons were as follows:

	To Great Britain	To Germany.
1914	1,611	31,891
1915	1,672	54,456
1916	923	96,931

The figures published by the German Steel and Iron Manufacturers Association for the first six months of each respective year show the following outputs, thanks to Sir Francis Oppenheimer's previous Netherlands Overseas Trust, which permits iron ore in millions of tons to proceed direct to Krupps' and other blast furnaces in Germany without let or hindrance to be used against us.

PIG IRON

	Tons
1915	5,530,000
1916	6,497,000

STEEL

1915	6,187,000
1916	7,756,000

The *Lokal Anzeiger,* July 28th, 1916, remarked: "These figures constitute a most gratifying state of affairs in respect of the *requirements of the German Armies.*" No wonder the captured German officer remarked: "You English will always be fools, whilst we Germans can never be gentlemen"!

In August[7] a Mr. E. Bell, of 12, Yarborough Road, Lincoln, wrote to the Press as follows:

The talk of tightening the blockade of Germany is rather futile in face of the following Board of Trade figures referring to cotton yarn exported from the United Kingdom to the following neutral countries:

---

7. *Daily Mail,* August 16th, 1916.

JUNE	Sweden	Norway	Denmark	Holland	Switzerland
1914	108,900	218,700	106,400	3,220,800	722,600
1915	260,800	348,300	204,700	4,493,300	1,788,800
1916	279,200	508,200	598,400	7,539,800	1,304,100

Germany is obviously getting the surplus.

The values[8] of New York exports taken for the week July 30th to August 5th are equally startling:

New York to	1915 $\pounds$	1916 $\pounds$
Norway	1,884	137,176
Holland	713	717,601
Holland and Scandinavia	123,327	970,255

On August 26th, 1916, an agreement was signed between the Dutch Fishing Association and the British Government regarding the release of some 120 to 150 Dutch fishing-boats laid up in Scottish ports, whereby not more than 20 *per cent.* of their catch shall be permitted to go to Germany. Of the remainder twenty *per cent.* was to be retained for home consumption, and sixty *per cent.* sold to neutral countries. On each barrel of this sixty *per cent.* the good, kind, benevolent British Government agreed to pay a subsidy of 30s. to the Dutch boat-owners.

Now the D.F.A. owned about 850 vessels and 1,000 barrels is a good average season's catch!

In addition to this arrangement the British Government agreed to pay full compensation for their loss of part of the season, to be calculated on the basis of the returns on an average season. They also agreed to pay for any damage which might have happened to the interned boats.[9]

One wonders what British fishermen whose vessels have been commandeered had to say when they were informed of these facts.

The *Hamburger Nachrichten* of August 23rd, 1916, published a telegram from its Hague correspondent declaring that the semi-official German Central Purchase Company was seizing Dutch food in enormous quantities; that local merchants were in a state of alarm and threatening government interference; and their correspondent defiantly stated: "The Netherlands Government will hardly dream of in-

---

8. *Evening News*, August 24th, 1916.
9. *Daily Mail*, August 28th, 1916.

terfering with the activity of the Dutch Bureau of the German Central Purchase Company, the operations of which are assuming larger and larger dimensions."

To add further proof of the utter futility and hollow sham of the alleged blockade safeguards, namely, the Danish Association Agreement and the Netherlands Overseas Trust, Sir Henry Dalziel informed the House of Commons on August 22nd, 1916, that in June Denmark imported *over ten times as much cotton yarn* as in June, 1913, and that in the first six months of the present year Holland exported to Germany *over twenty times as much butter* as in the first six months of 1914, nearly *eight times as much cheese,* and *over seven times as much meat.*

The unfortunate Lord Robert Cecil in mid-August gave quite a eulogistic report upon his stewardship as Blockade Minister, which was immediately followed by the arrival from New York of the Custom House returns showing that during the week ending August 5th the value of the exports to Holland, Norway, Sweden, and Denmark was *eight times* as *great* as in the corresponding week of the preceding year. To Holland the exports had increased in value *a thousandfold* and to Norway *seventy-fivefold.*

On September 1st, 1916, the government, through the War Trade Statistical Department, issued to the Press an official Memorandum on the question of the efficacy of the British blockade.

It barely amounted to the proverbial half-truth, and was pitiably feeble. It was more than unfortunate that the government should rush into print just before the United States export figures were due for publication—only a week later.

These latter reliable statistics showed an extraordinary state of affairs:

EXPORTS FROM U.S.A.

	1914. £	1915. £	1916. £
To Norway	1,813,400	7,815,000	10,735,600
„ Sweden	2,928,800	15,654,800	10,387,800
„ Denmark	3,134,000	15,964,800	11,132,400
„ Holland	22,443,200	28,653,400	19,852,600
„ Switzerland	204,000	547,200	1,631,200

The *Telegraaf*, Amsterdam's leading journal, on September 11th, 1916, quoted governmental statistics to account for the excessive rise in price of her home products, concluding by the statement that "Holland has sold her livelihood for greater war profits"; whilst all the Dutch Press seemed to deplore mildly the vast and unmanageable manner in which the smuggling of goods over the German frontier was permitted to continue.

The figures for meat, cheese, eggs, vegetables, and butter showed an average *increased export of seventy-five per cent.* on preceding years. Practically every ounce went to Germany or to territory under her rule.

On September 12th, 1916, Reuter's representative at the Hague was able to announce that: "The Dutch Overseas Trust had obtained the release of 420 tons of Kapok, Java cotton, and had also succeeded in removing the difficulties in the way of the importation of cocoa-beans."

Such paragraphs as the above could be found repeatedly by anyone who chose to search the Press. No wonder the smouldering wrath of the long-suffering British public became fanned to a flame and its confidence in its so-called representative ministers correspondingly decreased.

On September 9th, 1916, the Foreign Office issued a notice that no further export licenses or further facilities would be given by H.M.G. for the importation of certain specified commodities until further notice. The list embraced scores of foods, but, in fact, was merely another patch to the very ragged mantle covering the so-called blockade.

On September 12th, 1916, the War Trade Statistical Department made another feeble attempt in public to refute the statistics quoted by the Press. It set out specious and plausible arguments why general conclusions should be drawn in a light more favourable to our interests. It gave no denials nor suggested that the figures quoted were not correct. It was a fretful official apology, a tacit admission of weakness and inefficiency.

A casual remark was made by a really able German in the Wilhelmstrasse on English policy in regard to Germany, to Mr. D. T. Curtin, as reported by him in the *Times*, October 21st, 1916.

He said to me:
'When the war began we thought it would be a fight between the German Army and the British Navy. That was the cause of the outbreak of German anger against England on August 4th,

1914. As time went on we found that the English Government drew the teeth of its navy and enabled us to get in through the then so-called blockade supplies of cotton, copper, lubricating oil, wool' (here he named some twenty commodities) 'in a sufficiency that will last us many long months yet. How different would have been our position today if the British Navy had controlled the blockade as we had every reason to fear it would! We can and will hold out for a long time, thanks to their blunders.'

Blockade policy, prisoner policy, enemy trade control, the Zeppelin reprisal policy—all these are puzzles to the rulers of Germany. All are taken as part and parcel of their belief of your desire to curry favour with them and your fear of their after-the-war trade struggle.

The average German holds similar views as to America's fear of the *Kaiser's* army and navy after the war. They frankly tell us that it will be our turn next.

On October 25th, 1916, Mr. D. T. Curtin explained in the *Times* how, when he was in Germany, a neutral and pro-Ally resident of a certain port in Germany with whom he discussed things took him for a walk and showed him the quays. There were not hundreds, but thousands of barrels of fats. "It almost makes me weep," he said, "to know that every one of these barrels lengthens the war and destroys the lives of gallant soldiers and their officers." And apart from the public evasions of the blockade is the secret smuggling—difficult to deal with.

A day or so previously Mr. Curtin had written:

Every bar of chocolate entering Germany prolongs the war, which I know from my own personal necessities. The Allies and the government should realise the great value of the utmost pressure of the blockade.

It was not until December, 1916, that the rising tide of public feeling threatened to burst the banks of reasonable control.

On the first day of that month a crowded meeting of City business men was held in the Cannon Street Hotel under the presidency of Lord Leith of Fyvie to protest against the slackness of the government and terrible blunders which were far too serious to openly discuss; in particular to insist that "the British Navy be set free to exercise to the full all its lawful sea powers." Startling disclosures were made, and the government,

263

which had twice restored itself after its legal expiration, was characterised as worn-out and stale, unable to make peace any more than it was able to make war; sentiments which were unanimously acclaimed.

Almost the entire British Press echoed this condemnation, and the Haldane group, recognising that discretion was the better part, awoke at last from its delusions of the value placed by the nation upon their personal services, and after a few feeble remonstrances retired in favour of a new Cabinet. "Wait and see" was compelled to give place to "Do it now."

Mr. Asquith the Unready, Lord Grey of Falloden, the Irresolute, Lord Haldane, the friend of the *Kaiser,* and the Simonite group of backers, who for fifteen unlucky years had so grievously and disastrously led the country astray; who had cut down armaments, hoodwinked the nation, and when war was declared held back conscription, muzzled the Fleet and were too late for everything, were at last fallen from doing further mischief, and the nation breathed its prayers of thankfulness.

Of the late Prime Minister (Mr. Asquith) one able editor wrote:

Never before in all our history have such opportunities been given. He had no opposition; the nation was solid; the Empire was behind him. No country has ever given any leader such devotion and none has ever seen its devotion so carelessly wasted. Declaring he would 'stick at nothing,' he stuck at everything, and moved only when he was pushed.[10]

What Germany thought of the change is reflected in an extract from its Press when it first heard of the resignation of Mr. David Lloyd George from the War Office, and it was under the belief that the Haldane group had triumphed over him.

The Bavarian *Courier,* December 5th, 1916, said:

This is a terrible disaster for the war party in England.

Whilst the Leipzig *Tageblatt* said:

The British people have doubtless had enough of this war agitator. His fall from power brings nearer an honourable peace for Germany.

Within a few days of Mr. Lloyd George being created Prime Minister of England the *Kaiser* was seeking peace. *Res ipsa loquitur.*

---

10. *Daily Mail* leading article, December 6th, 1916.

★★★★★★

What has been given is merely a rough and very deficient *resumé* of England's sham blockade, which was permitted to muddle along its costly, tragic, and fatal course until the Americans joined the Allies in their fight for freedom and the rights of small nations. Washington at once swept aside maudlin sentiment by its practical common sense, get-right-there-quick decisions.

The nation's relief cannot be expressed in words.

Was it to be wondered at that from the soul of the Motherland prayers had so long and so often ascended?

Oh, for a man of the old, old Viking blood to lead and direct the battle in place of those poor craven lawyer politicians in the Cabinet of the never-to-be-forgotten twenty-three!

Indeed, this was the darkest hour before the dawn.

The autumn of 1916 saw the advent of the magic of the Wizard from Wales. To him all honour is due.

For some years prior to the war he had been perhaps the most hated man England had ever known. He had helped to minimise the army, the navy, and the House of Lords; he had led people to believe it was almost a crime to own land; he had descended to the lowest levels of vulgar abuse regarding our most sacred traditions; he had helped rob the Church in his native land; he had become despised by the noblest and best of his fellow-countrymen. His sole ambition, apparently, had been to gain the popularity of the masses—a transient glory which might fade in an hour. He had attained the position almost of a deity with the extreme Radical and Socialistic Mob.

But, in this hour of Great Britain's direst peril, he valiantly came forth. He buckled on his armour of undaunted courage and vast ability. He put his whole heart and soul into the fight, absolutely ignoring what effect his actions might have upon his recent followers, forgetting all his schemes of lifelong planning, and concentrating all his vast abilities and ceaseless, untiring energies upon one single concrete thought, one hope, one ideal—Victory.

Like that greatest of all the heroes of ancient Rome—*Venit, vidit, vicit.* Veritably he proved himself a man.

★★★★★★

What a pity it is that since those days he has not adjusted himself to this changed world and seized the opportunities for real statesmanship that lie in this era of reconstruction!

L'Envoi

Before parting with my reader I feel an apology is due from me, not for anything I have written, but for what I have left unsaid.

I admit this book is an amalgam, and far from being what it might have been, had circumstances not required the exercise of considerable restraint on the part of the writer.

Staunch loyalty to his native land is the least return every true-born British subject can make for his birthright; and just as in carrying out the investigations entrusted to me, I ever kept in mind that the one and only object of my existence for the time being was to help my country, so in compiling the preceding chapters I have been compelled, by what in a higher sphere would be called reasons of State, to suppress many facts and incidents which would, I make no doubt, have constituted interesting reading matter.

I have striven to give nothing away that could be construed directly or indirectly against my country. I have touched, lightly, yet I trust sufficiently, upon the canker spots that I so fervently hope and pray may in time be eradicated from our system of home and foreign affairs.

I may have added to my roll of enemies, yet I rejoice in the consolation that by my actions I know I have brought to me many true and great friends.

My readers may complain that the narrative portion of the book dealing with detailed adventures could well have been extended, and that the discursive semi-political portion could well have been curtailed.

I sympathise exceedingly with them to that extent, but if they knew all they would, I am sure, sympathise even more deeply with me in the difficulties which have arisen regarding the publication of these remnants of my knowledge which are now placed before them. The book, as it is, consists of but the fragments of a tale untold.

Had I been dealing with a foreign country as a foreigner, what a different word-film I could have unrolled!—whilst it must not be forgotten that I hope to re-visit in the future the countries mentioned. Were I permitted to record all the happenings of the past I might find such a return too eagerly awaited and the welcome accorded might be open to various interpretations by the powers-that-be.

It is extraordinary but nevertheless true that there are people who entertain doubtful feelings regarding anyone who has undertaken Secret Service work. Some even suggest that such a person, male or female, could only be classified as a spy, a person to be shunned and avoided. What ignorance! What little-mindedness!

When the country had declared war and we knew that the long-anticipated war with Germany had become an established fact, what Englishman, worthy of the name, could rest without dreams of active service? Who hesitated to question the service? When I failed again and again for enlistment by reason of age and was told to apply to Lord Grey direct, I had a tinge of suspicion that if I did have the luck to be found acceptable it would probably be for foreign intelligence work.

A bald statement of fact that such work was or is contemptible could only spring from a craven-souled individual who would probably shrink from his country's call in any event; from some narrow-minded, over-indulgent stay-at-home; or from some pompous, self-exalted incompetent, whose ideas of men and things are beneath contempt indeed.

Secret Service is essentially a service of isolated individuality. A member is not supposed to know, nor permitted if possible to know, other members, beyond those whom he must of necessity meet; yet I knew many more active members than my C.O. had any knowledge or any intention that I should know.

All those whom I had the honour of meeting I found to be men of honour, men whom I am proud to have met. I do not care to express any opinion concerning the ladies, because it is very certain that the more a man studies women the less he really knows of their true nature.

The men in responsible positions (I do not attempt to include the underlings employed in casual cases) I found in every instance to be unflinchingly loyal and true to their country over every other consideration. I will give an instance of this extremeness. An officer in the army, whom I would unhesitatingly have trusted with my honour and my life, was working with me in a dangerous undertaking. To safeguard us both, so far as I could, I suggested that we should form an absolute alliance, for life or death. He solemnly agreed, but he made one stipulation. It was that, if he received a peremptory order from home to put an effective stop to my further services, he should, very reluctantly indeed, but without the smallest hesitation, shoot me without warning. He hastened to add: "You know, old chap, I need not express my known feelings to you, but I am a soldier of the king. I have to obey my orders, and when my country is at war I would shoot my whole family without question, if so ordered from H.Q." I knew he meant it.

I read an account of the capture of this friend by the Germans in Finland—I knew what that meant. I mourned his loss for two whole years. Poor devil! How I pitied him and his fate! But the Secret Service is ever one of surprise and surprises. On April 7th, 1920, I received a letter from the much-lamented departed, "chipping" me in great glee, adding that he had left this branch of service only a few months after I myself had retired hurt, because, to use his own words, "the War Office refused to give me any honours of any kind."

As would be expected, he went straight out to France, where his valour in the field immediately earned some half-dozen mentions in despatches, the D.S.O. and other decorations. Knowing his bravery, skill, and marvellous work whilst abroad in the Secret Service, it seems unbelievable that Home Authorities (who apparently decorated every inmate of the Whitehall Offices, and even telephone girls who retained their stools whilst Zepps were about!) could wilfully ignore such services as his.

That this was not an exceptional case, I may add that I do not know, nor have I ever heard of, even one solitary honour or recognition being bestowed by our own government upon a soul who *actively served abroad in the Foreign Secret Service*; although I do know of highly-coveted decorations being offered and given from abroad, which would-be recipients declined, or dare not accept, because of those above and around them.

Personally I doubt whether any responsible member of the British Foreign Secret Service ever really troubled himself one iota about such trivial matters as decorations—as such. An ambition to climb to the highest rung of acknowledged service to one's country was another matter.

The sporting element of discomfiting and checkmating the Huns seemed to be the one thought uppermost in their minds, whilst, if any time for reflection was ever found, it was generally passed in cursing politicians at home for curtailing activities by shortage of funds, and ministers abroad for not following Nelson's patriotic ophthalmic action at the Battle of Copenhagen.

Speaking for myself, I can only say that my greatest joys in life have been consummated in successful big-game shooting. My employment in the Foreign Secret Service gave me opportunities at far bigger game than my wildest dreams had ever led me to hope for.

I enjoyed to the full every minute of those activities. I would not have missed them for a king's ransom; whilst now I rest in the consolation that if my past life thitherto had been useless and of little worth to the world at large or to anyone in it, I was, during the period of my then employment, striving to accomplish a better thing than I had ever done, to help to victory the noblest cause this world has ever known.

"Jim."

LEONAUR

ALSO FROM LEONAUR
AVAILABLE IN SOFTCOVER OR HARDCOVER WITH DUST JACKET

ZULU:1879 *by D.C.F. Moodie & the Leonaur Editors*—The Anglo-Zulu War of 1879 from contemporary sources: First Hand Accounts, Interviews, Dispatches, Official Documents & Newspaper Reports.

THE RED DRAGOON *by W.J. Adams*—With the 7th Dragoon Guards in the Cape of Good Hope against the Boers & the Kaffir tribes during the 'war of the axe' 1843-48'.

THE RECOLLECTIONS OF SKINNER OF SKINNER'S HORSE *by James Skinner*—James Skinner and his 'Yellow Boys' Irregular cavalry in the wars of India between the British, Mahratta, Rajput, Mogul, Sikh & Pindarree Forces.

A CAVALRY OFFICER DURING THE SEPOY REVOLT *by A. R. D. Mackenzie*—Experiences with the 3rd Bengal Light Cavalry, the Guides and Sikh Irregular Cavalry from the outbreak to Delhi and Lucknow.

A NORFOLK SOLDIER IN THE FIRST SIKH WAR *by J W Baldwin*—Experiences of a private of H.M. 9th Regiment of Foot in the battles for the Punjab, India 1845-6.

TOMMY ATKINS' WAR STORIES: 14 FIRST HAND ACCOUNTS—Fourteen first hand accounts from the ranks of the British Army during Queen Victoria's Empire.

THE WATERLOO LETTERS *by H. T. Siborne*—Accounts of the Battle by British Officers for its Foremost Historian.

NEY: GENERAL OF CAVALRY VOLUME 1—1769-1799 *by Antoine Bulos*—The Early Career of a Marshal of the First Empire.

NEY: MARSHAL OF FRANCE VOLUME 2—1799-1805 *by Antoine Bulos*—The Early Career of a Marshal of the First Empire.

AIDE-DE-CAMP TO NAPOLEON *by Philippe-Paul de Ségur*—For anyone interested in the Napoleonic Wars this book, written by one who was intimate with the strategies and machinations of the Emperor, will be essential reading.

TWILIGHT OF EMPIRE *by Sir Thomas Ussher & Sir George Cockburn*—Two accounts of Napoleon's Journeys in Exile to Elba and St. Helena: Narrative of Events by Sir Thomas Ussher & Napoleon's Last Voyage: Extract of a diary by Sir George Cockburn.

PRIVATE WHEELER *by William Wheeler*—The letters of a soldier of the 51st Light Infantry during the Peninsular War & at Waterloo.